A Buddhist Philosophy of Religion

Bhikkhu Ñāṇajīvako

A Buddhist Philosophy of Religion
by Bhikkhu Ñāṇajīvako

ISBN 0-88139-351-7

Printed in the United States of America.

First printing: July, 1992

For information address to:

The Internation Translation Institute
Dharma Realm Buddhist Association
1777 Murchison Drive
Burlingame, California 94010-4504

Telephone: (415) 692-5912
Fascimile: (415) 692-3017

Table of Contents

About the Author

Bhikkhu Ñaṇajīvako (Cedomil Veljacic) was born in Zagreb, Yugoslavia, in 1915. He took his Ph.D. in Indian and Greek philosophy and started his academic career as lecturer in Asian philosophy at the University of Zagreb. In 1966, after three years as a visiting professor in India, he was ordained a Buddhist monk in Sri Lanka where he lived as a hermit bhikkhu until 1989 when he moved to The City of Ten Thousand Buddhas in Northern California.

He is the author of many books on philosophy in his mother tongue. The bibliography includes History of Oriental Philosophy (two volumes, 1958), his principal work: At the Crossroads of Asian Philosophies (two volumes, 1978), and a large number of books on Buddhism based on his translations of Buddho's discourses and early Buddhist poetry.

He also has two books published in English: Studies in Comparative Philosophy, (Lake House Press, Sri Lanka 1983), and: Schopenhauer and Buddhism (Buddhist Publication Society, Kandy, Sri Lanka, 1971)

His writings in other languages have been published in philosophical journals, annuals and books in India, Germany, the U.K. and other western countries as well as in the U.S. A.

A Buddhist Philosophy of Religion further exemplifies Bhikkhu Nanajivako's understanding of the philosophies existence and the meaning of 'dhukkham' the Buddhist term for suffering and existential "anguish", as this term is often translated.

Without the devoted help of Snjezana Akpinar and Sarah Gilliatt who typed the manuscript and edited the initial draft this book would have never seen the light of day.

Part One

Why is Buddhism a religion?

Chapter One

Thera-vādo Texts

Introduction

In this introductory chapter a brief classification of texts taken from Buddho's discourses should help to clarify his attitude toward the general as well as the particular aspects of religion. A selection of texts taken from the *Pali: Sutta-piṭakaṁ* and a short explanation of the criteria used in their selection will serve as basis for analyzing problems that are implicit in their *prima facie* presentation.

The first group of selected texts is meant to indicate that Buddho's teachings on the specific aspects of religion abstract from any belief in 'revealed truths', beliefs beyond the reach of our direct knowledge and potential experience.

The second group consists of texts in which Buddho abstracts from the belief in an eternal, omnipotent, transcendent Absolute Being or God, while strongly rejecting his absolutist and eternalist attributes.

Finally, to the third group belong texts that are basic to the teaching of *anattā,* or negation of the permanent Self or Soul. (Sanskrit terms used in Buddho's time would be: *ātmā, jīvaḥ, pudgalaḥ)*

Even this brief classification brings out Buddho's critical, if not negative, attitude toward the traditional understanding of religion. It also elicits the following question: "Why is Buddhism a Religion?" - a question that the author has chosen as the heading for this introductory chapter. A necessary consequence of such a discussion on the primordial, essentially religious character of Buddho's teaching, would then be to revise the definition of religion. Implicitly, this also necessitates an analysis of religion and its relation to philosophy. Such an analysis will be attempted in the second part of this book in order to bring forth the artificiality of the earlier posed dilemma: "Is the *Buddha-dhammo* a religion OR a philosophy?" It is the author's hope to make evident that the religious dimension of the human mind is in this instance considered, not only essential, but also an existential and inseparable component of philosophical thinking.

In the more recent past, the same dilemma was aptly portrayed by Jean Paul Sartre. He delineated the merely descriptive negative attitudes of his skepticism, criticizing the naive "atheism" in "the purport of all that we in France call radicalism". "On the contrary," the tenet that "nothing will be changed if God does not exist, we shall rediscover the same norms of honesty, progress and humanity" proves to be extremely embarrassing for Sartre's existentialist, "for there disappears all possibility of finding values in an intelligible heaven..." This Sartre has learned not so much from Nietzsche as from Dostoevski. A fact that he admits in the just quoted famous lecture on "Existentialism and Humanism".

The Buddhist standpoint on which the present survey is based, also should be understood as a philosophy of existence. However, for Buddhism the severing of the religious aspect from the core of the philosophical quest is not admissible under any "pragmatist" or "practical" pretext - frequently attempted by those who do not wish to understand that a "no-religion" is possible without a metaphysical depth-dimension.

1

Texts indicating that Buddho's teachings about specific and personal aspects of religion abstract from beliefs in revealed truths, beliefs beyond the reach of our direct knowledge and potential experience.

1. Udānaṃ (V,3)

This text contains the standard formulation of an often repeated statement which Buddho used in order to mark the difference between his own teaching and the tenets of religiosity in general - here considered simply as a common cultural heritage. Buddho named this teaching: "The Teaching Specific to the Buddhas Par Excellence" (*yā buddhānaṃ samukkaṃsikā dhammadesanā*):

> Buddho "for the sake of Suppabuddho, the leper, gave a gradual instruction dealing with almsgiving, virtue, heaven; with the danger, debasement and defilement inherent in sensual pleasures; and the advantage of renunciation. And when the Lord knew that the mind of Suppabuddho, the leper, was ready, softened, freed from obstructions, elated and clear, then he explained those dhamma-teachings which are essential to the buddhas: suffering, its arising, its ending, the way."[1]

No matter how the *Buddho-dhammo* is defined, whether as philosophy or as religion, or else as victim of any other encyclopedic classification, it is essential for its proper understanding that positive and negative aspects of the defined term form an intrinsic part of the definition. Buddho conveyed this by promoting a sympathy for traditional religion and moral norms, while shunning dogmatic submission to them. He even encouraged critical scrutiny of his own teaching.

2. Brahma-jāla-suttaṁ (D.1)

The following text confirms beyond any doubt that the same rebuke to a blind dependence on religious norms, technically called *sīla-bbata-parāmāso* and best translated as 'restriction of moral and religious *heteronomy'*, also extends to a dependence upon moral precepts (*sīlam*). The basic text of the *Brahma-jāla-suttaṁ* makes this evident:

> "It is in respect only of such *less important and inferior* things concerning injunctions of moral conduct that a worldly man, when praising the Tathagato, would speak. And what are such less important and inferior things concerning injunctions of moral conduct which he would praise? - Giving up the killing of living beings *samaṇo* Gotamo abstains from the destruction of life...from taking what is not given...from unchastity...from lying words...from wrong means of livelihood... But there are other mental states, deep, difficult to perceive, difficult to understand, peaceful, subtle, not to be attained by means of mere logic, accomplished, to be comprehended only by the wise..."

3. Sabbāsava-suttaṃ (M.2.)

Direct reference to the technical term *sīla-bbata-parāmāso* as a "fetter" on the way to spiritual liberation is contained in a statement from the *Sabbāsava-suttaṃ* and is repeated in several other texts:

> "For him who has penetrated to the origin of suffering, to the origin of the arising of suffering, to the origin of the cessation of suffering, to the origin of the way leading to the cessation of suffering, three fetters are eliminated: the embodiment of views, uncertainty, and moral and religious heteronomy *(sīla-bbata-parāmāso).*"

In the following texts we shall see how Buddho succeeds in stressing the moral and religious prerequisites for the deeper understanding of his own teaching, while making it clear that religious elements are subordinate to rationally evident moral precepts.

4. Mahā-taṇhā-saṅkhayasuttaṁ (M.38)

While the preceding text stressed autonomy of *conscience* as a prerequisite for understanding Buddho's teaching on specific concepts of religion, the following one, *Mahā-taṇha-saṅkhayasuttaṁ* (*"Greater discourse on the destruction of craving"*, M 38), expands the same idea to the whole range of consciousness. It also formulates the *autonomy of intellectual understanding*:

- Would you, Bhikkhus, knowing and seeing thus, say: "The teacher is respected by us. We speak out of respect for the teacher"?

- No, venerable sir.

-...Or would you say: "A monk told us so, and other monks did too, but we do not speak thus"?

- No, venerable sir.

-...Or would you acknowledge another teacher?

- No, venerable sir.

-...Or would you return to the ordinary monks' and brahmans' practices and festival exhibitions, and consider these to be the essence?

- No, venerable sir.

- Do you speak only of what you have yourself known, seen and experienced?

- Yes, venerable sir.

- Good, bhikkhus. So you have been guided by me with this *dhammo* (true teaching) with effect visible here and now, not delayed, inviting inspection, onward leading, to be understood individually by the wise.

5. From the Dhamma-padaṁ

These statements from the *Dhamma-padaṁ* are considered to be the best known postulates on moral and intellectual autonomy:

Make an island for yourself, strive hard and be wise..."(238)
"You yourself should make an effort; the Awakened Ones can only show the way..."(276)

"A man defiles himself through his evil action. He purifies himself by avoiding evil. Purity and impurity depend on oneself. No one can purify another." (165)

"One oneself is the guardian of oneself. What other guardian would there be? With oneself fully controlled, one obtains a refuge which is hard to gain." (160)

6. Caṅkisuttaṁ (M.95)

An extensive analysis of "faith", "belief", "trust" or "confidence" - as the term *saddhā* is usually translated in Pali contexts - is found in this lengthy dialogue between Buddho and the young brahman Kapathiko:

"...The brahman youth Kapathiko spoke thus to the Lord:

- Master Gotamo, that which is an ancient mantram of the brahmans, transmitted by oral tradition, like a basket handed over from one to the other and with regard to which brahmans are unanimous in drawing the conclusion: "This alone is the truth, all else is falsehood" what does Master Gotamo say about this?
- But, Bharadvajo, is there even one brahman among them who speaks thus: "I know this, I see this; this only is the truth, all else is falsehood?"
- No, Master Gotamo.
- But, Bharadvajo, is there even one teacher of brahmans, even one teacher of teachers back through seven generations of teachers who speak thus: "I know this, I see this; this only is the truth, all else is falsehood?"
- No, Master Gotamo.
- But, Bharadvajo, those who were formerly seers of the brahmans, original makers and transmitters of mantras, whose ancient mantras are sung, taught and composed, the brahmans of today still sing, still speak; they still speak what was spoken, they still teach what was taught by Atthako, Vamako, Vamadevo, Vessamitto, Yamataggi, Angiraso, Bharadvajo, Vasettho, Kassapo, Bhagu. Do even these speak thus: "We know this, we see this; this only is the truth, all else is falsehood"?
- No, Master Gotamo.
- So it comes to this, Bharadvajo, that there is not a single brahman...not a single teacher of brahmans, not a single teacher of teachers back through seven generations of teachers who speaks thus: "I know this, I see this..." And those who were formerly seers of the brahmans, original makers of mantras..., not even these could affirm it...Bharadvajo, it is like a string of blind men holding one to another neither does the foremost see, nor does the middle one see, nor does the hindmost one see... What do you think about this, Bharadvajo? This being so, does not the faith of the brahmans turn out to be groundless?
- But, Master Gotamo, brahmans do not merely go by faith in this matter; brahmans also go by report.
- First you, Bharadvajo, set off about faith, now you are speaking of report. These five things, Bharadvajo, have a twofold maturing here and now. What four? *Faith, inclination, report, consideration of reasons, reflection on and approval of an opinion...*

Moreover, Bharadvajo, even although something may be thoroughly believed in...thoroughly inclined toward...well reported...well considered...well reflected upon, it may be empty, void, false. On the other hand, something not thoroughly believed in,... not thoroughly inclined toward,...not well reported...not well considered, ...not well reflected upon, it may be fact, truth, not otherwise. Preserving a truth, Bharadvajo, is not enough for an intelligent man inevitably to come to the conclusion: "This alone is truth, all else is falsehood."

- But to what extent, Master Gotamo, is there *preservation of truth*? To what extent does one preserve truth? We are asking Master Gotamo about preservation of truth.

- Bharadvajo, if a man has faith and says: "Such is my faith"' speaking thus he preserves truth, but not yet does he inevitably come to the conclusion: "This alone is the truth, all else is falsehood." To this extent, Bharadvajo, is there preservation of truth..., but not yet is there awakening to truth...

- But to what extent, Master Gotamo, is there *awakening to truth*?

- As to this, Bharadvajo, suppose a monk is living depending on a village or market town. A householder or householder's son, having approached him, examines him concerning three states: states of greed, states of aversion and states of confusion. He thinks: "Does the venerable one have such states of greed (of aversion, of confusion) that, his mind obsessed by such states..., although not knowing, he would say, "I know", or although not seeing, he would say, "I see", or would he incite another to such a course as for a long time would be for his harm and suffering?" While examining him, he recognizes: "This venerable one does not have such states of greed (of aversion, of confusion). As is that venerable one's conduct of body, as is his conduct of speech, so is it not that of a greedy person (of a person with aversion, of a confused person). And when this venerable one teaches *dhammo*, that *dhammo* is deep, difficult to see, difficult to understand, peaceful, excellent, beyond dialectic, subtle, intelligible to the wise..." After examining him and beholding that he is purified of states of greed, aversion, and confusion, then *he reposes faith in him*; with faith born *he draws close*; drawing close *he sits down near by*; sitting down near by *he lends ear*; lending ear *he hears dhammo*; having heard *dhammo he remembers it*; ...*he tests its meaning*,... *he approves* of it; from approval *decision is born*; having decided he *makes an effort*; having made an effort he *weighs it up*; having weighed it up *he strives*; being resolute he realizes with his person the highest truth; and penetrating it by wisdom he sees. It is to this extent, Bharadvajo, that there is awakening to truth.

- But to that extent, good Gotamo, is there *attainment of truth*?...
- There is attainment of truth, Bharadvajo, by following, developing and continually practicing these things...."

Thus Buddho reduces faith to a *minimum of reasonable trust*. One places this trust in a teacher for a limited period of training. It is instrumental like a "raft", justified by previous "examination", or test of the teacher's moral character and intellectual ability. It has no permanent value as a mood, in and for itself, since it is only the first step in a series of twelve (as enumerated in the underlined text above). It remains vain and fruitless ('like an empty basket') unless it leads one to "see, by means of intuitive wisdom" "in this very life", "here and now", "bodily". It is important to add that such religious training should not be understood as a "multipurpose" technique, but should remain focussed and dependent on "the only way" (*ekāyano maggo)* of *sati-paṭṭhānām* or mindfulnes, that of a moral purification which gradually leads to "purification from suffering" and attainment of "extinction" (nibbānaṁ). (Cf. Satipaṭṭhāna-suttaṁ, M. 10)

2

Texts abstracting from the belief in an eternal, omnipotent and transcendent Absolute Being or God, while rejecting his absolutist and eternalist attributes

The salient feature of the above quoted *Cañki-suttaṁ*, which overlaps into this second group of texts, is the absence of any reference to gods. In the discussion on the supreme *authority in religion*, Buddho does not mention a belief in gods, only the problem of a *teacher's trustworthiness*.

The very existence of gods forms a separate topic always treated as a problem of secondary importance. Buddho has been accused of being a disbeliever and a "destroyer" of gods and "the other world". It should be kept in mind, that among his contemporaries in India the existence of a strictly materialistic disbelief in such "supra-mundane" (*lokuttaram*) entities was nothing exceptional. Buddho documents such teachings in a number of his basic discourses and mentions several well-known masters (the best known reference is the *Sāmaññaphala-suttaṁ, D.2.*) who propagate such views. However, in rejecting accusations, Buddho makes it a point never to affirm the opposite view as his own. In this particular instance he does not deny his *belief* in the existence of gods or of the "other world" (*para-loko*). He insists, as always, and we shall see from the following texts, on emphasizing that we neither should nor reasonably can *believe* in such entities, and that *existence* as such should not be considered either as a matter of belief, or of reasoning, but can be grasped meaningfully and without contradiction only by immediate, pre-reflexive pure experience. Existence can only be *existed*. Where experience is not immediately present, one can believe only a trustworthy person; thus Buddho reduces the problem of belief to a problem of the trustworthiness of an *immediate witness*. Abstract beliefs in trans-human cosmic principles, necessarily based on rationally constructed ontological proofs are, therefore, considered mere attempts to infiltrate mediate grounds into the immediate *moral* experience and in this manner subordinate ethics to a heteronomous metaphysical "point of view". It is well known that Buddho, from his strictly and explicitly humanistic and acosmic standpoint, rejects all "views" (*diṭṭhi*).

In the *Caṅki-suttaṁ* the distinction of the "preservation of truth" from the "awakening to truth" characterizes the relation between heteronomous and autonomous attitudes to religion. In this context Buddho expressed the essential difference between the *sincerity* and the *facticity* of a belief. A faithful and reliable understanding of words or "propositions about ...", is in no way adequate, or even a guarantee, for the actual *existence*, or for a correct *representation of facts.* Therefore, statements of belief have to be very carefully distinguished and *very explicitly formulated* in a different manner than statements concerning facts. It is always with this principle in mind that Buddho rejects or reformulates *epistemologically incorrect questions*, or refuses to answer questions considered inadequate.

Buddho was far from ignoring the significance of "preserving the truth", and its social importance as a historical fact. The last two texts of this section will show how carefully he was able to evaluate both its negative and positive aspects.

7. The Saṅgārava-suttaṁ (M. 100)

The following text addresses itself to the existence of gods. The problem arises from a *wrong formulation of the question*. Buddho therefore, tries to establish its proper scope by separating the subjective element of sincerity found in the "preservation" of a heteronomous belief, from the facticity of an actual experience found in the autonomous "awakening to truth". These two incompatible values cannot be encompassed in *one* question and *one* answer without ambiguity.

At the beginning of the *suttaṁ* teachers of religious life (*brahmacariyā*) are divided into three types: 1. those who claim "perfection of knowledge in hearsay"; 2. the "masters of the three *Vedas*"; 3. the teachers of *takka-mīmāṁsā*, or "logical analysis" of the *Vedas*, their "perfection of knowledge", based on "mere faith alone", puts them into to the class of "preservers". "Awakening to truth" is peculiar only to the third type. Those who "know directly by themselves *alone*", "here and now".

-Bharadvajo, I say that there is a difference among those who claim to know the fundamentals of the religious discipline and to have attained here and now the integrity, the perfection of direct knowledge.

(1) There are some monks and brahmans who depend *on report;* these claim to know through report the fundamentals of the religious discipline and thus to have attained here and now the integrity, the perfection of direct knowledge. Such are the three-Vedabrahmans.

(2) There are some monks and brahmans who claim to have attained the same by mere *faith alone...* Such are the masters of logical analysis.

(3) There are some monks and brahmans who *by themselves alone* have attained direct knowledge of truth in matters that have not been heard before...I belong to the last of these (three groups)...

- Master Gotamo, are there gods?

(But the master anticipating that neither a question nor an answer on the existence of gods can be adequately formulated from the previous discussion and its standpoints, since identical terms do not exist, treats the question as an unacceptable criterion (*pramāṇam*). When carefully scrutinized it becomes obvious that this last "standpoint" of "direct knowledge" excludes the very idea of a belief in transmitted words. It is obvious from the context that this epistemological distinction has created in Bharadvajo's head a bewilderment out of which his question arose rather as an astonished exclamation.)

- The statement that there are gods (or, "statements about gods" (*adhidevā*, according to some manuscripts), Bharadvajo, is for me established by experience.
- But why do you, Master Gotamo, on being asked if there are gods say that for you statements about gods are established by experience? Even if this is so, is it not still empty and false talk?
- If on being asked, Bharadvajo, whether there are gods one should say: "There are gods", or: "The statement that there are gods is for me established by experience" then, for certain, an intelligent person can *draw the conclusion* that there are gods.
- But why did not Master Gotamo answer me thus at the beginning?
- Bharadvajo, it is *widely agreed* in the world that there are gods.

In this first, misunderstood, answer (*Thānaso me tam, Bhāradvāja, viditaṁyadidam atthi devā* [or: *adhidevā*] *ti*), Buddho attempts to *restrict the scope of the question* to the reasonable limits of the questioner's heteronomous purely verbal, belief. This intention becomes clearly visible only from the second, unequivocal and concluding answer: "It is *widely agreed* in the world that there are gods." Unfortunately, Buddho's first intention remained misunderstood both by Sangaravo and by the successive generations of pious exegetes and commentators, so that even today the text of this "critical" sentence creates a stumbling block. By now it is considered to be corrupted beyond repair and the blame falls on copyists. All this, however, does not affect the clear intention reaffirmed in the final answer: "...it is widely agreed that there are gods.".

8. Dhāñañjāni-suttaṁ (M.97)

The question in the following text, is the *inferiority of gods*, a consequence of Buddho's *acosmic standpoint*. Buddho considers the form of existence attributed to gods as temporary, intermediate in the cosmic process and therefore unimportant for the attainment of the ideal of "extinction" (*nibbānam*). We shall, therefore, have to define Buddho's acosmic position with a few additional texts (10-11).

> Requested by Buddho, venerable Sariputto visited the brahman Dhananjani who was gravely ill. ...Then the venerable Sariputto thought:
>
> - These brahmans are devoted to the world of Brahma. Let me show the brahman Dhananjani the way to Brahma's retinue.
>
> He said:
>
> - Dhananjani, I shall show you the way to Brahma's retinue. Listen and attend carefully to what I shall say... What is the way to Brahma's retinue? Here a bhikkhu abides in a state of mind imbued with loving-kindness, pervading one quarter of the world, and so the second quarter, and the third, the fourth..., and so the whole world everywhere in every way...he continues to pervade in a state of mind imbued with loving-kindness, far-reaching, wide-spread, immeasurable, without enmity, without malevolence... Again he abides in a state of mind imbued with compassion, with gladness, with equanimity...pervading the world... This is the way to Brahma's retinue.
>
> - Then, Master Sariputto, pay homage in my name with your head at the Blessed One's feet, and say: Venerable sir, the brahman Dhananjani is afflicted, suffering and gravely ill, he pays homage with his head at the Blessed One's feet.
>
> Then the venerable Sariputto went to the Blessed One, and after paying homage to him, he sat down at one side and said:
>
> - Venerable sir, the brahman Dhananjani is afflicted, suffering and gravely ill, he pays homage with his head at the Blessed One's feet...
>
> - But why did you, Sariputto, having established the brahman Dhananjani in the low world of Brahma, although still more could have been done, rise from your seat and depart?
>
> - Venerable sir, I thought thus: These brahmans are devoted to the world of Brahma. Let me show the brahman Dhananjani the way to Brahma's retinue.
>
> - The brahman Dhananjani is dead, Sariputto, and he has reappeared in the world of Brahma...

The whole question of gods in Buddhism is determined by a humanist attitude to religion. The following three texts will show how this attitude leads ultimately to an acosmic and consequently anti-ontological position, formulated through the *cātu-koṭikaṁ* (tetralemma) rule: "Neither being, nor non-being, nor both being-and-non-being, nor neither-being-nor-non-being" can express the existential quest and content of our human reality.

This rule Buddho applied to the *avyākātani*, or indeterminate questions, and to dialectical antinomies of speculative thought.[2]

Buddhist humanism is not metaphorical like the equivocal *Christian humanitarianism* of the merciful God-Savior. It goes down in a straight line to the ultimate ontological consequences. The acosmic essence of these consequences and the final antiontological attitude resulting therefrom, have been clearly elicited also by the existential humanism in contemporary European philosophy (K. Jaspers, G. Marcel, J. Wahl, N. Berdyaev).[3]

9. Brahma-nimantaṇika-suttaṁ (M. 49)

Brahma-nimantaṇika-suttaṁ (M.49) will also be significant for Buddho's argument against a permanent soul-entity (*anattā*) analyzed at the end of the chapter. In the text whose title has been translated as "Challenge to Brahma", Buddho is described as visiting the celestial assembly of the god "creator" Brahma Bako, who has conceived the false conviction that he himself is eternal (having forgotten the distant past when he came to his actual position), and that all other beings in his universe are his own creations a subject often recurring in the *suttas*.

> "...Then Maro, the Evil One, entered into a member of the Brahma's assembly, and he told me (Buddho):
> - Bhikkhu, bhikkhu, do not offend him, for this Brahma is the great Brahma, conqueror, unconquerable, all pervading overlord and creator endowed with highest power, chief, disposer, master and father of all that have become and ever will be. Bhikkhu, there were monks and brahmans in the world before you who condemned earth through disgust with earth, water through disgust with water, fire through disgust of fire, air through disgust of air, beings through disgust with beings, gods through disgust with gods these at the breaking up of the body, when their breath was cut off, were established in an inferior body. Bhikkhu, there were monks and brahmans in the world before you who praised earth through delight in earth,... gods through delight in gods these after breaking up of the body,...were established in a superior body. So, bhikkhu, I tell this: Be sure, good sir, to do only what Brahma says to you, do not go beyond Brahma's word...

(To all this Buddho's answer was:)

- Brahma, having had from earth direct knowledge of earth, from water (fire, air, beings, gods), and having had direct knowledge also of what cannot be adequately experienced as the earthiness of earth, the waterness of water, the fireness of fire, the airness of air, the beingness of beings, the godliness of gods I realized by the same direct knowledge that I was not earth, ..., that I was not god, that I was neither in earth nor apart from earth, I did not claim earth to be mine, I did not affirm earth; ... that I was neither in gods nor apart from gods, I did not claim gods to be mine, I did not affirm gods.
- Brahma, having had from all direct knowledge of all, and having had direct knowledge also of what cannot be adequately experienced as the allness of all I realized by the same direct knowledge that I was not all, that I was neither in all nor apart from all, I did not claim all to be mine, I did not affirm all.
- Thus, Brahma I am not standing on the same level with you as regards direct knowledge, and it is not less that I know, but more than you."

At the end, Buddho summarizes his attitude in the *gāthā*:

"I have seen anguish in being
and being in those who seek to disjoin from being;
I have nothing to state on being,
I don't enjoy being, I don't cling on being."

10. Dhammapadaṁ(153-4)

The most impressive and explicit declaration of Buddho's acosmic attitude is contained in his first utterance after the Awakening:

"Through many births I wandered in the stream of existence
seeking but not finding the builder of this house (the world).
It is sorrowful to be born again and again.
But now, o House-builder, you have been seen.
You will not build the house any more (for me).
All your rafters are broken, your ridge-pole is shattered.
The mind is beyond doubt, attained is the end of craving."

11. Aṅguttara-nikāyo (iv,5,5)

The best known statement of the same humanistic principle is here expressed in such a sober philosophical explicitness that it would be rather difficult not to presume that Schopenhauer was acquainted with it when he expressed the identical basic idea using Buddho's comparison in his *"Criticism of the Kantian Philosophy.'*[A]

> Indeed, friend, I declare there is no world wherein there is no birth, death, decay or repeated deaths and rebirths, and end whereof it is possible to know, see or reach by walking. But, friend, I do not declare that without reaching the end of the world one can make an end of sorrow. My friend, I do proclaim that in this very fathomlong body, with its feelings and mind, is the world, and the path leading to the world's ceasing.

12. The Apaṇṇaka-suttaṁ (M.60)

This text has not been selected to serve as a further illustration of the same problem of gods, of their existence, nor of their inferior position in the universe, although Buddhist theologians use it regularly for that purpose. In this text and in the following one we shall concentrate our attention on the next problem of our inquiry - *the problem of social facticity or moral and religious heteronomy:* the "fetters" which Buddho affronted in order to bring out the *superiority of moral criteria over religious injunctions.* Whenever practical conflicts and aporias arose within social and conventual circumstances Buddho pointed to this issue. The title of this *suttaṁ* has been translated as the *"correct criterion"* (or 'mature' - *apaṇṇako dhammo* in the text). It is a norm that the worldly-minded man (*puthujjano*), who is guided in his affairs by average common-sense, needs to apply when faced with social conflicts and conventional aporias:

On the occasion of his visit to the brahman village Sala, in the country of Kolsala, Buddho asks the brahmans:

- Householders, have you any dear and trustworthy teachers?
- No venerable sir.
- If you have no such teacher, then you can take a correct criterion and apply it in the following manner: There are, householders, some monks and brahmans who maintain and teach the following opinion: "There is nothing given, nothing offered, nothing sacrificed, no fruit or ripening of good and bad action, no this world, no other world, no mother, no father, no spontaneously arising beings, no monks and brahmans whose conduct and behavior are correct and who have themselves realized by direct knowledge and made known this world and the other

> world." But, there are some other monks and brahmans whose theory is directly opposed to those...Now of those monks and brahmans whose theory and opinion is that there is nothing given,...no fruit or ripening of good and bad action, no this world, no other world..., it is to be expected that they will avoid these three righteous criteria, namely, good bodily conduct, and they will adopt and apply these three wrongful criteria, namely, bodily bad conduct, verbal bad conduct, and mental bad conduct.

What is the reason for it? It is that those reverend monks and brahmans do not see the danger, the degradation and the defilement in doing wrong, nor the advantage and the purifying effect of renunciation for the sake of doing good... About this a wise man considers: "If there is not another world, then, on the dissolution of the body, this venerable person will be safe. But if there is another world, then, on the dissolution of the body, after death, he will reappear in a state of deprivation, on a sorrowful way, in perdition, in hell... But, if there is indeed another world then this venerable person comes under wise men's censure *here and now* as an unvirtuous person with wrong view and theory that there is *nothing given.* But, if there is indeed another world then this venerable person has had an unlucky throw on both counts: since he has come under wise men's censure here and now, and since on the dissolution of the body, after death he will reappear in a state of deprivation... He has wrongfully taken and applied the correct criterion in such a way that while it extends only to one side it excludes the profitable count... There are some monks and brahmans who maintain and teach that there is no *integral cessation of being.* But, there are also some monks and brahmans whose theory is directly opposed to those, and they say: "There is integral cessation of being." About this a wise man considers: "When these venerable monks and brahmans maintain and teach the opinion that there is no integral cessation of being, *that has not been seen by me.* And when these other monks and brahmans maintain and teach the opinion that there is integral cessation of being, *that has not been known by me.* If I, not knowing and not seeing, were to take one side and decide: 'Only this is true, anything else is wrong' that would not be correct. Now if the monks and brahmans who maintain and teach the opinion that there is no integral cessation of being are right, then there is a certain possibility that the state of gods consisting of formless perception may be attained by me. But, if the monks and brahmans who maintain and teach the opinion that there is integral cessation of being are right,

> then it is possible that I might *here and now attain complete extinction (nibbanam).* Thus the opinion of those venerable monks and brahmans who maintain and teach that there is no integral cessation of being is *tending to lust,* to bondage, to defilement, to cleaving, to grasping - while the opinion of those... who teach that there is integral cessation of being is tending to the absence of lust, of bondage, of defilement, of cleavage, of grasping. After reflecting thus, he practices *the way of aversion, dispassion and cessation of being.*

Granted that there are "blind" people in the world, Buddho in this discourse tries to help them with a seeing man's advice, as far as he can. Another detail worth mentioning from the standpoint of comparative religion: it is those who believe in the "cessation of being", and not those who believe in its eternity, that behave in conformity with Buddho's teaching. From the viewpoint of any cosmically minded religion or maybe of any religion "in the proper sense" (in accordance with the classical western Biblical standard) just the opposite should be considered as obvious.

13. Kandaraka-suttaṁ (M.51)

This is an often repeated classification of human characters and corresponds to *religious superstitions* which are used as means for justifying man's inborn cruelty - in its masochistic and sadistic forms as they are termed today.

- These four kinds of persons are found in the world:

(1) a person who is a *self-tormentor,* intent on the practice of self-torment;

(2) a person who is a *tormentor of others...;*

(3) a person who is *both a self-tormentor and a tormentor of others;*

(4) a person who is *neither a self-tormentor nor a tormentor of others...* The neither self-tormentor nor tormentor of others is *here and now allayed,* extinguished, cooled; he abides experiencing pleasure as one become divine in himself...

> ... And which, bhikkhus, is the self-tormentor?... In this case some person comes to be unclothed... He does not consent to accept food offered or specially prepared for him or to accept an invitation to a meal... He comes to be a one-house man or a one piece man or a two-house man or a two-piece man... or a seven-house man or a seven piece man. He subsists on one little offering... on seven little offerings. He takes food only once a day, only once in two days...

once in seven days. Then he lived intent on such a practice as eating rice at regular fortnightly intervals... He is one who subsists on forest roots or fruits, eating the fruits that have fallen... He is one who plucks out the hair of his head and beard; and he is one who stands upright, refusing a seat; and he is one who squats on his haunches..; he makes his bed on covered thorns... Thus in many a way does he live intent on the practice of mortifying and tormenting his body. Bhikkhus, this is the person who is a self-tormentor...[5]

And which is the person who is a tormentor of others...? In this case, bhikkhus, some person is a cattle-butcher, or pig-killer, fowler, deer-stalker, hunter, fisherman, thief, executioner, jailer, or one of those others who follow a bloody calling. This is a person who is called a tormentor of others...

And which is the person who is both self-tormentor, and also a tormentor of others?... In this case, bhikkhus, some person is a noble anointed king or a very rich brahman. He, having had a new sacrificial hall built to the east of the town, having had his head and beard shaved, having put on a shaggy skin, having smeared his body with ghee and oil, scratching his back with a deer-horn, enters the sacrificial hall together with his chief consort and a brahman priest... Then he says:

"Let so many bulls be slain for the sacrifice, let so many steers, heifers, goats, rams be slain for the sacrifice, let so many trees be felled for the sacrificial posts, let so much kusa-grass be reaped for the sacrificial spot." Those who are his slaves or messengers or work people, they, scared of the stick, scared of danger, with tearful faces and crying, set about their preparations. This, bhikkhus, is called the person who is both a self-tormentor and a tormentor of others...

And which is the person who is neither a self-tormentor nor a tormentor of others..., and who is here and now allayed, extinguished,cooled; who abides experiencing pleasure as one become divine in himself?... (This is the follower of) a perfect one, fully awakened, endowed with right knowledge and conduct, well-fairer, knower of the world,...teacher of gods and men - a *buddho*..."

3

Texts basic to the teaching of anattā, or negation of the permanent Self or Soul

14. Brahma-jāla-suttaṁ (D.1)

A series of discourses analyze and reject all aspects of the *soul theory* under its Vedantic designation of *ātma-vāda* (for the Pali term *attā-vādo*, e.g., S. 38, 4, 12). The best known and most extensive is the *Brahma-jāla-suttaṁ* (D.1). In it there are forty seven theories representing specific positive views on the nature of the self (*attā*). These are classified in seven groups. Three dealing with "the Self and the World", another three with the self-conscious aspect and one with the substance aspect of its being. Sub-classes of these main groups are: *sassata-vādo* (eight "eternalist theories"), *adhicca-sanuppannikā* (two theories on "spontaneous generation" analogous to the Christian dogma on a "created" soul), *saññi-vādo* (sixteen theories on a conscious soul), *āsaññi-vādo* (eight theories on an unconscious soul), *n'eva-saññi-nāsaññi-vādo* (nine theories on a neither conscious nor unconscious soul), and *uccheda-vādo* (seven theories affirming the "destructibility" of a substantially existing soul).

15. Sabbāsava-suttaṁ (M.2)

"Six kinds of views", concerning the permanence of soul or self-principle are specified and rejected as follows:

> In him whose mind does not penetrate to the origin, one of these six views arises: the view, "For me there is a Self", arises in him as true and established; or the view, "For me there is no Self"..., or the view, "I cognize the Self by the Self"...; or the view, "I cognize the Non-Self by the Self"...; or the view, "I cognize the Self by the Non-Self"...; or else he has some such view as, "It is this my Self that speaks, knows and experiences here and there the ripening of good and bad actions; this my Self is permanent, stable, eternal, not subject to change, and will endure as long as eternity". - This is called pursuance of views, adherence to views, thicket of views, contortion of views, vacillation of views, fetter of views. No untaught ordinary man, bound by the fetter to views is freed from birth, aging and

death, from sorrows and lamentation, from pains, griefs and despairs; he is not freed from suffering, I say.

16. Mahā-nidāna-suttaṁ (D.15)

Four "statements on the Self" are reported with respect to its form and limits:

> "Either in the words, 'My Self has form and is minute'... or in the words, 'My Self has form and is boundless'..., or in the words, "My Self is formless and minute'..., or in the words, 'My Self is formless and boundless';...: - The refutation of these theories is indicated in reference to other analogous cases: "We have said enough about the case of one who is given to (such speculative) theories..."

17. Poṭṭhapāda-suttaṁ (D.9)

One of the most remarkable texts for the critique of the soul theory is based on a fine and extensive analysis of the functional nature of consciousness. Here Buddho refers to "these three assumptions on the Self: that it has a material shape, or a mental one, or that it is shapeless... Now I teach a doctrine that leads to the abandonment of (each of these three) assumptions on the Self."

Buddho's main argument against the soul theory has found its explicit formulation in a number of texts in the *Khanda-saṁyuttaṁ* of the *Saṁyutta-nikāyo (S.XXII)*. We shall conclude our survey with two quotations from that section whose typical argument, that there is no soul "apart" from the psycho-physical formations (*khānda*), is often repeated.

18. Anurādho (S.XXII, 86)

- What do you think, Anuradho: Do you regard the body as the *tathāgato*? (According to the generally applied commentarial explanation, the attribute *tathāgato* is understood in such contexts as designating a human being in the widest sense.)
- Surely not, venerable sir.
- Do you regard the feeling, the perception, the activities, the consciousness as the *tathāgato*?
- Surely not, venerable sir.
- Do you regard the *tathāgato* as being apart from the body (feeling, perception, activities, consciousness)?
- Surely not, venerable sir.

- Do you regard the body, the feeling, the perception, the activities and the consciousness taken together as a whole as the *tathāgato*?
- Surely not, venerable sir.
- Do you regard the *tathāgato* as being without body, feeling, perception, activities and consciousness?
- Surely not, venerable sir.
- Then, Anuradho, since in this very life a *tathāgato* cannot be identified by you as existing in truth, in reality, is it proper for you to state that a *tathāgato* is the superman, the most excellent man who has attained the highest aim, and that a *tathāgato*, if he has to be designated in other than these four terms: "The *tathāgato* exists after death"; or, "he does not exist after death"; or, "he both does and does not exist after death"; or "he neither dies nor does not exist after death"?
- Surely not, venerable sir.
- Good, Anuradho. Both formerly and now, it is just suffering that I proclaim, and the ceasing of suffering.

(The best known *suttaṁ* where the whole argument is repeated is the *Yamako-suttaṁ* in the same section of the *Saṁyutta-nikāyo*, Sect.85.)

19. Upāyo (S. XXII, 53)

- Bhikkhus, should one say: "Apart from body, from feeling, from perception, from the activities, I shall explain how consciousness comes and goes, or how it disappears and emerges, or how it increases, unfolds and attains its full expansion" he would not be able to do so.
- If desire for body is abandoned by a bhikkhu, as well as desire for (the mental formations of) feeling, perception, activities and consciousness, by the abandonment of desire its object is eliminated, too, and can no longer serve as a support of consciousness. Without that support consciousness cannot develop nor generate action and is freed.

The criteria used in selecting these texts are meant to emphasize Buddho's *negative attitude* to some religious beliefs prevalent in India at the time. In this light, it is obvious that the Buddhist theory of 'no-self', *an-attā*, is simply a corollary of the more relevant and wider encompassing principle of 'nullity' or 'nothingness' (*suñña-vādo and ākiñcaññ'āyatanam*) which will be our concern in the third part of this book. Our texts, however, will remain focussed on the problem of the religious aspects of the *Buddha-dhammo* in the attempt to point out its relevance to the development of differential studies in comparative philosophy.

Chapter Two

Buddhist Influences on Western Philosophy of Religion

Criteria used in selecting the preceding texts were meant to emphasize Buddho's negative attitude to some traditional religious beliefs prevalent in India at the time. The same texts will be used in the further analysis of this point. However, the question formulated in the heading (Why is Buddhism a Religion) still remains unanswered: we merely outlined its limits and cleared the ground by eliminating the traditional aspects of heterogenous religious beliefs.

The negative effects of such beliefs will appear more salient if we try to determine Buddhism in contradistinction to modern western encyclopedic definitions of religion. Universal as these may claim to be, their critical proceedings appear inadequate in our case, both in their essential and historical dimensions. Today, the Bible is still assumed (although in a generalized form) to be the fundamental standard. A comparative approach shows to what extent different cultural heritages can be applicable to our texts. Such an attempt demonstrates the incapacity of the Bible to serve as the predominant positive determinant for a general definition of religion. Within such limits religion remains restricted to the morphological varieties and possibilities of a belief in God (or "gods") and the immortality of the soul. Both of these entities denote the principles of a transmundane and eternal life, or an Absolute Being, as the widest possible range of the encyclopedic concept of "religion".

The most unprejudiced judgment on this shortcoming, to my knowledge, was pronounced by Swami Vivekananda, as a spontaneous reaction of religious feeling, at the Congress of Religious Unity in Chicago (1893):

> "Now, there are sects that do not admit of the existence of God, that is a Personal God. Unless we wish to leave these sects out in the cold,... we must have our platform broad enough to embrace all mankind... I think we should love our brother whether we believe in the universal fatherhood of God or not, because every religion and every creed recognizes *man as divine*.[6]

If the *Buddha-dhammo* is to be defined as a religious teaching, it must be on entirely different terms: those of religious experience. All premises of theological speculation have to be left behind.

1. A. Schopenhauer

The first to address the *problem of revising the definition of religion* in the West was Schopenhauer. He did this from a position influenced to a considerable extent by Buddhism:

> "The fundamental difference in religions is not to be found in the question "whether they are monotheism, polytheism, Trimurti, Trinity, pantheism, or atheism (like Buddhism)", but "in the question whether they are optimism or pessimism" - as Schopenhauer tries to define the whole problem of a new, more adequate criterion in terms of his own system of philosophy:
>
> "...The knowledge of God, as the personal ruler and creator of the world who made everything well, is found simply and solely in the religious doctrine of the Jews and in the two faiths derived therefrom (Christianity and Mohammedanism) which in the widest sense might be called Jewish sects, but it is not found in the religion of any other race, ancient and modern." - "Even the other two religions existing with Buddhism in China, those of Laotse and Confucius, are just as atheistic... Incidentally it should be observed that the word atheism contains a surreptitious assumption, in that it assumes in advance that theism is self-evident."[7]

2. William James

Schopenhauer addressed the problem, but the actual question of defining religion in specific terms was approached systematically only towards the end of the nineteenth century by William James. His friendship with Swami Vivekananda whom he met in New York in 1895, encouraged James to research the existential component of religion. When the first volume of Vivekananda's American lectures on *Rājā-Yoga* was published, Swami Tejasananda, the Principal of Belur Math, in his biographical study on *Swami Vivekananda and His Message*, wrote:

> "The book was enthusiastically received by the American intelligentsia and the demand became so great that it ran into three editions within a few weeks of its publication. Even the eminent psychologist Prof. William James of Harvard University became interested in the subject.....
>
> ...that he personally came to meet the great Swami at his residence in New York, became one of his ardent admirers... In his classical work, *The Variety of Religious Experience*, he specially refers to the Swami..."

In his *Gifford Lectures on Natural Religion* in 1901-2 [8], James refers to the Swami's Address, (No. XII, "Practical Vedanta") and to his "Lectures". The questions and ideas on Vedanta, as formulated by Vivekananda, which impressed James were, among others:

> "Why does man go out to look for a God?..."
>
> "I am Thee and Thou art Me... Assert it, manifest it..." "Knowledge is, as it were, a lower step, a degradation. We are It already; how to know It?"

Impressions evoked by Buddhism:

> "I am ignorant of Buddhism and speak under correction..., but as I apprehend the buddhistic doctrine of Karma, I agree in principle with it. All supranaturalists admit that facts are under the judgment of higher law, but for Buddhism as I interpret it, and for religion generally so far as it remains *unweakened by transcendentalistic metaphysics* the word 'judgment' means no such bare academic verdict or Platonic appreciation as it means in vedantic or modern *absolutist systems;* it carries, on the contrary, *execution* with it, is *in rebus* as well as *post rem*, and operates 'causally' as *partial factor* in the total fact." (my underlining.)

Underlined statements indicate the salient points on which a new conception of religion emerges from the philosophy of William James, defined solely in terms of religious experience, abandoning all premises of theological speculation. Interestingly enough, he opposed Buddhism to the "Vedantic or modern absolutist systems", showing his understanding of the role Buddhism played in history.

The observation, however, does not yet offer a sufficient and adequate basis for comparison of the Vedanta with Buddho's acosmic turn of thought. As we have seen, Buddho's thought has implications and consequences which necessitate a deeper quest than the empiricist pragmatic dimensions of practical philosophy are capable to evoke. James' anti-absolutist attitude taken in the Pluralistic Universe[9], however, does imply the basic phenomenological structure of the world as a "stream of existence" (bhavāāga-soto) as well as its momentariness (*khaṇika-vādo*). Also implied is the necessary denial of a substantial and statical ontological status of self-consciousness. All of this bears a striking similarity to Buddho's "radical" idea of *an-attā*. Thus James' basic theory of "pure experience" eliciting the "stream of consciousness" or "stream of thinking" (which when scrutinized, 'reveals itself to consist chiefly of the stream of my breathing'), is defined as "the instant field of the present...this succession of an emptiness and fullness that have reference to each other and are of one flesh" - a succession "in small enough pulses", which "is the essence of the phenomenon". In a similar manner, James reduces "the result of our criticism of the absolute", the metaphysical and metapsychical idea of a "central self" to "the conscious self of the moment".[10]

Information on Buddhism and comparative remarks on this subject in the Gifford Lectures reach far beyond the references suggested by the direct or indirect influence of Vivekananda. James realized, for example, that "in strictness the Buddhistic system is atheistic" and compared "Emersonian optimism, on the one hand, to Buddhistic pessimism, on the other."[11] References to Vivekananda and to Buddhism appear to follow each other closely, although from different sources (of which the Buddhist source is much older). They refer to the state of *samādhi*, the highest state of meditative concentration, and the stages of meditative experience in *dhyānam*, subjects in which James was most interested. Quoting Vivekananda's *Rājā-Yoga* on *samādhi*, he underscores the importance of such experiences in stating "there is no feeling of I...", or that the yogi "comes face to face with facts which no instinct or reason can ever know". Then he compares the way "the Buddhists used the word '*samādhi*' as well as the Hindus; but '*dhyāna*' is the Buddhists' special word for higher states..." - There follows a detailed and correct description of these stages (*rūpa* - and *arūpa* - *jhāna*) "following the account of C.F. Koeppen: *Die Religion des*

Buddha, Berlin, 157 - a book quoted with appreciation already by Schopenhauer."

There are no direct references to Swami Vivekananda in James' *The Will to Believe.* Yet, on the occasion of the Vivekananda Centenary (1963), an American scholar, Vincent Sheean, interested in the Swami's activity in America, suggested that the result of Vivekananda's discussions with James "may be seen in many things that don't have anything to do with Hinduism. When James is discussing mysticism in general I think he is relying to some extent on Swami Vivekananda.[12]

Without venturing to analyze further such suggestive associations, I wish to underscore another characteristic statement found at the beginning of *The Will to Believe*, which will turn our attention in a new direction no less significant. Again we see James' openmindedness and enthusiasm for the broadening of the universalist dialogue: "I have long defended to my own students the lawfulness of voluntarily adopted faith."

3. Henri Bergson

This trend in James's thought, which brings us out of our restricted and necessarily biased religious molds, continues to suggest an analogy with a later analysis of the problem of "closed" versus "open", and "static" versus "dynamic" religion brought forth by Henry Bergson in his *The Sources of Morality and Religion.* (1935)

When Bergson's main work, *Creative Evolution*, appeared in 1907, one of the first emphatic congratulations came from W. James: "Oh, my Bergson, you are a magician, and your book is a marvel, a real wonder..." Respect was mutual, for when *Pragmatism* by W. James was translated into French in 1911, Bergson wrote the preface, *On the Pragmatism of William James - Truth and Reality*. At the outset of his interpretation Bergson seems to insist on a new, spiritual, dimension without which "one would have a mistaken idea of James's pragmatism if one did not begin by modifying the idea usually held of reality in general."[13]

Analyzing this "modification", Bergson reached the following conclusion: "According to James, we bathe in an atmosphere traversed by great spiritual currents." This thesis corresponds (of course implicitly and explicitly) to the Buddhist "theory of momentariness" (*khaṇika-vādo*), described above in connection with James's refutation of a permanent self-consciousness. Bergson argues:

> "But the relations are fluctuating and the things fluid. This is vastly different from that dry universe constructed by the philosophers with elements that are clear-cut and well-arranged... and coordinated to the whole. The "pluralism" of William James means little else than this."

In his *Oxford Lectures*[14] he went a step further and affirmed:

> "There are changes, but there are underneath the change no things which change: change has no need of support... movement does not imply a mobile."

In the *Introduction to Metaphysics*[15] Bergson formulated his most significant thesis concerning the reversal of thought inward ("torsion") which brought him a step closer to Buddho's acosmic approach to religion.

> "To philosophize means to reverse the normal direction of the working of thought."

The significance of this claim for our discussion becomes more clear in the *Creative Evolution*[16]:

> "But has metaphysics understood its role when it has simply trodden in the steps of physics, in the chimerical hope of going further in the same direction? Should not its own task be, on the contrary, to remount the incline that physics descends, to bring back matter to its origins, and to build up progressively a *cosmology, which would* be, so to speak, a *reversed psychology*?"

> "Things and states are *only views*, taken by our mind, of becoming. There are no things, there are only actions."

In his introductory essay to James' *Pragmatism* Bergson seems to have extended the scope of this humanistic tendency to the "atmosphere traversed by great spiritual currents":

> "But the importance of man himself, the whole of man, will thereby be immeasurably enhanced."

These ideas are often strikingly similar to basic Buddhist tenets: that of "views", diṭṭhi; "momentariness", *khaṇika-vādo*; and "no-self", *anattā*. For both authors such ideas are a corollary of the wider aspects of the general acosmic theory of "nothingness", suñña-vādo. The final expression of such concepts is found in Bergson's *Two Sources of*

Morality and Religion[17], in 1935. However, in spite of these similarities Bergson himself does not offer many direct references to India, nor to Buddhism. Although less prominent here than in William James, it is important to state that such references do reflect the favorable atmosphere created in America and in Europe, since Vivekananda's breach of the restrictions imposed by British colonial interests.

In the chapter on "Dynamic Religion" (p. 211-216) Bergson mentions Ramakrishna and Vivekananda, but only as "the most recent examples" of "that enthusiastic charity, that mysticism comparable to the mysticism of Christianity... And it was industrialism, it was our Western civilization, which unloosed the mysticism of Ramakrishna or a Vivekananda."

There is little doubt that Bergson's comparison here seems to be motivated by Romain Rolland's The Life of Ramakrishna[18], yet another example of the recently awakened sympathy for India. Grounds for the comparison are partial and incomplete, and do bear a certain naiveté on the part of Bergson. It is interesting to note that Bergson added the quoted reference to Ramakrishna and Vivekananda at the end of a slightly more extensive presentation of the development of early Indian religious thought:

> "a set of practices... systematized into the yoga, on the one hand, and on the other to "the road of deliverance... more accurately traced" along the line of historical development of "Brahmanism, Buddhism, even Jainism." They "preached with increasing vehemence the extinction of the will to live, and this preaching strikes us at first as a call on intelligence, the three doctrines differing only in a greater or lesser degree of intellectuality. But on a closer look, it is clear that they aimed at implanting a perspective which was far from being a purely intellectual state." (p. 212-13)
>
> As for "the significance of the practices which culminated in yoga, in one aspect at least,... mysticism was no more than outlined; but a more marked mysticism, a purely spiritual concentration, could utilize the yoga in its material elements, and by that very operation spiritualize it." (p. 212)

In the same context, in the chapter on "open" "dynamic religion", Bergson compares Greek mysticism with the Indian prototype. He states that it may have "undergone the influence of Eastern thought, so very much alive in the Alexandrine world" and wishes to "let us first remark that India has always practiced a religion similar to that of ancient Greece." (p. 20-211)

This statement is further clarified through his explanation of the criterion used for the comparison and the hypothesis. Accordingly, Alexandrine (neo-Platonic) mysticism emerges from "the relation between two currents, the one intellectual, the other extra-intellectual" and "it is only by placing ourselves at the terminal point that we can call the latter supra-intellectual or mystic." This statement complies with his broader context of "closed" static and "open" dynamic religion as well as the reversal of thought, and from this point he elicits his definition of mysticism:

> "One may give words whatever connotation one likes, provided one begins by defining that meaning. In our eyes, the ultimate end of mysticism is the establishment of a contact, consequently of a *partial coincidence*, with the creative effort which life itself manifests... The great mystic is to be conceived as an *individual being*, capable of transcending the limitations imposed on the species by its material nature, thus continuing and extending the divine action. Such is our definition. We are free to posit it, provided we ask ourselves whether it ever finds its application, and then whether it fits such and such a particular case." (p. 209-10. Italics are mine.)
>
> Analyzing Indian and Greek thought Bergson clarified the relation of mysticism to philosophy. He chose Plotinus as the central model on the western side of this equation, stating that in his case: there is a radical distinction... between the mystical and the dialectical; they only come together at long intervals. Elsewhere, on the contrary, they have been constantly intermingled, in appearance helping each other, perhaps in actual fact mutually preventing each other from attaining full maturity. This is what appears to have happened in Hindu thought... Its development extends over a considerable period of time. Being both a philosophy and a religion, it has varied with time and place." (P. 210-11)
>
> "In defining mysticism by its relation to the vital impetus, we have implicitly admitted that true mysticism is rare... It is not by chance, then, it is by reason of its very essence that true mysticism is exceptional." (P. 202)
>
> "In this sense, religion is to mysticism what popularization is to science... In reality, the task of the great mystic is to effect a radical transformation of humanity by *setting an example*... So then mysti-

cism and religion are mutually cause and effect, and continue to interact on one another indefinitely." (P. 227-. Italics are mine.)

The concluding chapter, *"Mechanics and Mysticism"*, elucidates the *necessarily elitist character* of the "open" (non-dogmatic) religion which Bergson identifies with mysticism. Ethical dependence is essential to an authentic mystical experience viz. not mechanically and technically profaned. This purity he finds only in *asceticism*:

"For, be it static or dynamic, we take religion at its origins. We have found that the first was foreshadowed in nature; we see now that the second is a leap beyond nature, and study the leap in those cases where the impetus was insufficient or thwarted." (p.212)

"Throughout the Middle Ages, an ascetic ideal had predominated. There is no need to recall the exaggerations to which it led, here already you had frenzy. It may be alleged that asceticism was confined to *a very small minority*, and this is true. But just as mysticism, *the privilege of a few*, was popularized by religion, so concentrated asceticism, which was doubtless exceptional, became diluted for the rank and file of mankind into a general indifference to the conditions of daily existence. "There was for one and all an absence of comfort which to us is astonishing. Rich and poor did without superfluities which we consider necessities." (p.27)

"...since the great expansion of industry, we demand material comfort, amenities and luxuries. We set out to enjoy ourselves. What if our life were to become more ascetic? *Mysticism is undoubtedly at the origin of great moral transformations.* And mankind seems to be as far away as ever from it. But who knows? In the course of our last chapter we fancied we had caught sight of a possible link between the mysticism of the West and its industrial civilization." (P. 20)

In the second half of the twentieth century this prophecy of Bergson's appears to be more and more confirmed from day to day.

"It will not be long before science enlightens us on all these points. Let us suppose that it does so in the sense we foresee: the mere reform of our food supply would have immeasurable reactions on our industry, our trade, our agriculture, all of which it would considerably simplify. What about our other needs? The demand of the procreative senses are imperious, but they would be quickly settled if we hearkened to nature alone... Thus the senses are constantly being roused by the imagination. Sex-appeal is the keynote of our whole civilization.

Here again science has something to say, and it will say it one day so clearly that all must listen: there will no longer be pleasure in so much love of pleasure." (P. 290-1.)

Today the constructive aspect of Bergson's prophecy appears much too optimistic even as a science-fiction utopia. Despair on account of losing love of pleasure, is incommensurably too strong to be challenged by any better prospects of a science politically enslaved in technological subservience. But through the destructive symptoms of Bergson's prophecy - analogous to Nietzsche's prophecy concerning "the European form of Buddhism, this active negation... spiritual exhaustion... the reduction of all problems to the question of pleasure and pain... and the catastrophe of nihilism which will put an end to all this Buddhistic culture...[19]. there transpires a steady ossification ghastly in appearance.

Leaving such dark thoughts aside, let us reconsider from this end our initial analogy with James. Both Bergson's similarity and his divergence from James can be found in the concept of morality and religion. Bergson sees them as two distinct sources. 'Religion' is taken as the "closed", "static", "traditional religion". James formulated this distinction in different terms, no less important. Thus in the text quoted above, he identifies Buddhism, as he understands it, with a particular aspect of religion stressing his appreciation of Buddhism, and of "religion generally, so far as it remains unweakened by... such bare academic verdict... as in Vedantic or modern absolutist systems", but "carries... execution (deliberate action) with it... and operates... as partial factor in the total fact." For Bergson the fundamental task was "to find out whether mysticism was no more than... an imaginative form such as traditional religion is capable of assuming in passionate souls, or whether, while assimilating as much as it can from this religion, while turning to it for confirmation, while borrowing its language, it did not possess an original content, drawn straight from the very well-spring of religion, independent of all that religion owes to tradition, to theology, to the Churches."

"In the first case, it would necessarily stand aloof from philosophy, for the latter ignores revelation which has a definite date, the institutions which have transmitted it, the faith that accepts it: it must confine itself to experience and inference. But, in the second case, it

> would suffice to take mysticism unalloyed, *apart from the visions, the allegories, the theological language which expresses it,* to make it a powerful help-meet to philosophical research. Of these two conceptions of the relation that it maintains to religion, the second seems to us indubitably the right one... All the information with which it would furnish philosophy, philosophy would repay in the shape of confirmation." (p. 239. Italics here and in the sequel are mine.)

Bergson's more explicit agreement with James can be found further in the stress he lays on "terms of experience" and "experimental approach". Such investigation will bring him necessarily to reduce problems of theological cosmology and of soul-entity to questions of secondary importance so that they may be relayed to "a mixed religion".

> The mystics "had to tell all men that the world perceived by the eyes of the body is doubtless real, but that there is something else, and that this something is no mere possibility or probability, like the conclusion of an argument, but the certainty of a thing experienced: here is one who has seen, who has touched, one who knows... The enterprise was indeed discouraging: how could the conviction derived from and experience be handed down by speech? And, above all, how could the inexpressible be expressed? But these questions did not even present themselves to the great mystic. He has felt truth flowing into his soul from its fountainhead like an active force. He can no more help spreading it abroad than the sun can help diffusing its light. Only, it is not by mere words that he will spread it." (P. 222)

On the other hand, in approaches closer to the interest of James in methods of parapsychological investigations, Bergson considers also the question:

> "How can we help seeing, however, that if there really is a problem of the soul, it must be posited in terms of experience, and in terms of experience it must be progressively, and always partially, solved?" (P. 251)

> "If mysticism is really what we have just said it is, it must furnish us with the means of approaching as it were experimentally... Indeed we fain to see how philosophy could approach the problem in any other way." (P. 229)

Considering the bottom line which was also reached, historically speaking, in ancient Greece with the eruption of oriental mysteries and the cult of Dionysos, Bergson seems to look for an excuse and justification for his friend James, who, descending to such a primitive and barbarian level of "mysticism," started experimenting, perhaps for the first time for scientific purposes, with hallucinogenic drugs:

> "As a foreign god from Thrace, Dionysos was *by his violence a sharp contrast* to the serenity of the gods upon Olympus. He was not originally the god of wine, but he easily became so, because the intoxication of the soul he produced was not unlike that of wine. We know how William James was treated for having described a mystical, or at least having regarded as such for the purpose of study, the condition induced by inhaling protoxide of nitrogen. People took that to be a profanation..." (P. 207)

Today we may judge more seriously on this danger and the moral, social and biological consequences provoked by it.

4. A.N. Whitehead and Julian Huxley

The bio-genetic aspect of mysticism was first seriously researched by A.N. Whitehead and Julian Huxley. In their books *Religion in the Making* and *Religion without Revelation* they carry Bergson's quest a step further: the vitalistic analyses, their historical aspects, as well as the mission of mysticism in its bio-genetic perspective.

Whitehead's "philosophy of organism," contains salient points of agreement with Bergson. Among the more outstanding comparisons: "the operation of mentality is primarily to be conceived as a diversion of the *flow of energy*." (Cf. Bergson's "torsion".[20]

Similar to James' "vitalist" interpretation of philosophy, the "pulses of existence," whose succession forms "the essence of phenomena," are here designated as "actual entities" or "actual occasions". They "are the final real things of which the world is made up. There is no going behind actual entities to find anything more real. They differ among themselves...[21]

Applying his "vitalist" orientation to the definition of "Religion in the Making"[22], Whitehead implicitly agrees with the Indian fundamental designation of religion as *"force of belief cleansing the inward parts"*. His explanation of this statement contains the following reasoning:

> "Life is an internal fact for its own sake, before it is an external fact relating itself to others... Religion is the art and the theory of the internal life of man... This doctrine is the direct negation of the

theory that religion is primarily a social fact... Religion is what the individual does with his own solitariness... Thus *religion is solitariness* and if you are never solitary, you are never religious."

Julian Huxley, in his *Religion without Revelation*[23], refers to the quoted statements of Whitehead, though he is not satisfied with Whitehead's "neglecting the highly social nature of almost all religions". This disagreement brings us implicitly back to its better formulation in Bergson's distinction between "closed" and "open" religion.

On the other hand Huxley, singles out very adequately references to Buddhism, both in an explicit as well as in an implicit form:

"There are whole religions which make no mention of God. The most notable example... is that of Buddhism." (P. 44)

"But if religion is not essentially belief in a God or Gods and obedience to their commands or will, what then is it? It is a way of life, an art like other kinds of living, and an art which must be practiced like other arts if we are to achieve anything good in it." (P.6)

Living in an ex-colonial Buddhist country I have often heard the same statement, "Buddhism is a way of life," used particularly by Christians with the intention of dismissing Buddhism as a "religion" *sensu proprio* from the "friendly dialogue" among religions, and to leave open to Buddhists, along with the high praise of their "way of life", also the access to the farther belief in God. Personally I do not wish to enter into discussions concerning the surreptitious shortcoming of such compliments on my "way of life," except for the remark that this "way of life" has to be understood as a "philosophy of existence" with a specific deeper foundation in ontology and metaphysics[24]. It is obvious that most Buddhists, in gladly accepting the compliment, do not think of going any further, and do not even understand the tendency of my rejoinder.

This is probably not the place to enter further into a Buddhist interpretation of adequate statements by J. Huxley, nevertheless I shall mention the following:

"In place of eternity we shall have to think in terms of an enduring process..." (P. 7;25)

In order to avoid possible misunderstandings due to superficialities concerning the Buddhist "way of life", I shall try to show why I agree with a more essential statement by J. Huxley on the deeper intention of Buddhist asceticism:

> "And the relation to practical existence may be one of escape, as in asceticism or pure Buddhism; or of full participation, as in classical Greece or the city-states of ancient Mesopotamia..." (P.152)

I have endeavored to elicit the meaning of asceticism in "pure Buddhism" using as model of the most beautiful (and the most neglected) of Buddho's poems, "The Rhinoceros" (*Khaggavisāṇa-suttaṁ, Sutta-nipāto* 35-75;[26]

> *"Do not wish a son and still less a friend.*
> *Go alone as the rhinoceros.*
>
> *Be like a king who has abandoned his conquered country.*
> *Go alone as the rhinoceros.*
>
> *Wise in selfish aim, men are dirty.*
> *Go alone as the rhinoceros."*

5. George Santayana

George Santayana also analyses the vitalistic orientation of "faith". This brings him close to Buddhism which correlates to his own brand of skepticism. For Santayana skepticism is conceived as a "system of philosophy" steeped in ancient Stoicism. However, the connection between skepticism and Buddho's criticism of dogmatic views (*diṭṭhi, Sk. dṛṣṭiḥ*, Greek doxa) will be shown in the second part of this book more explicitly. Here it suffices to say that Buddho's "thicket of views, wilderness of views, scuffling of views, and fetter of views"(M.72) - corresponds to the original skeptical attitude of Pyrrho's ethos of knowledge and his teaching of epoché as "refraining from judgement" which he brought back to Greece from India and its religions founded in *ahiṁsā*, or abstention from violence. "The Indian Origin of Pyrrho's Philosophy of Epoché" was revived in the twentieth century in the transcendental logic of Husserl. Santayana also touched upon the same concepts.

Santayana's philosophy of skepticism arises from his basic analysis of "Animal Faith"[27]. Revealing some Indian influence, Santayana defines "animal faith" as follows:

> "I suspect, or I like to imagine, that what the Indians mean is rather that the principle of my existence, and of my persuasion that I exist,

is an evil principle. It is sin, guilt, passion, and mad will, the natural and universal source of illusion - very much what I am here calling animal faith; and since this assertiveness in me (according to the Indians) is wrong morally, and since its influence alone leads me, to posit existence in myself or in anything else, if I were healed morally I should cease to assert existence..." (P.52)

With explicit reference to India, Schopenhauer formulated essentially the same problem of the "mad will" as the "natural and universal source of illusion", a "morally wrong" motive "to posit existence". "Moral healing" of this disease is attained by "ceasing to assert existence". Santayana's method of healing corresponds implicitly to the ethical motive of Pyrrho's Epoché.[28]

However, Schopenhauer was not satisfied with the attainment of this "natural" level of the "universal source of illusion". His criticism of the Stoical ethos of knowledge shows how for him the metaphysical problem of the "right knowledge" (*sammā-diṭṭhi*, as formulated on the Indian side by Buddho) arises first on the natural level, while the moral obligation to solve it constitutes its "ground" (*bhūmi* - terminology for the gradual progress on the path of katharsis in meditation [*visuddhi-maggo*]) which is on a higher level of the ethos of knowledge[29]. Neither Schopenhauer who found it wrong to posit existence, nor Santayana's vitalistic orientation of "Scepticism" in "ceasing to assert existence" were able to bring us further than the Stoical response to the Pyrrhonian formulation of ethical skepticism: refrain from judgement.

Schopenhauer found a solution to this central problem in the justification of a soteriological "reversal of the normal working of thought" (Bergson's *"torsion"* as defined in his *"Introduction to Metaphysics"*;[30]). This, then, become the target of Christian, mainly Lutheran, criticism of Schopenhauer's theory of knowledge. A recent author has summed it up as follow[31]:

"A deep chasm divides the reformer (Luther) from the anti-theistic will-metaphysician of the 19th century (Schopenhauer)... And yet, there remains a fundamentally common feature, which should not be sought in the result, but in the starting point of both thinkers... Both Schopenhauer and Luther share the same concrete fundamental experience."

"On one deciding point of their doctrine of release they both agree to such an extent that the parallelism must not any longer be considered as merely formal-schematic, but as grounded in the contents... According to Schopenhauer, who considers the fact of individuation as guilt, the release results from the absolute inhibition of individuality through negation of the will-to-live in the voluntary renunciation to all individual willing, ultimately attainable in death..."

Luther's "doctrine of justification" of the "possibility of turning the will against itself," and the "change in the direction of cognizing" - in contrast to Schopenhauer's "philosophy of the duplicity of consciousness"[32] - has to serve the purpose of "the individual, who in his individuality is of divine origin, to renounce his egocentricity by virtue of an act of God, though not in order to be extinguished in his individuality, but rather to be redeemed in it: in the image of God himself, which each individual is in a different corporeal manner."

"The duplicity of consciousness" arising from the possibility of "turning the will against itself" might be explained in both cases by a reduction to a gnostic theory of knowledge. Schopenhauer sought and found an explanation on the empirical level. He analyzed a psychology of crisis in existential situations. Such interest which Schopenhauer focussed on persons sentenced to death[33], can also be compared to Dostoevski's moral gnosticism where the same intention was further dramatized.

An existential experience of this magnitude elicits a radical divergence. In it a solution was sought both in the East and in the West. Martin Luther found it in an act of God, while India stuck to the intuitiveness of gnosticism. This is seen as an alternative to the metaphysics found in both systems of moral and religious philosophies.

Santayana was no less aware of this dilemma which rests on the "duplicity of consciousness" and on a primeval religious gnosticism which could be considered as the last biological root of metaphysics. Its lowest level appears in "animal faith". In light of this complex background of historical antecedents Santayana, albeit with a skeptical smile, began the preface of his book by saying, "Here is one more system of philosophy." Let us now consider the actual value of Santayana's re-examination of the fundamentally biological source of "religion without revelation" in his *Scepticism and Animal Faith.*

Bearing the above statement in mind, we could deduce the definition of Santayana's skepticism directly from his affirmation of the Indian *māyā-vāda*. The same is also clearly implied in Pyrrho's ethical doctrine of epoché. In Santayana's "watershed of criticism" (title of ch. XI, p. 99) he sums up these precedents in what he calls "a clearer meaning of this old adage":

> "Therefore, if I regard my intuitions as knowledge of facts, all my experience is illusion, and life is a dream. At the same time I am now able to give a clearer meaning of this old adage; for life would not be a dream, and all experience would not be illusion, *if I abstained from believing in them*. The evidence of data is only obviousness; they give no evidence of anything else; they are not witnesses... If I hypostatise an essence into a fact, instinctively placing it in relations which are not given with it, I am putting my trust in animal faith..."
>
> "Belief in substance, taken transcendentally, as a critic of knowledge must take it, is the most irrational, animal, and primitive of beliefs: it is the *"voice of hunger."* (P.190-1)

Buddho's basic Noble Truths reveal suffering as the essential root of all existence, not only human. Thus the "theory of momentariness" (*khaṇika-vādo*) explains the arising of suffering as stemming from the intuition of change of all appearances[34] and from the intuition of ineluctable evanescence of phenomena as the basic law of their structure. In Santayana's terms, this theory could be designated as the "survey" of "a biography of reason, in which I should neglect the external occasions on which ideas and beliefs arise and study only the changing patterns which they form in the eye of thought, as in a kaleidoscope." (P.109)

In the chapter on "doubts about change" (V, p.27 f), Santayana starts by reminding us both of Buddho's criticism of "belief" (*saddhā*) and of Pyrrho's ethics of epoché:

> "The intuition of change is more direct and more imperious than any other. But *belief* in change... asserts that before this intuition of change arose the first term of that change had occurred separately.
>
> This no intuition of change can prove. The belief is irresistible in animal perception, for which reasons biology can plausibly assign; and it cannot be long suspended in actual thinking; but it may be suspended for a moment theoretically, in the interest of a thorough criticism. The criticism too may prove persuasive..."

The *ephectic* "abandonment of good and evil"[35] (puñña-pāpa-pahāyaṁ in the words of Buddho) is reduced to the natural error of transcendental illusion:

> "Nor is there any *moral offence* any longer in the contingency of my view of it, since my view of it involves no error. The *error came from a wild belief* about it; and the possibility of error came from a wild propensity to belief. Relieve now the pressure of that animal haste and that hungry presumption; the error is washed out of the illusion." (P.73)

Thus a primeval motive of religion is revealed in "the insecurity inseparable from animal faith, and from life itself". (P. 107)

> "Animal faith being a sort of expectation and openmouthedness, is earlier than intuition... and perhaps primitive credulity, as in a dream... yields its whole soul to every image. Faith then hangs like a pendulum at rest; but when perplexity has caused that pendulum to swing more and more madly, it may for a moment stop quivering at a point of unstable equilibrium at the top; and this vertical station may be likened to universal skepticism. It is a more wonderful and more promising equilibrium than the other, because it cannot be maintained; but before declining from the zenith and desisting from pointing vertically at zero, the pendulum of faith may hesitate for an instant which way to fall, if at that uncomfortable height it has really lost all animal momentum and all ancient prejudice." (Ibid.)

The problem of the gnostic duplicity of consciousness-and-conscience arising from the ethos of knowledge is ultimately conceived under the heading of "Sublimations of Animal Faith." (Ch. XXI):

> "Animal faith, being an expression of hunger, pursuit, shock, or fear, is directed upon *things*... In other words, animal faith posits substances, and indicates their locus in the field of action of which the animal occupies the center. Being faith in action and inspired by action, it logically presupposes that the agent is a substance himself... Ultimately, however, the spirit may come to wonder why it regards all things from the point of view of one body in particular, which seems to have no prerogative over the others in their common realm. *Justice and charity* will then seem to lie in rescinding this illegitimate pre-eminence of one's own body: and it may come to be an ideal of the spirit... an effort which, by a curious irony, might end in *abolishing all interests and all views*. Such *moral enlightenment* is dangerous to animal life, and incidentally to the animal faith... If the qualms and ambitions of spirit prevailed in anybody altogether, as they tend to do in the *saint and even in the philosopher*, he would not be able to halt at the just sympathy... He would be hurried on to rebel against these natural interests in himself, would call them vain and sinful,... and would initiate some disciplines, mortifying the

> body and *transfiguring the passions,* so as *to free himself* from that *ignominy and bondage...* What would occur? He would be happier fasting than eating, freezing than loving... His sympathy, if it survived at all, would be sublimated into pity..." (P.214-215)

Out of similar considerations the Buddhist theory of nothingness (suñña-vādo), instead of turning to God and the Absolute Being, found its immediate way of insight through dread and pity into the nullity of man's 'nihilating' existence (to use a term coined by Sartre for "human existence.... as useless passion...for man is not what he is, man is what he is not.";[36]

Santayana, when speaking of "the mind of another man or god or an eventual self of one's own" (P. 283), is not far from a transcendentalist interpretation of the Buddhist theory of no-self (*anattā*). Speaking of music, in a manner reminiscent of Schopenhauer, and "its play with pure essence, " which, "in the objective direction, ... is full of trepidation, haste, terror, potentiality, and sweetness," he comes to the question:

> If mere sound can carry such a load, why should not discourse do likewise, in which images of many other sorts come trooping across the field of intuition? This is no idle doubt, since the whole Buddhist system is built on accepting it as a dogma; and transcendentalism, though it talks much of the self, denies, or ought to deny, its existence, and the existence of anything; the transcendental self is pure spirit, incoherently identified with the principle of change, preference, and destiny which this philosophy calls Will... The Buddhists too, in denying the self, are obliged to introduce an ambiguous equivalent in the heritage of guilt, ignorance, and illusion which they call Karma. (p. 148)

In another context Santayana, out of pure phenomenological observations, comes, in a way astonishingly close for a Buddhist, to the Jainist doctrine of "karmic matter," consisting of "polluting influxes" of passions - *āsavā*. This is an archaic theory of matter taken over also by Buddho. Santayana also approaches a theory that action creates matter in its primordial "viscose" appearance (as Sartre depicted it in one context of Being and Nothingness):

> "Such a thought or passion, while evidently animating the body and expressing its situation, does not exactly lie within the body; to localize it there with any literalness or precision is absurd; and a man feels in his own case that they are *influences* visiting him, perhaps demons or obsessions... Hence the notion of *spiritual sub-*

stances ... Feelings and thoughts pass for the principles of action... The spirit can be confused with substance only when it is spirit incarnate..." (P.217. Cf. the Indian belief in *avatars,* a term used by Sartre.)

Such considerations ultimately bring the skeptic to the essential question:

"Why should I have awaked at all?"

Yet the possibility of awakening is an obvious existential faculty concealed in the roots of "animal faith," as embarrassing as the investigation in its nature may appear. In the same connection Santayana defines Spirit "the wakefulness of attention" (cf. the central importance of *sati-paṭṭhānaṁ in Buddho's teaching of contemplative life) which "contains no bias, no principle of choice, but is an impartial readiness to know." (P. 283—4)*

No less authentically Buddhist is the impression of Santayana's meditation found on the concluding pages of the book on the same subject of "the discipline of my daily thoughts":

"My criticism is not essentially a learned pursuit...it is not a choice between artificial theories; it is the discipline of my daily thought and the account I actually give to myself from moment to moment of my own being and of the world around me...Merely learned views are not philosophy... I should like, therefore, to turn to the ancients and breathe again a clear atmosphere of frankness and honor... The Indians were poets and mystics; and while they could easily throw off the conventions of vulgar reason, it was often to surrender themselves to other conventions... such as the doctrine of transmigration of souls; and when, as in Buddhism, they almost vanquished that illusion, together with every other, their emasculated intellect had nothing to put in its place..." (P. 305-6)

This consideration reminds me strongly of Nietzsche's criticism of "Buddho and Schopenhauer" in *Beyond Good and Evil* (ch. 3, "The Religious Mood," section 56):

"(I) have looked with an Asiatic and super-Asiatic eye, inside and into the most world-renouncing of all possible modes of thought - beyond good and evil, and no longer like Buddho and Schopenhauer, under the delusion of morality.[37]

Agnosticism is rejected no less resolutely by Santayana than by Buddho[38]:

> "The interest in truth for its own sake is not a worldly interest, but the human soul is capable of it; and there might be spirits directed on the knowledge of truth as upon their only ultimate goal, as there might be spirits addressed exclusively to music; ... and an agnosticism which was not merely personal, provisional, and humble would be the worst of dogmas[39]. A sinking society, with its chaos of miscellaneous opinions, touches the bottom of skepticism in this sense, that it leaves no opinion unchallenged. But as a *complete suspense of judgment* is physically impossible in a living animal, every *sceptic of the decadence* has to accept some opinion or other... Nevertheless, among Greek sceptics there were noble minds. They turned their scepticism into an expression of *personal dignity* and an *argument for detachment*. In such scepticism everyone who *practices philosophy must imitate them...*" (P. 307)

On the last page of this book, comparing his skepticism with "other criticism of knowledge," Santayana comes to the conclusion:

> "Living when human faith is again in a state of dissolution, I have imitated the Greek sceptics in calling doubtful everything that, in spite of common sense, any one can possibly doubt... There are many opinions which, though questionable, are inevitable to a thought attentive to appearance, and honestly expressive of action. These natural opinions are not miscellaneous, such as those which the Sophists embraced in disputation. They are superposed in a *biological order, the stratification* of the life of reason... Belief in them, however, is not grounded on a priori probability, but all the judgments of probability are grounded on them... This natural faith opens to me various realms of being, having *very different kinds of reality* in themselves *and a different status in respect to my knowledge* of them." (P. 308-9)

A comparative analysis of this post-Kantian skepticism with the Kantian criticism (to which on several occasions it seems to allude more or less vaguely) would not bring us far, especially not beyond the regions of practical reason. I wish however, to conclude with an analogy remaining within the historical limits of Santayana's last reference to the origin of his renewed attempt to base "one more system of philosophy" on the "imitation of Greek sceptics."

The idea of this analogy was suggested by a critical remark of Max Scheler about Kant's ethics as an un-Christian return to the rationalism of the ancient Stoics and Skeptics with an explicit allusion to their affinity with Buddhism. In rejecting the views of "the Stoa and the old Skeptics who considered apathy, i.e. dulling of the sensuous feelings, to be good," Scheler reproaches all pre-Christian "ancient ethics... an arbitrary misinterpretation of suffering as a judgment of 'reason' (the Stoic: 'Suffering is not an evil'), i.e. a sort of illusionism and autosuggestion against pains and suffering of life. The Buddhist doctrine, on the other hand, knew only the method of objectifying suffering through the knowledge of its (presumed) ground in the very essence of things and a resignative settlement therewith.[40]

Kant himself anticipated a deeper meaning of the modern (implicitly Christian in Scheler's opinion) misinterpretation of *apatheia* (*upekhā* in Buddhism) in these systems of ethics. In the *Preface to the Metaphysical Elements of Ethics*, under the heading "Virtue Necessarily Presupposes Apathy (considered as strength)[41]:

> "This word (apathy) has come into bad repute, just as if it meant want of feeling, and therefore subjective indifference with respect to the objects of the elective will; it is supposed to be weakness. This misconception may be avoided by giving the name *moral apathy* to that want of emotion which is to be distinguished from indifference. In the former the feelings arising from sensible impressions lose their influence on the moral feeling... The true strength of virtue is the *mind at rest*, with a firm, deliberate resolution to bring its law into practice. This is the state of health in the moral life.

6. Karl Jaspers

In a different perspective, in the middle of the 20th century, the central conception of a contemporary *philosophy of culture* focussed on the critical position of religion in its analysis of the problem of "philosophical faith" (*Der philosophische Glaube*) by Karl Jaspers[42].

> "It is questionable whether *faith* is possible *without religion*. Philosophy originates in this question.[43] Faith is "hope grounded in reason itself and not in some other guarantee coming from outside." Consequently, "religion is not an independent source of truth," and doctrinal belief remains always "insecure." - These are conclusions drawn by Jaspers in his interpretation of Kant's *Religion Within the Limits of Mere Reason*[44]. Kant's philosophy as a whole has for Jaspers the value of a "revolution in man's *way* of thinking." "What we know is not the world but only our ways in the world": "Philosophy as a way" had to be "found by a turnabout." By following this way "we gain no knowledge of an object, but our consciousness of being is transformed. The *non-knowledge* of philosophical exploration transcends the understanding and transforms our awareness of

being."[45] Expressed in classical terms, the way of philosophy is not a way of *cosmic knowledge (doxa, diṭṭhi)* but a way to *human wisdom.* This is why, in terms of Kantian criticism as understood by Jaspers, even rational "dogmatism always leads ultimately to skepticism and unbelief, while critique leads to *science and faith.*[46]

Already in his interpretation of the religious thought of St. Augustine, Jaspers defined philosophy as "a thinking that penetrates and makes for awareness," while "philosophical faith stands in the concreteness of its always unique, noncatholic, historical actuality, through which it is able to ascertain the true reality, for which there is no guarantee except in the freedom of man and its communicative realization on the *brink of the abyss* of failure in the reality of the world.[47]

The religion of the philosophical faith is thus a religion of continual risk, acceptable and bearable only for those who have already conquered the existential fear of failure and death.

Penetrating still deeper in the history of philosophical faith, in his interpretation of Buddho's fundamental religious wisdom, Jaspers formulates the well-known characteristic of this most aristocratic faith as follows:

"By his inexorable either-or Buddha seizes hold of the whole man. But the *faith* required for this path of salvation *is a knowledge...* salvation itself is a knowledge, redemption is insight achieved simultaneously with it.[48]

Chapter Three

The Path of Purification: Visuddhi-Maggo

In the preceding chapters I underlined expressions which are significant for the Buddhist approach to the problem of defining religion. In this chapter such broader philosophical problems are only implied. Its aim is to bring out the purely religious aspect of the "philosophical faith," here understood as the path of purification (*catharsis*, Buddhist *visuddhi-maggo*), and thus to add a new orientation to our quest for a broader definition of religion.

In the following discussion about essential trends extant in such new, 20th century conceptions, I have singled out certain aspects of systematic wholes. They range from the basic biological "animal faith" to its ultimate critical sublimation in "philosophical faith." The post World War II situation brought with it a seed of decadence and a destructive attitude towards global culture. This further separated the already tenuous integrity between East and West exposing an archeological skeleton whose ever more ossified structure protrudes out of the expanding wastelands and deserts menacing the future of our planet.

Deeper than the problem of "religion without revelation" is the problem of religion without "soul," "self," or even a permanent "I." Among the higher, philosophically relevant religions, Buddhism is the only one fundamentally steeped in transcendental criticism. While having the same radical meaning as Kant's philosophy, it does not only sporadically conjecture a distant analogy, but goes further than Kant's own philosophy of religion.

William James was the first and most explicit among the authors here discussed to underscore the importance of the question: "Does consciousness exist?" - and to answer it negatively. Yet he did not extend it to the central problem of re-evaluating and redefining the notion of religion as a whole in its contemporary actuality. In their investigations of the biological grounds of religion "as a diversion of the flow of energy", A.N. Whitehead and J. Huxley came even closer to this problem. While mysticism in its bio-genetic aspect also interested G. Santayana, it found a more extensive analysis in the prophetic work of H. Bergson. The decisive turn to the philosophical core of religion in the actual crises of our world-culture became possible only by the middle of the century, and was diagnosed then and there by K. Jaspers. And now, what is it that remains pertinent for our analytical endeavors in establishing an analogy with the *Buddha-dhammo*, the quintessential acosmic religion?

(A) Religion is defined as a way of *meditative reduction* of mental structures and of their contents (*noesis* and *noema* in the terminology of Husserl's phenomenological method), an *ephectic* way of purification. This process is still not differentiated from the fundamental philosophical attitude of *epoché* as preached by Pyrrho of Elis and his disciple Timon. Their main concern was a moral and even a religious attitude. Husserl, in his reinterpretation of *epoché* brought forth only its noetical significance, nevertheless, he saw in it a method of phenomenological reduction meant to serve the purpose of a "science of phenomena which lies *far removed from our ordinary thinking*... so extraordinarily difficult... a new way of looking at things, one that contrasts at every point with the *natural attitude* of experience and thought."[49]

Jaspers, in *The Great Philosophers*, refers on several occasions to ancient and mystical "experiences in meditation", insisting on their essential difference from modern methods of "suspension" in the transcendental analysis of the "subject-object relationship." He formulates the difference most clearly with reference to "Buddha's doctrine of redemption by insight". It "springs from experience in the transformation of consciousness and the stages of meditation." While modern "science and philosophical speculation remain within our given form of consciousness... this Indian philosophy may be said to take consciousness itself in hand, to raise it in higher forms by exercises in meditation."[50]

In whatever way the intrinsic connection between the presumed two aspects of *epoché* may be construed - as a philosophical method of transcendental analysis, or as the way for a transcending consciousness to attain "ek-static" wisdom - its religious purport can be encompassed only from a still higher level of existential experience, to which all "suspension" attained by *epoché* points (already in the case of Pyrrho's original doctrine). It does not aim - in either case - at a "mundane" transcendence; its essential attainments have always remained in the service of a *via negativa*. (Even Husserl was very consequent in stressing that his reductive method does not and ultimately cannot lead or even point to any further transcendence, beyond the "transcendence in the immanent". Sartre, in his critique of Husserl on this ground, was no less adamant.)

It seems that Jaspers (similar to the whole existential trend in contemporary philosophy) overemphasizes the importance of "ecstasis" and of its "all-encompassing" aim. From a European bias, this remains a specifically ontological aim or ideal. From the Indian bias the same ideal seems to be peculiar just to the *Advaita-Vedanta*. Here I cannot enter any farther into its differential analysis. Buddho's anti-vedantine standpoint is equally anti-ontological: "Neither being, nor non-being, nor both being-and-non-being, nor neither-being-nor-non-being" can express the existential purport and content of our human-reality.

When utilized for religious aims of *catharsis* (Buddhist *visuddhi-maggo*), the method of *epoché* remains far from being exhausted in any "ecstatic" vision (not even in the meaning of Buddhist *vipassanā* in and for itself, whose proper primal significance cannot be successfully severed from its original location in the reductive structure of the way of jhānaṁ). The deepest motivation of philosophical faith is *release*, not only as "suspension", and not even as "freedom!" The proper religious meaning of "suspension" has been elicited most adequately for our context, in Schopenhauer's aesthetic approach to the problem of pure contemplation: "And we know that these moments, when, delivered from the fierce pressure of the will, we emerge, as it were, from the heavy atmosphere of the earth, are the most blissful that we experience. From this we can infer how blessed must be the life of a man whose will is silenced not for a few moments, as in the enjoyment of the beautiful, but forever, indeed completely extinguished..."[51]

On the Indian side, *mokśa* (Pali *vimutti*) is not equivalent in its *ephectic* or *cathartic* meaning to a positive attainment of "freedom to...". It is a *release from* the "suspended" existential affirmation of being. It does not indicate any positive idea of "freedom to..." as its aim, but simply and purely abandonment of, leading to further realization of revulsion and escape (Pali *paṭikkūlaṁ* and *nis-saraṇaṃ*) from any whatsoever "mundane" and "cosmical" intention. To what purpose? - To *none*. Where *release-from* does no longer constitute a *freedom-to,* "extinction" (*nibbānam*) can no longer serve any purpose either. This process of release through *suspension* of existential judgment (*epoché*) contains its moral and spiritual value in itself.

Why do we designate it - also in the Buddhist sense - merely as suspension? The reason has deep ontological implications. The same as Pyrrho's apatheia, Buddho's *upekkhā* cannot be considered as "annihilation" (*uccheda-vādo*).

Thus meditative reduction on the *via negativa* of religious experience cannot admit to any structural limitation of its intention. There is a fundamental mistake, from the standpoint limiting the "higher religion" to the aspect of mystical ecstasy, in taking the distinction between "mundane" and "transmundane" "levels" as an ultimate differential criterion. The *via negativa* proceeds originally, in all attitudes of *epoché,* irrespective of intentional differentiations in their noematic aims, from an *attitude to consciousness,* from the "*terminus a quo*" of "all theoretical, axiological or practical attitudes" of my "*Cogito*" or "*sum cogitans,*"[52] and not from an *attitude to the world*. The merely ecstatic conception of religion and of the "mystical" *epoché* (as envisaged by Jaspers) disregards, besides that, the ultimate *acosmic intentness on the ascetic religion*. I shall try to base my definition of religion from the Buddhist standpoint, precisely on such an acosmic intent.

(B) Postulated by this acosmic attitude, the ideal of the ascetic practice, of hermitic life, is *escape* from the world. Only as deeply irreligious times of "*idola fori*" as the twentieth century could so grossly misunderstand the highest religious ideal of escape for social "unhealthiness" as it is brandmarked today.[53]

Regardless of any *consensus gentium* sanctioned by all "closed religions" (Bergson), and understood as an integral social formation quite apart from our interest in philosophical faith, Buddhism can be considered a religion among others only in so far as a definition of religion can comprise the idea of hermitic life as a way to the ultimate attainment of its goal - beyond any transcending metaphysical justification. To this effect the philosophical aspect of the *Buddha-dhammo* is limited to the gnoseological scheme: *sīlaṁ-samādhi-pañña*, or to the belief that no attainment of wisdom (*paññā*) is possible for the introvert seeker (*sāvako*, "listener" becoming a *muni*, or "silent sage") without the existential prerequisite of purification through moral virtue (*sīlaṁ*) and mental discipline (*samādhi*)[54]. The latter refers to the *sati-paṭṭhānam* method which proceeds in the following manner: "contemplation of the body in the body; of feelings in feelings; of mental states and their contents in mental states and contents;" thus *strictly excluding* all ecstatic transcending in "transmundane" experiences. Without these preconditions all knowledge remains mere *diṭṭhi* (Greek *doxa*), consisting of "views," "opinions" or "beliefs" concerning extrovert ("extensional," *āyatanam*) objectified facts of scientific knowledge-about-the-world (*lokāyatam*). Rationality or irrationality of knowledge have here no more bearing on the criteria of distinction between philosophical and religious knowledge.

In the selecting elements for the classification of religions, with respect to the limits here postulated, careful consideration should be given to the following trends in religious experience:

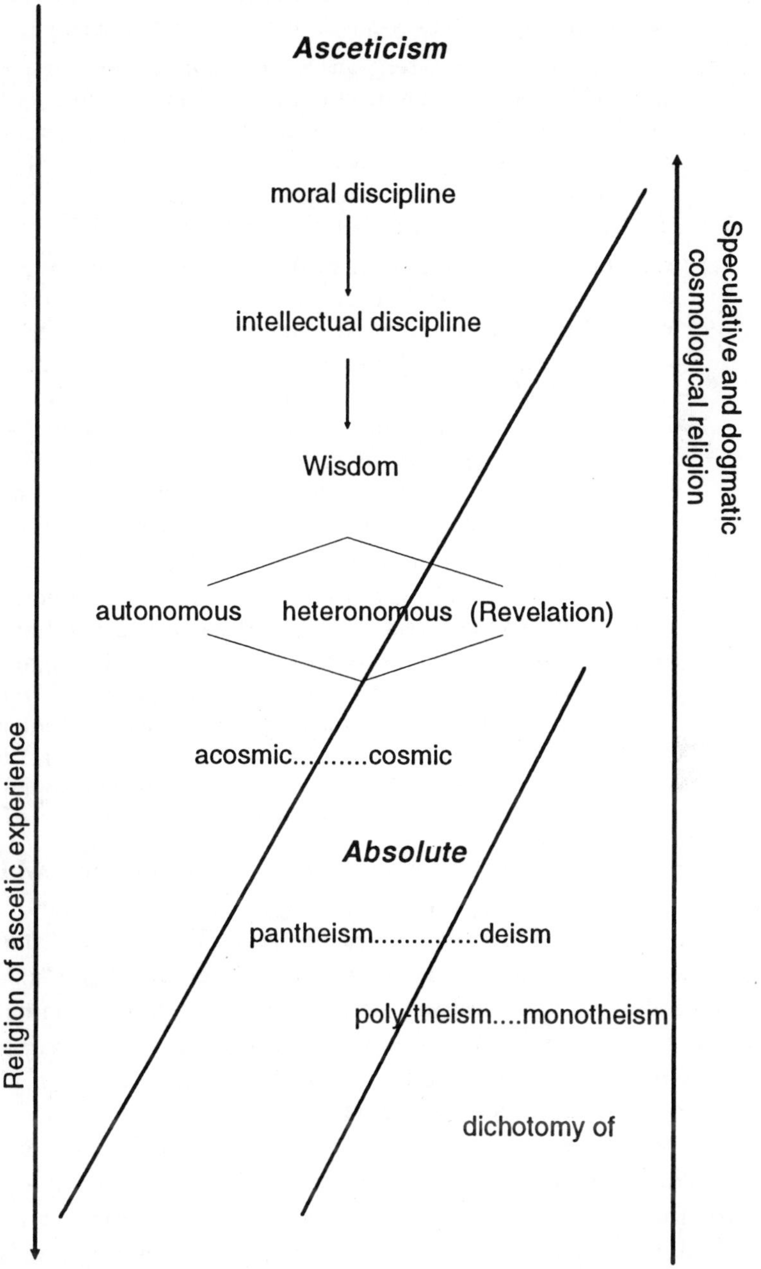
Asceticism
moral discipline
intellectual discipline
Wisdom
autonomous
heteronomous
(Revelation)
acosmic..........cosmic
Absolute
pantheism..............deism
poly-theism....monotheism
dichotomy of
Religion of ascetic experience
Speculative and dogmatic
cosmological religion

(a) The diagonal line may serve to delimit Buddhism from any other type of Indian or European religion. (In this case I would like to leave open the problem of classifying Chinese religions.)

(b) When the definition of religions is elicited from the lowest specific difference, from the dichotomic belief in God and soul, it appears applicable only to the three Biblical religions: Judaism and its offshoots, Christianity and Islam. (In primitive polytheism, as well as in its extant forms found in popular Indian religions, the dichotomy of God and soul is rendered doubtful.)

(c) Even European pantheism, which could be considered in the least as a potential trend of philosophical belief, along with the Indian Vedantic belief in the Absolute as "one without a second" (*advaita*), would obviously remain excluded and "left out in the cold," as Vivekananda put it. Thus the area between the main diagonal and the broken line parallel to it, forms a disputed area for an adequate application of the pseudo-inductive method which starts from the "surreptitious assumption that theism is self-evident" and taking theism as its basic *differentia specifica*.

(d) At the same time we can consider this middle area, less artificially, as a historically given field of transitional formations, mainly between the acosmic and the cosmic trend, resulting, as it seems, from a more or less consequent and explicit recognition of *the ideal of asceticism* as the fundamental phenomenon of religious experience. In the formation of genuine religious mentality cosmic orientation will consequently appear as a "natural" impediment. A permanent dialectical tension in the development of historical religions seems to confirm this estimate.

In the early cryptic stages of Graeco-Roman religions, which arose from oriental backgrounds of magic and mystery cults, the selective principle of *individual religious vocation* was still confirmed. Yet the ascetic discipline had already been replaced during an "axial" epic period by a bond (*"religio"*) whose "yoke" (*yoga*) was originally not less rigorous, but whose ultimate aim had been expanded into epic attainments of magic powers (*siddhi*). (Here *Ramāyāna* and *Mahābhārata* are considered as archetypes of "axial" history.) On the western soil the secularization of the sacerdotal office was a rapid process of emerging from the *decorum* of occult mysteries and abandoning them as unnecessary and even suspect to social morality.

A number of hymns in the extant collection of the *Rig-veda* are clearly marked by a fine irony of intellectual criticism denoting a not less rapid degeneration of the brahmanic religion, down to the immoral conditions exposed by the Buddho in the *Kandaraka-suttaṁ*(our text 13 above). On the other hand, the *ascetic religion* re-emerges first as an immediate social reaction in heterodox mendicant orders (*Sannyāsins*, Buddhist *samaṇā*), and then recedes, always and again, to its primal stability in the hermitic diaspora of "Old Believers" (Pali *thero*, Sanskrit *sthavira*, Russian *starets*), where it continues to survive and to reaffirm itself morally invigorated by hardship and persecution. When approaching the recesses of any hermitic religion, the first ambiguous figure that we may meet is *"le prophete qui crie dans le desert et refuse d'en sortir"* (Camus).

Thus the area between the two lines on our scheme marks the epic "battlefield" (*dharma-kṣetraṁ* in the *Bhagavad-gita*) of the two antagonistic tendencies influencing the formation of religious mentality throughout historical processes.

Chapter Four

Pacceka-buddho and Bodhisattva

Now, what might be considered the actual contents of the *Buddha-dhammo* in authentic Pali terms? This question we can answer only after isolating the superfluous outgrowth of traditional religion. Traditional Buddhism in Sri Lanka was instituted at the time of Asoka. This oldest lineage is considered preserved in the Sinhalese *thera-vādo* heritage in spite of Hinduized offshoots (prevalently of *Vaiṣṇava* origin) which are common in popularized Buddhism.

The emphasis in this chapter is on the limits set by the "negative", non-aggressive, character of the Sinhalese pre-Buddhist magic religion. An emphasis that becomes more obvious when compared with the exuberance of the imported *Mahāyānam* layers from the north eastern expanses of Mongolian Asia. It is worthwhile to remember some early observations of this point which also attracted Schopenhauer's attention. Aboriginal cults still exist in Sri Lanka sharing the island with the "positive" Hinduized culture imported by Asoka. They are the *devala* cults of inferior village godlets who need to be appeased at the telluric source of their magic powers.

> There are a few races who, as it were, prefer the minor key to the major and have, *instead of gods,* merely evil spirits; through sacrifice and prayer these are persuaded not to do harm... Similar races appear to have been the original inhabitants of the Indian peninsula and Ceylon before the introduction of Brahmanism and Buddhism; and even now their descendants are said to have to some extent such a cacodemonological religion, just as do many savage races. Hence springs the Cappuism that is mixed with Sinhalese Buddhism.[55]

Apart from all these historical permutations in the organic development of our *genus* within the *species* of Asian religious life and its culture, there remains the principal task of assessing its essential value and absorbable dosage, in order to establish whether its potential import could strengthen the biological root of Western religious life as well as fill the exhausted sources of Christianity, since both are in urgent need of regeneration.

The origins of *māhayānam* Buddhist religions diverged from the *thera-vādo* tradition by reconstructing the archetypal ideal of *bodhisattvaḥ* as a savior[56]. In the original Pali, the process of a *bodhisatto* throughout long ages was visualized in *historical retrospect* as a process of ripening (*kamma-vipāko*). The purpose of reconstructing such legendary models of "great men" (*mahā-purisā*) in Pali *suttas*[57], or "supermen" (*adhi-puruṣa*) in Brahmanic texts[58] was purely pedagogical.

Already in Buddho's time, the earliest scholastic schematization of the teaching classified the end of a bodhisatto's thorny way of *catharsis* (*visuddhi*), very characteristically, into two karmically accidental possibilities of ramification. The importance of this original dilemma appears to have depended on historical circumstances alone - on ebbs and flows of historical events present in the momentariness of the flux accompanying a bodhisatto's inner detachment in his maturing to buddhahood. The ultimate attainment always remains essentially the same (*akaliko*): independent of the momentary situation in the world, and following its own purely intimate and personal rhythm of inner maturing which always leads to the final detachment - *mokṣa*. It was an event of exclusively introvert *acosmic* importance aiming at his individual extinction (*nibbānaṁ*) which is the *liberation from*, and *not liberation-to* any transcendent or even "extatic" attainment of being, or Being in any absolute or Absolute sense, but on the contrary, it led to annulment (*suññatā*, Sk. *śunyatā*).

A parallelism, karmically accidental and pertaining to this "low world", can be drawn between the Hindu *Brahmā-sahampati* or divine fellow traveller on a world stream, and a *buddho* whose detachment consists of a less conspicuous intimately esoteric introversion of a *muni* a non-preaching silent sage. In Pali he is designated as *pacceka-buddho*; the other being the preaching buddho known and glorified as the supreme *sammā-sambuddho*.

The alternative of preaching a "doctrine" was for a *buddho* the worse karmic finale for reasons psychologically understandable already from the *prima facie* documentation. After his spiritual awakening, one of the first things that Gotamo Buddho became aware of was:

> "When I was staying at Uruvela, near the shore of Neranjara, under the banyan tree of the goatherd, at the first place after my awakening where I went for seclusion, the following thought arose in my mind: 'He lives unhappily who has nothing to venerate and obey. But what recluse or brahman is there under whom I could live, honoring and respecting him?...' Then this thought arose in me: 'But there is this law (*dhammo*) into which I have awakened. Should I live under its rule alone, honoring and respecting it?' " (A.IV,21)

Such was the beginning of the first five weeks of Buddho's meditative hesitation after his awaking[59]. The first seven days he "sat at the root of the Bodhi tree, the tree of awakening, in one session."- "At the end of seven days the Blessed One rose from that absorption and went from the root of the Bodhi tree to the root of the Ajapala-nigrodha, the goatherd's banyan tree... and sat there for seven days in one session, feeling the pleasure of deliverance." After that he spent the third week at the root of the Maculinda tree. Maculindo was the royal Mago serpent who "came out of his realm and wrapped the Blessed One's body seven times in his coils... since on that occasion a great storm arose out of season with seven days of rain, cold winds and gloom." After seven days when Maculindo "saw the sky bright and cloudless again, he unwrapped his coils from the Blessed One's body," and the Buddho gave him the following teaching:

> *Seclusion is happiness for one contented,*
> *By whom the Law is learnt, and who has seen;*
> *And friendliness towards the world is happiness*
> *For him that is forbearing with live creatures.*
> *Disinterest in the world is happiness*
> *For him that has surmounted sense desires.*
> *But to be rid of the conceit 'I am' -*
> *That is the greatest happiness of all.*
>
> *(Udānaṁ II,1)*

The fourth week was spent at the root of the *Rājāyatana*-tree. From there he went in the fifth week back to the Goatherd's *banyan* tree.

"Then, while the Blessed One was alone in retreat this thought arose in him: 'This Law that I have attained to is profound and hard to see, hard to discover; it is the most peaceful and superior goal of all, not attainable by mere rationalization, subtle, for the wise to experience. But this generation relies on attachment, relishes attachment, delights in attachment. It is hard for such a generation to see this truth, that is to say, specific conditionality, dependent arising. And it is hard to see this truth, that is to say, stilling of all formations, relinquishing of the essentials of existence, exhaustion of craving, fading of lust, cessation, *nibbānaṁ*. And if I taught the Law (of *dhammo*), others would not understand me, and that would be wearing and troublesome for me.'

Thereupon there came to him spontaneously these stanzas never heard before:

Enough of teaching of the Law
That even I found hard to reach;
For it will never be perceived
By those that live in lust and hate.
Men died in lust, and whom a cloud
Of darkness laps, will never see
What goes against the stream, is subtle
Deep and hard to see, abstruse.

Considering this, his mind favored inaction and not teaching the Law. Then it occurred to Brahma Sahampati, who became aware in his mind of the thought of the Blessed One's mind: 'The world will be lost, the world will be utterly lost; for the mind of the Perfect One, accomplished and fully awakened, favors inaction and not teaching the Law.'

.... Then Brahma Sahampati appeared before the Blessed One... and said: 'Let the Sublime One teach the Law. There are beings with little dust on their eyes who are wasting through not hearing the Law. Some of them will gain final knowledge of the Law...

-Proclaim the Law; for some,
O Blessed One, will understand."

(M.26, S.VI,1)

Thus enticed by the divine fellow-traveller of an unfortunate world, Buddho agreed to preach a doctrine. But how, and to whom? This was his next crucial question and cause of further delay, which until today has remained unnoticed and overseen by all enthusiastic followers of his "Law." Two of his former meditation teachers, Alaro Kalamo, who taught him about the attainment of nothingness (*ākiñn-caññāyatanaṁ*) and Uddako Ramaputto, who taught him about the attainment of neither-perception-nor-non-perception (the highest level of "formless" *arūpa-jhānaṁ*) had already died.

> Then he thought: 'The bhikkhus of the group of five who attended me while I was engaged in my struggle were very helpful. Suppose I taught the Law first to them?... Where are these bhikkhus living now?'- And with the divine eye, which is purified and surpasses the human, he saw that they were living at Benares in the Deer Park at Isipatanam, the Resort of the Seers."
>
> On his way he met first a wandering ascetic, Upako, who was impressed by Buddho's radiant appearance and asked him:
>
> "Your senses are serene, friend; the color of your skin is clear and bright. Under whom have you gone forth? Who is your teacher? Under whose Law do you confess?"
>
> The answer was:
>
> - *I have overcome all, I am the knower of all,*
> *Unsullied in all ideas, renouncing all*
> *By craving's ceasing freed. And this I owe*
> *To my own wit. To whom should I ascribe it?*
> *I have no teacher, and my like*
> *Exists nowhere in all the world*
> *With all its gods, because I have*
> *No person for my counterpart..."*
>
> When this was said, the wandering ascetic Upako remarked:
>
> - May it be so, friend - and shaking his head,
> he took a side track and departed.

The same happened when he met again the five ascetics, his old friends, at Isipatanam. It was only his outward appearance, characterized by the biological strength of a superman (*adhipuruṣa*) which fascinated them and ultimately broke their resistance. Earlier these five ascetics were waiting on him while he was emaciated by too severe penances. They thought:

- If the monk Gotamo achieves something, he will tell us. But as soon as he ate again the solid food, they were disgusted and left him saying:

- The monk Gotamo has become self-indulgent, he has given up the struggle and reverted to luxury. (*M.36*)

Now, when they saw him coming again in Isipatanam (modern Sarnath, near Benares), they agreed among themselves:

- Friends, here comes the monk Gotamo who became self-indulgent, gave up the struggle and reverted to luxury. We ought not to pay homage to him or receive his bowl and outer robe. Still a seat can be prepared. Let him sit down if he likes. But as soon as the Blessed One approached, they found themselves unable to keep their pact. One went to meet him and took his bowl and outer robe; another prepared a seat; another set out water, footstool and towel..."

On several occasions Schopenhauer commended St. Francis of Assisi by comparing his ways to those of Buddhist asceticism[60]:

"The most famous passages of the Sermon on the Mount state in an indirect manner just what the Buddho directly commands to his followers to do and confirmed by his own example, namely, to cast away everything and become bhikkhus, that is to say mendicants... These precepts afterwards became the foundation of the mendicant order of St. Francis... I say therefore that the spirit of Christian morality is identical with that of Brahmanism and Buddhism."

"... it is noteworthy that the turning of St. Francis from prosperity to a beggar's life is entirely similar to the even greater step of the Buddho Sakya-muni from prince to beggar, and that accordingly the life of St. Francis, as well as the order founded by him, was only a kind of sannyasi existence. In fact, it is worth mentioning that his relationship with the Indian spirit also appears in its great love for animals, and his frequent association with them, when he always calls them his sisters and brothers..."

More important for our context on the dilemma of silent and preaching *buddhos* is the following confession of St. Francis, (according to St. Bonaventura):

"Moreover, prayer purifies the heart and the affections, it unites with the highest and true Good; to virtue it gives vigour and solidity. The preaching, on the contrary, soils with dust the feet of a religious man. It is a dissipating and distracting occupation in the sense that it induces to the relaxation of discipline... Thus preaching compels us to condescend many times to the exigencies of people. In order to live among them, to hear them, the preacher feels fatally induced to think and to speak as they do, that is in a worldly manner... And yet, it seems to me that it must be more agreeable to God if I abandon the restful tranquility of aloneness and go to preach to the crowd."

Buddho did not feel committed to any heteronomous obligation to do anything only because "it must be more agreeable to God." He was always doubtful of the arguments encouraging teaching brought forth by such divine "fellow-travellers" who were committed to that very world from which he looked for an *escape in the acosmic direction.*

"You yourself should make the effort.
The Awakened Ones can only show the way." (*Dhammapadaṁ*276)

In modern terms: A *buddho* should not be mistaken for a tourist guide. A consequence of this autonomous attitude towards "gods-and-men" (*devā-manussā*) was that he always remained ready to give up and abandon the monastic community which had gathered around him. He did so and not only in the famous case of "the quarrel at Kosambi" (supposed to have occurred in the ninth year of his preaching):

Then he went to those bhikkhus and said to them: 'Enough, bhikkhus, no quarrelling, no brawling, no wrangling, no disputing." - When this was said, a certain bhikkhu replied: 'Let the Blessed One, the Master of the Law wait; let the Blessed One live devoted to a pleasant abiding here and now and not concern himself with this..."

- A second time and a third time the Blessed One said the same thing and received the same answer. Then he thought: 'These misguided men seem obsessed. It is impossible to make them see.' He got up and walked away. *(M. 128)*

The most radical expression of his "disgust with the whole world" (*sabba loke anabhirati*) remained sublimated in the poem on "The Rhinoceros" (*Khaggavisāṇa-suttaṁ*, Sn. 35-75;[61] The core of the whole poem is here condensed to its first, middle (21) and last (41) stanzas:

Put aside the rod, and do not harm any living being.
Do not wish a son and still less a friend.
Go alone as the rhinoceros.
....

"I have overcome the sophistry of views,
found the right method, reached the way, attained wisdom.
Nobody is my guide" Realizing this,
go alone as the rhinoceros.
....
People will join and serve you for their own purpose.
Friends who seek nothing are rare today.
Wise in selfish aim, men are dirty.
Go alone as the rhinoceros.

According to the later institutionalized commentaries, this most beautiful poem of ancient Buddhist literature has been vivisected arbitrarily and, bereft of its organic whole, distributed piecemeal into forty-one "sayings" ascribed to various *pacceka-buddhas*, setting each "saying" into some naive hagiography, mainly of mythological "kings of Benares." Once they have attained their *pacceka-bodhi*, they are disposed of by a collective transfer to a specific *bhūmi* ("ground") between heaven and earth, a mythical area called Nandamūlaka-slope of Mount Gandhamādanam "beyond the seven mountains" of the Himalayas, reminding us rather of the heaven of the completely purified souls of Jain *kevalins*. And sometimes the whole poem is still "critically" considered by "modern" scholars as a Jain infiltration (rather than "interpolation") into the early Buddhist canon.

In a careful reconstruction by a conscientious scholar, interested more seriously in this case and its actual value, Dr.Kloppenborg[62], the *pacceka-buddho* "model" appears now, according to its commentarial degradation, as follows:

A *pacceka-buddho* is a "silent sage" or *muni* (as Jain monks are still called today;[63]). Consequently, the only possible way of instructing for them is by *personal example* without intention to be a model for others.

"The way of instructing which is followed by *pacceka-buddhas* is typical for them: most times it is done indirectly by means of an example, a few clever remarks or a gesture, by which a person who is able to understand the deeper meaning of this, is helped to take an object of meditation. In this connection the *pacceka-buddhas'* teaching is called 'by means of body' (*kāyikā*) and not 'by means of words' (*vācikī*)."

This "shortcoming" has been used by some commentators first of all to deduce for the sake of the popular tradition the inferiority of the *pacceka-buddho* ideal in the hierarchical order of institutional religion:

> "...it is clear that even if a *pacceka-buddha* intends to teach, he is thought not to be capable of revealing the essence, i.e. to teach what he thinks is unteachable."

Having taken this dogmatic position, the commentary proceeds to obliterate one by one the specific differences distinguishing the noble silence (*ariyo tuñhībhāvo*) and meditative solitariness (*viveko*) of the ideal *muni*. *Pacceka-buddhas* have to be ordained, instructed by a guru, and even to preach as ordinary socially minded mendicant monks or *loquentes* (in medieval Christian terminology). Their misfortune consists only in having been born in some dark "period in which no *buddho* exists."

Besides all such misfortunes -

> "To find an adequate English equivalent of the term *pacceka-buddha*... is almost impossible... It has the meaning of: 'one who is enlightened by himself, or for himself,' and also of: 'an enlightened one who is single, who is on his own.'"

In the *thera-vādo* Pali tradition the remaining lives of a *bodhisatto* to be lived for the welfare of the suffering humanity is proportional to the purely human and individual progress of a single mind, "striving with diligence" towards the attainment of his own goal, whereas in the later *mahāyānaṁ* cosmical dimensions they were reintegrated into the mission of a *buddho* and still more enhanced in the metaphysical proportions of *bodhisattvas*. The *human* ideal of salvation was replaced by a *cosmical* and even divine conception. *Buddho*, the human being, was transfigured into a divine trinity. Some essentially philosophical implications of this transformation will be worked out in the third part of this book in the section on the mahayanic philosophy dealing with "The Limits of Buddhist Nihilism."

Thus the cosmological turning towards a Divine Plan in the world was reintegrated and at the same time subordinated to the specifically Buddhist aim of ultimate "extinction" (*nirvāṇaṁ*) of Cosmic Life in one particular cycle of world evolution-and-involution. Now there arises for us the critical question: Wherefrom has it been reintroduced in the *mahāyānaṁ* religions and philosophies. On the one hand, initially it came from the readjustment, in a long historical process, in the invigorated brahmanical tradition in India. The historical circumstances must be presumed here as broadly known. On the other hand, in popular *mahāyānaṁ* religions of Central and East Asia, Buddhism was so transformed that the authentic teaching of the historical Buddho Gotamo was progressively covered with heterogeneous layers of exuberant cults of numberless mythological *buddhas* and *bodhisattvas*. Thus there arose a peculiar Buddhist Pantheon populated by creatures overlapping their own Indian origin.

Among the *Mahāyānaṁ*sutras *Vimalakīrti nirdeśa* became the most popular in China. Prof. Paul Demieville, in an appendice on "Vimalakirti en Chine", to the French translation of this text by Etienne Lamotte[24] finds its presentation of "the doctrines of *prajñā-pāramitā* in some respects so close to those of the ancient Taoism...."

We are certainly not less estranged from the *thera-vādo* model of the "golden age" of Asoka's cultural and moral imperialism, older at least by a few centuries, and appearing perhaps so much better, than from a *bodhisattvaḥ* ideal - according to Schopenhauer's pessimistic proposition:

> It almost seems that, as the oldest languages are the most perfect, so too are the oldest religions. If I wished to take the results of my philosophy as the standard of truth, I should have to concede to Buddhism pre-eminence over the others."[65]

Today, one and a half centuries later, to estimate such distances has become so much more inhibitory that we might rather attempt to understand the pressure which the ripening of our personal crises exerts, as well as grasp the deeper meaning of the injunction to get rid of our historically rooted "selves", by facing "the truth that cannot be repeated" (Krishnamurti). From the traditional religions' retrospective point of view, two modern Indian reformers in search of "the reconstruction of religious thought" - one Hinduist, Swami Vivekananda, and one Muslim, Mohammad Iqbal - may help us on this point to readjust, perhaps less forcefully, our attitude to Buddhism, conceived from the outset of our investigation in its *peculiar religious aspect*.

Swami Vivekananda[66]:

> "I reject the Vedas!" is the last word of the Vedanta philosophy... Our fundamental idea is that your doctrine cannot be mine, nor mine yours.

Mohammad Iqbal[67]:

"In Islam prophecy reaches its perfection in discovering the need of its own abolition... (It is) the belief that all personal authority, claiming a supernatural origin, has come to an end in the history of man."

With the help of the last one in any historical lineage of prophets humanity comes of age, at least in its cultural cycle. The same principle is also valid for Jainism which considers itself with sufficient reason, to be the oldest religion on the highest universalist level of *ahiṁsā*, satisfying Schopenhauer's postulate, still extant not only in India but clearly traceable, both in its moral and archeological remainders in and beyond the cultural area of the ancient *Arabia Felix* where it was directly succeeded - and suppressed by the last prophet of another alien lineage, Muhammad.

In Buddhism, a direct offshoot of Jainism, the explicit stress on the postulate of moral and religious autonomy (as we have seen in texts 3-6 of our first chapter) has made superfluous and obsolete the apology for a similar principle. Nevertheless, the lineage of 24 preceding *buddhas* in cosmological world-cycles (*kappa*, Sk. *kalpah*) has been taken over in some mythological texts in very close analogy to that of the 24 Jain *titthagaras* (Sk. *tīrthaṅkarāḥ*). However, on Buddhist lists unlike the Jain ones, future *buddhās* are foreseen (as in some Hinduist traditions).

The *mahāyānaḥayanist* ideal of *bodhisattvaḥ* and its antagonism with the "hinayanist" (i.e. lower, lesser) level of the historical Buddho appears even more polarized today when viewed from a perspective aimed at renewing Buddhism on a broader universal basis - a point of view prevalent in the western world. Here the crucial issue often ends up being a confrontation between a *bodhisattvaḥ* as an ideal against the primeval ideal of the "silent sage" (Jain *muni*), or *pacceka-buddho*, whose archaic emblem is the rhinoceros.

The fatal predicament in the turning of "the second appearance of Buddhism" in its "European form", foretold by Nietzsche as "the catastrophe of nihilism" that "will put an end to all this Buddhist culture"[68], incites us now to reconsider the *pacceka-buddho* alternative as a model, not only of some more or less fictitious neo-Buddhist "sects", but rather as the archetype of the most ancient universal religion still extant in a few varieties between the Near and the Far East.

In this context there arises the following question. What is really relevant for us in the ideal distinction of the noble personality of a *pacceka-buddho*? It is necessary to carefully eliminate all of the common virtues praised by serial clergymen and "high priests of the Buddhist Church" preaching for "the greatest possible happiness of the greatest possible number." Also, we must sift the professional preachers' words through the filter of Lao-tse's criterion: "Who knows does not talk, who talks does not know."

In my attempts to survey the range of this essential notion[69], the following aspects arose as the most conspicuous points toward its attainment:

(1) The classification of various sorts of *buddhās* in and for the rank and file of any institutional religion should be discarded. First of all one should discard the superfluous tendency towards *irrational disintegration* - or "those *dhammo*-teachings which the awakened ones have themselves discovered when establishing the ideal personality of a *pacceka-buddho*. Whereas one should include the disclosure of specific aspects, relevant for each single (*paccattam*) personal and historical situation which a *pacceka-buddho* faces directly and solves thanks to his own experience and ripened wisdom.

The archetypal model of personal perfection "thus transmitted" (*tathāgato*), should not be conceived by us as "irrational", but rather understood from the deeper scholastic background of European religious philosophy. The meaning of "individual universals" is here considered as analogous to the phenomenological analysis of "material values" found in Max Scheler's ethics.[70] With the same intention in mind, we might indicate in our model, the cognizing faculty of "intuition of essence" (*Wesens-Schauung*) in its "material *a priori* contents", granted that "the essence itself... is neither general nor individual" and that it is "just therefore meaningful to speak also of the individual value-essence (*Wertwesen*) of a person."

(2) It would be even less suitable to designate a *pacceka-buddho* as being "exclusively pragmatic", in the style of preachers of various "multipurpose" yoga-methods and "techniques of meditation".[71] In contradistinction to this, the model of *pacceka-buddho* excels in the lucidity of his *paradigmatic rationality*.

(3) The attainment of a *pacceka-buddho* should be understood essentially as a "truth that cannot be repeated" (Krishnamurti), a truth which refers always to "one's own" existential condition, in the meaning which Heidegger gives to the "*Charakter der Jemeinigkeit.*"[72] The rational dimension of each personal existence-situation always points, with archetypal adequacy, to the law which in Indian philosophy is indicated as *karma* and *karma-vipāka*, "the ripening of the fruit."[73]

Such a model implies the unimpaired, rational importance of the method of purposeful exertion of will. It is designated by *buddho* as *sammā-vāyāmo*, the sixth level on "the eightfold path leading to the cessation of suffering". Known as " The Right Effort" [74] it is also the first element of the triad leading to the ultimate state of *samādhi*.

(4) The pedagogical value "for others" (*parārtha* in the theory of syllogism of the later Buddhist epistemological logic)[75] should never be reduced to a superficial "sceptical" attitude against dogmatic "views" (*diṭṭhi*). It is true that *buddho* often designated dogmatic viewpoints and the whole dialectics of the antinomies as "the pursuance of views, adherence to views, vacillation of views,fetter of views." (M.2.Cf. text 15 in Ch. I of this part.) But, at the same time he also excluded (in his first discourse on the four antinomies, D.1, corresponding both in basic terms and in their sequence to the Kantian scheme, in an intermezzo between the first and the second half; cf.n. 38 in the Ch. on Santayana) the attempt of an agnostic evasion of "*samaṇā* and *brāhmaṇā* who wriggle like eels... because they do not realize things as they are; they do not realize what is good and what is bad."

(5) A "bodily" (*kāyikā*) example as the paradigm of the *rational perfection of an ideal personality* should be, as I understand it, the very opposite of those who keep their irrational secret "esoterically" closed "in a clenched fist."[76]

(6) The perfect model of a *pacceka-buddho* which also fits the precepts of the universal *philosophia perennis* (*sanātana-dharma*) is manifested as a personality whose values could not ripen or even subsist on merely "pragmatic" and "irrational" terms, which are far from the genuine insight of pure reason. Kant elucidated such

precepts as "the idea of the perfect man" in his comparison of Plato's rational ideal with the moral ideal of the Stoics[77]:

> "What to us is an ideal was in Plato's view an ideal of the divine understanding... Without soaring so high... the wise man (of the Stoics) is, however an ideal, that is, a man existing in thought only, but in complete conformity with the idea of wisdom. As the idea gives the *rule,* so the ideal in such a case serves as the *archetype* for the complete determination of the copy; and we have no other standard for our actions than the conduct of the divine man within us, with which we compare and judge ourselves, and so reform ourselves, although we can never attain to the perfection thereby prescribed. Although we cannot concede to these ideals objective reality (existence), they are not therefore to be regarded as figments of the brain; they supply reason with a standard which is indispensable to it, as they do, with a concept of that which is entirely complete in its kind, and thereby enabling it to estimate and to measure the degree in the defects of the incomplete..."

It appears that also in our "modern" world the "ripening of fruits" (*phala-samāpatt*) happens on the paths of solitariness and spiritual estrangement. In silencing the "broken gong" of belief in this or in any "better" world - at the ultimate turning toward "extinction without remainder" (*an-upādisesa-nibbānaṁ*) - there remains faintly perceptible and audible echo of "the voice crying from the desert, but refusing to come out of it" (Camus). Sri Ramakrishna expressed it less dramatically one hundred years earlier, on the new year 1883:

> "When the log burns, it makes a crackling noise and one sees the flame. But when the burning is over and only ash remains, then no more noise is heard. Thirst disappears with the destruction of attachment. Finally comes peace."[78]

This can be taken as the measure of all *pacceka-buddhās'* distance from all cosmic and divine worlds and human worldliness.

Chapter Five

Ahiṁsā: The Place of Nonviolence in Buddho's Teaching

Nekkhamma-saṅkappo avyāpāda-saṅkappo
avihiṁsā-saṅkappo,
ayam vuccati bhikkhave sammā-saṅkappo.
Mahā-satipaṭṭhāna-suttantaṃ

(The intention of renunciation the intention free of ill-will,
the intention of nonviolence,
This is called, bhikkhus, the right intention.)

In Pali, *nonviolence* is designated by the term *ahiṁsā*, the same as in Sanskrit, or by *a-vi-hiṁsā*, stronger form of the same stem, as is used in defining the second component of the Eightfold Path Leading to the Cessation of Suffering.

In the short definition quoted above, as in most texts on the Noble Eightfold Path, *ahiṁsā* is the pinnacle of a threefold gradation of the basic virtue known as *the right intention.*

In Jainism, the religion closest to Buddhism, "*ahiṁsā* is the highest law" (*ahiṁsā paramo dharma*). This is the only essential tenet which could be considered its exclusive dogma. All the rest is normative teaching consisting of maxims deduced from this categorical imperative. Exceptions are tolerated since Jainism is a religion of extreme tolerance, defined as "tolerance of many modes of truth":

> "The faith in one truth or even a plurality of truths, each simply given as a determinate, would be rejected by it as a species of intolerance.[79]

Buddho's Eightfold Path starts from the stance taken against "the pursuance of views, adherence to views, jungle of views, contortion of views, vacillation of views, fetter of views." (M.2 and several other texts). This critical prerequisite is the reason why the sifting of world-views (*diṭṭhi*) and dogmatism are placed before *ahiṁsā* as a preliminary step of Buddho's Path.

His "right views" do not consist of any whatsoever dogmatically infallible propositions or beliefs, the likes of which are dismissed in the often repeated warning *against* the affirmation that "this only is true, all the rest is false." The best analysis of the shortcomings of his authoritarian opponents is given in the *Cañki-suttaṁ*(M.95).[80] The basic definition of "right views" (*sammā diṭṭhi*) in our context underscores the purely existential *restriction* of the *problem* referred in the following passage:

> The understanding of suffering, the understanding of the origin of suffering, the understanding of the cessation of suffering, the understanding of the path leading to the cessation of suffering; this bhikkhus, is called the right view." (D.22 and other texts)

Buddho often warned his worldly minded interlocutors (*putthujjanā*) against "untrustworthy teachers" who "take and apply the correct criterion in such a way that, while it extends only to one side it excludes the other... right criteria address good bodily conduct, good verbal conduct, and good mental conduct." Buddho taught the method used for detecting such "unripe criteria" through independent thinking (*apaññaka-suttaṁ*, M.60)[81]. The best known example of such advice is the *Kālāma-suttaṁ* (A II,65) where Buddho gives the following answer to a complaint:

- Some *samaññā* and *brāmaññā*... expound only their own tenets while they abuse and rend and censure and rail at the tenets of others.
- *Kālāmā*, do not be satisfied with hearsay or with tradition or with legendary lore or with what has come down in your scriptures or with conjecture or with logical inference or with weighing evidence or with linking for a view after pondering over it or with someone else's ability or with the thought 'the monk is our teacher'. When you know in yourselves 'these things are wholesome, blameless....then you should practice them and abide in them.

Such was the original teaching of Buddho's Noble Truth on acquiring correct standpoints at a historical epoch of Indian culture which is still considered comparable to the highest standards of Europe, and often referred as an age of "Renaissance".

Swami Vivekananda, in a talk on "Buddha's Message to the World", in San Francisco in 1900, boldly affirmed that in 600 B.C. "the Indian civilization had already completed its growth."[82]

A few decades later the same assessment was confirmed by the well known European sociologist, Max Weber, who considered the atheist and caste free Jain and Buddhist movements of that period as "intellectualist heterodox soteriology" characteristic for the drawing room elitist ideology and the cultural ambience of royal courts and cities.[83]

Historically speaking, the origin of Buddhism can be considered an apostasy of Jainism at the time of Mahaviro's conservative reforms. These were aimed at a purely formalist rigorism. Buddho, on the other hand, in his discussions with and about the Jains underscores a resolute break from their overloaded tradition and the often disgusting commentarial explanations about background stories. In comparison to this, Buddho's criticism of the Brahmins and their traditions takes the form of mild irony, or rebuke aimed at some more or less dangerous stupidity.[84]

However, most of the penances which Buddho practiced before his spiritual awakening in *Uruvelā* (cf. *Ariya-pariyesana-suttaṁ*, M.26) were specifically and peculiarly typical to the Jains:

> "This was my asceticism. I went naked, rejecting conventions,.... not coming when asked, not stopping when asked; I did not accept a thing brought, or a thing specially made, or an invitation; I received nothing from out of a pot, from out of a bowl, across a threshold, across a stick, across a pestle, from two eating together, from a woman with child, from a woman giving suck, from where a woman was lying with a man, from where food was being distributed, from where a dog was waiting, from where flies were buzzing; I accepted no fish or meat, I drank no spirits or wine or fermented liquors. I kept to one house, to one morsel; I kept to two houses, to two morsels;... I kept to seven houses, to seven morsels. I lived on one saucerful, on two saucerfuls. ... on seven saucerfuls a day; I took food once each day, once each two days, ... once each seven days; and so up to one each fortnight, I dwelt pursuing the practice of taking food at stated intervals... I was one who pulled out hair and

beard .... I was one who stood continuously... I was one who squatted continuously.... This was my roughness. Just as the bole of a tinduka tree, accumulating over years, caked in my body and flaked off.... This was my scrupulousness. I was always mindful in stepping to and fro: so much so that I was full of pity even for a drop of water thus, 'Let me not hurt the tiny creatures in the crevices of the ground..."
(M. 12, *Mahā-sīhananda-suttaṁ*)[85]

The similarities of both teachings, Jain and Buddhist, are most strikingly presented in two beautiful poems included in *Sutta-nipāto*: *The Rhinoceros* (*Khaggavisāṇ-suttaṁ*, Sn. 35-75) and *Muni-suttaṁ* (Sn. 207-221), describing according to many Buddhists, rather the ascetic attitude of a Jain *Muni* (silent sage) than the traditional and institutionalized Buddhist "priest".

The most characteristic Pali texts describing Buddho's discussions with and about Jains are:

a. Buddho's witnessing of animosity in the sharpness of their controversies *(vitañḍa-vāda)*.

According to the Jain exegetic work *Niśitha-cūrṇi*[86], "the highest aspiration of a monk was to be bestowed with the title of *Vādian* monk, one who came out successfully in a literary affray where he was to defend his own religion from the active onslaughts of rivals."

The Buddhist commentary on *Therī-gāthā* verses 107-111, attributed to *Bhaddā Kundalakesā*, describes her as a Jain nun who

> *"...travelled in a single cloth,*
> *with hair torn out by the roots, covered in dust,*
> *thinking of faults in the faultless,*
> *while in the faulty seeing no faults...."*

She visited many spiritual teachers, thereby obtaining an excellent knowledge of religious scriptures and philosophies becoming one of the most famous debaters. When she entered a town, *Bhaddā* would make a sand pile and stick a rose-apple branch into it announcing that whoever wished to engage in a discussion with her should trample the sand-pile.

Upāli-suttaṁ (M.56) and *Abhaya-rājakumāra suttaṁ* (M.58) contain some standard phrases attributed to such disparaging challenges and threats of Jaina dialectitians, premeditated to defeat Buddho in sophisticated disputes. As a counter-move from the Buddhist side there is a description of the situation after Mahavire's death among his followers in the *Sāmagāma-suttaṁ* (M.104), as a well as in the *Sangīti-suttaṁ* (D.33). On that occasion "Sariputto addressed the bhikkhus:

- Friends, the *Nigaññho Nāthaputto (Mahāvire)* has just died at Pava. Since his death the *nigaṇṭ* (Jains) have become divided and have fallen into opposite parties and onto strife. Disputes have broken out and they go on wounding each other with wordy weapons...; so badly has their doctrine and discipline been set forth... and now wrecked of his support and without a protector. - But to us, friends, the principles have been well set forth and imparted by the Exalted One..... Herein there should be a chanting by all of us in concord...."

In the same text, where under the guidance of Sariputto the basic tenets of Buddho's teaching were "compiled as catechisms"[87] the teaching of *ahiṁsā* is included in three groups of principles (*dhammā*):

In the group of "double principles" (1,9) *ahiṁsā* and moral purity (*soceyyaṁ*) are praised as two perfect virtues.

In the group of "triple principles" (1,10) belong the "three good thoughts": "thoughts of renunciation, thoughts free of ill-will, and thoughts of no-violence (*avihiṁsā*)".

In the group of twenty-six "fivefold principles", the twenty-fourth set contains "Five elements tending to deliverance (*nissāranaṁ*) from sensous desires, ill-will, cruelty (*vihesā*), external objects (*rūpaṁ* and egotism (*sakkāyaṁ*). The third of these five principles refers to *a-vi-hiṁsā* (*avihesā* in this text):

"When a bhikkhu contemplates violence, his mind does not rush violently into it, nor enjoy it, nor remain seized by it. His mentality is properly directed by him, well developed, *well turned away and detached from violence, he is freed from those destructive, passionate intoxicants (āsavā)* which break out due to violence. He is not affected by such feelings. - This is called the *deliverance from violence.*"

b. Critique of the Jaina doctrine of the unlimited and always present total and absolute knowledge of a *titthagaro* (*Tīrthañkara*), his *kevala-nāñam*, is sometimes exposed with a cynical acerbity[88].

c. Buddho's descriptions of his austerities in meditation (*jhānaṁ*) in (*Mahā-Saccaka-suttaṁ*), when

> "with my teeth clenched and my tongue pressed against the roof of my mouth, I beat down, constrained and *crushed my mind with my mind* .... tireless energy was aroused in me, and unremitting mindfulness established....; *but such painful feelings as arose in me, gained no power over my mind."*

Notwithstanding all such testimony of the same kind of ascetic penances as described often in terms *identical* to the practices of the Jain *Munis*, Buddho's renunciation even to this ultimate extreme of ascetic effort *immediately before he attained his final liberation in awakening*, is today more than ever understood and explained away as an episode of exclusively negative and even misleading Jain influence on *samaṇo* Gotamo who, before he became a *buddho*, had to break through and liberate himself from this last "error" after all the "eons" of strenuous endeavors to attain his ultimate perfection.

But Buddho himself explicitly denied the tendency of such erroneous explanations in the classic description of this final event of his awakening:

> "Then the future Buddho turned his back to the trunk of the Bodhi-tree and faced the east. And making the mighty resolution: - Let my skin, and sinews, and bones become dry, and let all the flesh and blood in my body dry up, but never from this seat shall I stir until I have attained the supreme and absolute wisdom! - he sat down cross-legged in an unconquerable position, from which not even the descent of a hundred thunderbolts at once could have dislodged him."[89]

It appears obvious from several other texts of a less hagiographic character, describing actual and directly reported experiences of Buddho's ascetic heroism up to the utmost limits of self mortification, that the result of his attainment of unshakable control of mind and wakeful alertness was in *strict proportion*, up to the last moment of his struggle, to the climax of such extreme efforts, - and not simply a simple result of the presumed realization of his worst "mistake" committed at the last moment. This he explicitly admitted and underscored as being the essential pre-requisite in the discourses on braving "the fears and terrors" of forest-life in *Bhaya-bherava-suttaṁ* (M.4):

> "Suppose some ascetic or brahman is unpurified in bodily, verbal or mental conduct... is subject to fright and horror... unconcentrated and confused in mind, devoid of understanding.... When such an ascetic or brahman resorts to a remote jungle-thicket abode in the forest, then owing to those faults he evokes unwholesome fear and dread. But ... I have none of these defects. I resort to a remote jungle-thicket as one of the *Noble Ones,* who are free from these defects. Seeing in myself this freedom from such defects, I find great solace in living in the forest.... I thought: But there are the specially holy nights ... Suppose I spent those nights in such an awe-inspiring abode ... which make the hair stand up - perhaps I should encounter that fear and dread. And later, I thought: Why do I dwell in constant expectation of the fear and dread? Why not subdue that fear and dread while maintaining the posture I am in when it comes to me? - And while I walked... sat .. lay ..., the fear and dread came upon me; but I neither stood nor sat ... till I subdued the dread."

In the archaic poem ascribed to Buddho, on the symbol of the rhinoceros, the first, the middle(21) and the last (41) *gāthās* form the essential knots on which the whole texture is harmoniously woven. The pinnacle is the central statement:

> *Escaped from the exhibition of views,*
> *arrived to the clearing, take the straight way:*
> *"I have attained the wisdom not guided by others."*
> *- Go alone as the rhinoceros. (Sn.55)*

Without having reached this point of clear orientation at the *end* of the thorny and tortious pathless passage through the "jungle of views" and misleading opinions, one will necessarily be lost in the vicious circle of eternal reproduction and renewal of interdependent causes and intricate relations of *paṭicca-samuppādo;* torn by all the currents of the stream of samsaro, unable to swim across and ultimately, stranded: "pine away like old cranes in a lake without fish." (Dhp.155) Even a casual visit to a Buddho and a talk with him will remain useless and annoying - as described in the classic case of Malunkyaputto (M.63), or, recently, in the well-known and romantic "model" skillfully shaped by Herman Hesse in the *bodhisattva* ideal of his *Siddhartha*.

Texts:

1. Upāli-Suttaṁ

In Buddho's discourses on the subject of *ahiṁsā* with Jain *nigañtā*, followers of his opponent Mahaviro, the most conspicuous topic was "the modes of action in doing evil deeds, namely: action of body, word and mind" (analyzed most extensively in the *Upāli-suttaṁ*, M.56).

Diga-Tapassi, the naked ascetic, follower of Niganṭho Nataputto, the Mahaviro, visited on one occasion Buddho in Nalanda and Buddho asked him:

- Well, Tapassi, how many modes of action does Nigagantho Nataputto declare there are in evil acting and behaving?
- No, friend Gotamo; the performed action is not declared by Nigantho Nataputto to be an action, it is declared to be an offence.
- Well, Tapassi, how many modes of offence does he declare there are in evil acting and behaving?
- .... offence of body, of word, and of mind... Of these three offenses ... bodily offence is the most blameable. Verbal offence and mental offence are not so blameable.

But according to Buddho, on the contrary,

- of these three actions (*kammāni*), thus analyzed and differentiated, mental action, I declare, is the most blameable. Bodily action and verbal action are not so blameable....

When on a later occasion another follower of Mahaviro, Upali, insisted again on the same standpoint as Tapassi, Buddho asked him:

- what do you think, householder? Suppose there were a naked ascetic with four kinds of restraint; restrained as regards all evil .... He, while walking up and down, inflicts destruction upon many tiny creatures. Now, what does Nigantho Nataputto declare is the result of this?
- He declares that what is unintentional is not blameable....
- And in which offence does Nataputto recognize intention?

- In mental offence.
- Householder, householder, think carefully before you reply. This latter does not agree with your former statement that bodily offence is the most blameable, and not so the mental and the verbal offenses...

In my own attempts to verify this statement on the gradation of evil deeds in Jaina scriptures or oral tradition I have never come across any confirmation of the sequence insisted upon by Digha-Tapassi in the above quoted text which is often repeated in other Buddhist references. The sequence confirmed in the subsequent Jaina tradition is always identical to the Buddhist one: mind-word-body, and there is no mention of its discutability at any time. As this was a time of deep religious reforms in several Jaina communities, we should not exclude the possibility that such discussions with Buddho and his followers might have influenced the Jaina reformers - a problem that may be worth further investigation in comparative studies of these two closely related and therefore historically antagonistic religions of *ahiṁsā*.

In the Jaina *Ayaranga-suyaṃ*[90], its first book, *Bambha-ceräiṃ* (3,4,3), dealing with the training in ascetic discipline *(brahma-caryā)*, concludes:

"There are degrees in injurious act, but there are no degrees in nonviolence." - indicating, in its context, a deeper approach to the whole problem taken from the standpoint of the vicious circle of morally reprehensible effects.

2. The Dhammapadaṁ

is the most popular collection of aphoristic verses attributed to Buddho, some of which have been culled out of his more extensive discourses. Like the *Jātaka* tales, some of these verses convey archetypal symbols and meanings of ancient Indian wisdom placed in a Buddhist context. In Jainism the *Uttarajjhayaṇa suyaṁ*(Sk.*Uttarādhyayana-sūtraṁ*) in its thirty-six chapters comes closest to the *genre* of both the twenty-six chapters of the *Dhammapadaṁ* and the more extensive collection of 1149 stanzas, interwoven with tales and dialogues in the *Sutta-nipāto*. Some of these verses, sometimes in chapters under analogous headings in both the *Dhammapadaṁ* and the *Uttarajjhayaṇa-suyaṁ*, correspond to each other not only in analogous but also in homologous sequences of several stanzas. The following selection following selection from the *Dhammadapaṁ* can serve as an illustration of this analogy. It is the eighth chapter, known as "The Thousands" (*Sahassa vaggo*). The following stanzas correspond closely to the same style and contents of utterances ascribed to king Nami, a *Patteya-buddha (Pāli: Pacceka-buddho)* of Jaina tradition, after his *pavajjā (Pāli: pabbajja*, 'escapefrom the world) at the beginning of the ninth chapter of the *Uttarajjhayaṇa-suyaṁ*:

Dhammapada	**Uttarajjhayaṇa**
If a man were to conquer a thousand times a thousand men and another conquer himself. he indeed is the greatest of conquerors.	Though a man were to conquer in battle thousands and thousands of enemies, greater will be his victory, if he conquers only himself
Conquest of self is indeed better than the conquest of other persons; one who has disciplined himself who always practices self-control. (103-104)	Fight with yourself; why fight with other enemies? He who conquers himself through himself, will obtain happiness. (34-35)
If a man month after month for a hundred years should sacrifice a thousand offerings and if he only for one moment would honor a man with a developed self, that honor is, indeed better than a century of sacrifice. (106)	If a man should offer every month thousands and thousands of cows, better will be he who controls himself, though gives no offering. (40)
Let a fool month after month eat his food with a kusa grass blade; nevertheless he is not worth the sixteenth part of those who have well understood the Truth (Dhammaṁ). (70)	If a fool should eat with a kusa grass blade, the merit of his penance will not be equal the sixteenth part of his who possesses the Truth as it has been taught. (44)

The last, XXVI, chapter of the Dhammapadaṁ, Brāhmaṇa-vaggo, contains a sequence of stanzas ending with the refrain: " him I call a brāhmaṇa" (tam ahaṃ brūmi brāhmaṇam). In the XXV chapter of Uttarajjhayaṇa-suya*ṁ* a sequence of sixteen stanzas (19-34) end with the refrain : Him we call brāhmaṇa". The following few samples are characteristic for the analogy:

Him I call a brahman who does not hurt by body, speech or mind who is controlled in these three things. (391)

Him I call a brahman who has laid aside the rod with regard to beings, whether weak or strong, who neither kills nor lets others kill. (405)

Him we call brahman who thoroughly knows living beings, whether they move or not, and does not injure them in any of the three ways (by thoughts, words, and acts). (23)

Independently of such implications, the word *ahiṁsā* occurs in the following aphorisms of the *Dhammapadaṁ*:

The silent sages abstaining from violence (*ahiṁsakā*),
Always restrained in body, go to the state
from which they never relapse,
whither gone they never grieve. (225)

He in whom dwell truth, virtue, nonviolence, restraint, control, he who is free from impurity and is wise, he is called and elder (*thero*). (261)

A man is not noble because he harms (*hiṁsati*) living beings.
He is called noble because he does not harm any living being. (270)
The disciples of Gotamo are always well awake;their mind, day and night, delights in abstinence from harm (*ahiṁsā*). (300)

3. Lakkhaṇa-suttaṁ

In *Dīgha-nikāyo* the following references are worth singling out: In *Lakkhaṇa-suttantaṁ* (D.XXX,1,6), on the "marks of the great man" (*mahā-purisa-lakkhaṇāni*), the first section of verses praising the virtues of a *buddho* states:

Harming no living being (pāṇe ahiṁsāya), not violent,
delighting in almsgiving, with no violence (ahiṁsā),
shunning force, consequent in principles,
wholehearted in action, he always proceeds impartially...

In the second part of the same discourse (D.XXX,2,7) it is said that

"in whatsoever former birth, former state of being, former sojourning, such a man (*tathāgato*), as a human being acquired the virtue of not harming any living being, either by hand or clod or rod or sword, he by doing and by accumulating of that *kamma,* by its fulfillment and abundance, after his death was reborn happily in a heavenly world."

4. Brāhmaṇa-saṁyuttam

In *Saṁyutta-nikāyo,* VII (*Brāhmaṇa-saṁyuttaṁ,* the title of the fifth discourse is *Ahiṁsa-suttaṁ*:

> "The brahman Bharadvajo, dedicated to nonviolence (*ahiṁsako*) visited the Blessed One ... and said:
>
> - I am dedicated to nonviolence, friend Gotamo, I am dedicated to nonviolence.
>
> Buddho's answer was:
>
> - In accordance with your name, may you be nonviolent! He who does not commit violence either by body, or by word, or by mind is nonviolent; he does not hurt any other being."

5. Itivuttakaṁ

Itivuttakaṁ (IV,8), describes three bad (*akusalā*) and three opposite, or good, thoughts (*kusala-vitakkā*). This group is the same as the previous quote in D.XXXII, in section 3. The context in the *Itivutakkaṁ* is as follows:

> Three virtuous kinds of thought do not cause blindness, but sight, knowledge, strength of wisdom. They are not on the side of destruction, but leading to extinction (*nibbānam*). These three thoughts are the thought of renunciation, the thought of goodwill, and the thought of nonviolence (*avihiṁsā vitakko*).
>
> *"Three virtuous thoughts should be pondered over,*
> *and three unvirtous thoughts should be avoided.*
> *Who in this way is able to appease his grasping and*
> *eliciting thought,*
> *even so will reach the state of appeasement."*

6. Sutta-nipāto

In *Sutta-nipāto,* chapter II, the seventh section contains Buddho's sermon to the brahmans from Kosala who wished to know better the traditional way of righteous living as it was followed by brahmans (*brāmaṇa-dhammikā*) at the time of "rishis of old, austere, restrained of self". Their virtue of *ahiṁsā* is praised in stanza 292:

> "They praised chastity and virtue and righteousness, ascetic ardor, gentleness, nonviolence and forbearance."

7. Jātaka tales.

Some *Jātaka* tales were also motivated by the same virtue and intention to illustrate the application of *ahiṁsā* to daily life. The most poetic text on the subject is the *Cakkavakā - jātakaṁ* (451), or the fable of the "ruddy goose" in its didactic dialogue with the crow[91]:

The Crow:

Fine colored art thou, fair in form, stout and ruddy,
O goose, thou art beautiful, thy face and senses are clear!
Sitting on the bank of the Ganga thou feedest for sure on pike and bream and dark fish swimming around the reed.

The Ruddy Goose:

I do not eat anything that lives in the jungle or water.
Friend, my food is only that what does not contain animal life.

The Crow:

I cannot believe that this is food of the ruddy goose
While I eat in the village food seasoned with salt and oil,
And yet my color, O ruddy goose, cannot be compared with yours.

The Ruddy Goose:

Realizing the connate hatred and violence in human nature,
You eat your food in fear and fright; therefore your color is such.
You have erred in all the world by sinful deeds,
you have pleasure in no bit of food, therefore your color is such.
But I, friend, eat without hurting any living being;
I have little to trouble and no regret with nothing to fear from anywhere.
Thus you should do and thrive and renounce your evil ways.
Live in the world without violence and be as friendly as I am.
He who neither kills nor incites slaughter,

Who neither conquers nor incites conquest of power,
But extends his love to all beings - he has no reason for hate.

The last three verses are repeated also in *Iti-vuttakaṁ* I,3,7. The first of them -

yo na hanti na ghāteti

- translated here with "He who neither kills nor incites slaughter", is repeated in other texts as the definition of *ahiṁsā*. Radhakrishnan translated it in the same terms in the *Dhammapadaṁ*

"Likening others to oneself, one should neither slay, nor cause to slay." (Dhp.129)

"Him I call a Brahmin who lays aside the rod with regard to creatures, moving or unmoving, and neither kills nor causes (their) death." (Dhp.405)

8. Milinda-pañho

In *Milinda-pañho*, "The Questions of King Milinda", VII,5,10[92] the Buddhist sage *Nāgaseno* mentions the *Cakkavāka-jātakaṁ* to his Greek interlocutor the Indo-Greek king Menandros:

"And again, O king, as the Cakkavaka bird does no harm to living beings; just so, O king, should the strenuous follower of yoga, earnest in effort, laying aside the rod, laying aside the sword, be full of modesty and pity, compassionate and kind to all living beings. For it was said in the *Cakkavāka jātakam* tale:

- He who neither kills nor incites slaughter,
Who neither conquers nor incites conquest of power,
Is not violent (ahiṁsā) to any living being,
he has no reason for hate.

Notes to part I

1. Quotations of Pali texts have been adapted prevalently from the Pali Text Society Translations Series (London). For the *Majjhima-nikāyo* the unpublished translation by the late Nanamoli (Island Hermitage, Ceylon) has often been consulted. For the collections of texts conventional abbreviations are used. (A for *Aṅguttara-nikāyo*; Dhp. for *Dhammapadaṁ*; D. for *Digha-nikāyo*; M. for *Majjhima Nikāyo*; S. for *Samyutta-nikāyo*.)

2. An astonishingly close analogy between the formulation of the four antinomies of the dialectical reason by Kant and the same basic structure of the four groups of 'views(*diṭṭi*, cf. *doxa*) in the *Brahma-jāla suttaṁ*(D. 1) has been singled out in my papers: *Dependence of punar-bhava on karma in Buddhist philosophy*, and *My Approach to Indian Philosophy*, in *Indian Philosophical Annuals*, Vols. I and II (1965,1966, University of Madras, under my lay name Chedomil Veljachich).

3. A parallel on this point is elicited in brief in my essay on *Aniccam*, Buddhist Publication Society, Kandy, Sri Lanka, 1973.

4. "We therefore compare all the dogmatists to people who imagine that, if only they go straight forward long enough, they will come to the end of the world, but Kant had then circumnavigated the globe, and has shown that, because it is round, we cannot get out of it by horizontal movement, but that by perpendicular movement it is perhaps not impossible to do so. It can also be said that Kant's teaching gives the insight that the beginning and the end of the world are to be sought not without us, but rather within." *The World as Will and Representation*, transl. by E.F.J. Payne, Dover Publications, New York, 1966; vol.I, pp.420-1. Cf. My book, *Schopenhauer and Buddhism*, pp. 84-87, Buddhist Publication Society, Kandy, Sri Lanka, 1970.

5. Practices singled out in our condensation of the above text are those most prominently characteristic to the Jain *munis*.

6. *The Complete Works of Swami Vivekananda*, vol. VII, P.199. (ED. Advaita Ashrama, Calcutta, 3rd ed.1959)

7. Cf. *Parerga und Paralipomena*, vol.II (P. Deussen's ed. *Arthur Schopenhauer's Samtliche Werke*, Munchen, 1913), p. 422, Section 181, and *Uber den Satz vom Grunde* (2nd. ed., Deussen, pp.233,237). Compare also my book, *Schopenhauer and Buddhism* pp.11ff, 22, 31-33.

8. The following references are from the edition of the *Gifford Lectures on Natural Religion,* delivered at Edinburgh in 1901-2, New York, The Modern Library, 1936, p.503 n.2
9. Cf. ref. in *Classic American Philosophers,* N.Y., Appleton-Century Crofts, 1951, p.163-4
10. Cf. op. cit. pp.160, 155, 161, 163n.
11. Cf. Gifford Lectures, pp. 32,34.
12. *Swami Vivekananda Centenary Memorial Volume,* Calcutta 1963, p.527.
13. *The Creative Mind* by H.Bergson, transl. by M.L. Andison, N.Y., Philosophical Library, 1946, p.248
14. *"The Perception of Change"* in Bergson's Oxford lectures, op. cit. p.173. Cf. in my essay "Karma - the Ripening Fruit" (in *Kamma and its Fruit,* Kandy, P.B.S., 1975) Chapter II, on Bergson, pp. 27-40
15. *The Creative Mind,* p.224
16. *Creative Evolution,* translated by A. Mitchell, N.Y., The Modern Library, 1944. p.227f.
17. Quoted in the sequel to the English translation by R. Ashley Audra and C. Brereton, N.Y., H. Holt Co., 1946
18. Since the first edition of the English translation of *The Gospel of Sri Ramakrishna* by the Sri Ramakrishna Math in Madras, 1944, detailed first hand documentation on this period of his life gives not only broader, but also essentially different picture of his relations with the extreme pro Christian fraction of the Brahmo-Samaj and the miniature importance of its leader Kashab Chandra Sen, enlarged in Rolland's imagination beyond any conceivable possibility of a realistic assessment of the cultural and political situation in Bengal at that time (about 1875). Notwithstanding such inaccuracies, still possible and pardonable in 1928, the Ramakhrishna Mission in its reprints of Rolland*Life of Ramakrishna* is still limiting its reserve concerning "the author's views and interpretations" which "have to agree in *toto* with those of the Ramakhrishna order" to a note at the end of the book on just this particular subject, supported by numerous bibliographical data of first hand documentation, on "Sri Ramakhrishna and Keshab Chandra Sen" (a consumptive devotee who died before Ramakhrishna, repentant and reconciled with him).
19. See on this subject my paper "The Philosophy of Disgust - Buddho and Nietzsche" in *"58. Schopenhauer-Jahrbuch, 1977",* Verlag W. Kramer, Frankfurt/M.
20. The following quotations are from *Classic American Philosophers,* N.Y., Appleton-Century-Crofts, 1951. *Modes of Thought* (1938), p.437.

21. *Process and Reality*, op. cit. p.400.

22. Macmillan 1926. Op. cit. p.452 f.

23. London, Watts, The New Thinker's Library, 1967, pp.47.

24. Cf. the chapter on "Buddhism and Modern Philosophies of Existence" the III. part of this book (published earlier in *Buddhism and Western Philosophy*, edited by Nathan Katz, New Delhi, Sterling, 1981)

25. Cf. my essay "*Aniccam* - The Buddhist Theory of Impermanence" in the *Basic* Facts of Existence, I. Impermanence. Kandy, B.P.S., 1973

26. Cf. a more extensive selection in my essay quoted in note 19 above.

27. G. Santayana, *Scepticism and Animal Faith*, quoted from Dover Publications, N.Y. 1955. Underlinings are partly mine.

28. See on this subject the chapter on "The Indian Origin of Pyrrho's *Epoché*" in Part II of this book.

29. Cf. the first chapter of my forthcoming book "The Ethos of Knowledge in European and Indian Philosophies", dealing with the Stoic heritage in Kant's moral philosophy.

30. In *The Creative Mind* English transl. Philosophical Library, N.Y. 1946. p. 224.

31. R. Malter, *Schopenhauer Verstandis der Theologie Martin Luthers*, "63. Schopenhauer-Jahrbuch", 1982, pp. 39, 38. This study refers also to a rich bibliography of earlier studies on the same subject, since Schopenhauer's life-time till today.

32. In Schopenhauer-literature this problem has been singled out specifically in two articles by the second president of the Schopenhauer Gesellschaft, Hans Zint: "Schopenhauers Philosophie des doppelten Bewusstseins", and "Das Religiose bei Schopenhauer", 14. and 17. Schopenhauer-Jahrbuch,1921 and 1930.

33. Cf. *The World as Will and Representation*, Vol.I, Sect. 68; p. 393 f.. in E.F.J. Payne's transl., Clarendon Press, Oxford 1974.

34. Cf. my article "Aniccam - The Buddhist Theory of Impermanence" in *The Basic Facts of Existence I*, B.P.S., Kandy 1973.

35. Nietzsche, in the *Genealogy of Morals* (II,24) uses both terms, Skeptics and Ephektics, as derivatives from the same Greek verb *ephein*, to refrain from.

36. *L'etre et le neant*, Paris, Gallimard, NRF, 1943, pp. 708,97. For the essentially mutual relation of the spontaneous feeling of compassion (*karuna*)

and the insight in nothingness according to the Buddhist authors (mainly from Tibetan sources) see Part II, ii,2, of this book.

37. Cf. my article "The Philosophy of Disgust - Buddhho and Nietzsche" in *58. Schopenhauer-Jahrbuch*, 1977, p.118, and the context on pp.120-1, concerning Nietzsche's wider critical attitude to the Buddhist nihilism and its relevance.

38. The *Brahma-jala-suttaṁ*, the first of the long discourses in *Digha-nikayo*, Buddho discusses extensively theories corresponding, also in their sequel, to the four antinomies (concerning the endlessness of the world in time and space) and the second two (concerning causality and the problem of God and soul) - Buddho has interpolated and *intermezzo* excluding the agnostic alternative:

    "There are *samana* and *brahmana* who wriggle like eels... who resort to equivocation... because they do not realize things as they are, they do not realize what is good and what is bad."

39. Cf. Nagarjuna's caution against the misunderstanding of his theory of nothingness in such an agnostic way:

    "Annulment (*śunyatā*) of all (world-) views is postulated by the Victorious Ones (*buddhas*) as the way to release. Incurable indeed are those who take *sunyata* itself as a view." (Madhyamaka *kārikā* XIII, 8)

40. Max Scheler, *Der Formalismus in der Ethik und die Materiale Wertethik.* (4th ed. Bern, Francke, 1954) p.358.

41. Quoted from Kant's *Critique of Practical Reason and other Works on the Theory of Ethics*, transl. by Th.K. Abbot. London, Longman's, 1923. p. 258 (Rosenkranz edition). Cf. my book *The Ethos of Knowledge in European and Indian Philosophies*, Part I, Theses 1 and 3, texts corresponding to footnotes 5 and 36.

42. *Man in the Modern Age*. London 1959, p.142.

43. *The Great Philosophers*, London 1962, pp. 313, 311.

44. Op. cit., pp. 316, 279, 317, 316, 321.

45. Id. 351.

46. Id. 216.

47. Id. 45.

48. E. Husserl, Ideas: *General Introduction to Pure Phenomenology*, English transl. by W.R. Boyce Gibson, New York, Macmillan, 1931, pp.41-43.

49. *The Great Philosophers*, p. 36.

50. *The World as Will and Representation*, vol. I, 68 (Payne's transl. p.390)

51. Cf. Husserl. Ideen, vol. II, Haag, Nijhoff, 1952, p. 105.

52. The protest against imposing imperatives of social subserviency to religion is becoming more and more acute as an issue of central importance also in the actual crisis of Christian dogmatism. Paul Tillich, in his book *The Eternal Now* (London, 1963) formulates this question in a sermon on St. Paul's Epistle, "Do not be conformed", and also with reference to the saying of Jesus, "I have come to set a man against his father...", as follows: "Why does Paul attack conformism? Why does he not call the Christian the perfectly adjusted man?... His thought is far from this, and certainly he could not have been called a good educator according to the criterion of 'adjustment'.... Every Christian must be strong enough to risk non-conformity, even in the radical sense that Jesus describes with respect to one's family..." (pp. 115ff, 144)

53. Cf. my forthcoming book *The Ethos of Knowledge in European and Indian Philosophies.*

54. See my article on "Buddhismus: Religion oder Philosophie in *60. Schopenhauer-Jahrbuch 1979.*

55. Schopenhauer, *Parerga and Paralipomena,* vol. I, 13, p. 118 in Payne's translation (Oxford, Clarendon Press, 1974).

56. See on this subject Har Dayal, *The Bodhisattva Doctrine in Buddhist Sanskrit Literature,* London, Kegan Paul, 1932; and, on the Bodhisatta tradition in *Thera-vā* (Pali) Buddhism, Narada Thera, *The Bodhisatta Ideal,* Colombo, Vajirarama, 1963.

57. Cf. *Dīgha-nikayo,* discourse 30.

58. *Mīmāṁsa-sūtraṁ,* VI,2, 16.

59. The following account is based on texts referring to it in Bhikkhu Nanamoli's *The Life of the Buddha,* Kandy, B.P.S 1972, pp.30-40 (HC. II, "After the Enlightenment")

60. *The World as Will and Representation,* Vol. II, CH. XLVII, pp. 633 and 614 in Payne's transl. Also see my *Studies in Comparative Philosophy,* Vol.I, Colombo, Lake House, 1982.

61. A more extensive selection is included at the end of my study *The Philosophy of Disgust - Nietzsche and Buddho,* In *Studies in Comparative Philosophy* I. For a complete translation Cf. E. M. Hare, *Woven Cadences of Early Buddhists,* in *The Sacred Books of the Buddhists,* Vol. XV, Oxford University Press 1947. A scholarly translation including commentarial literature is contained in the dissertation of M.A.G. T. Kloppenborg, *The Paccekabuddha, A Buddhist Ascetic, Leiden, Brill, 1974.*

62. Op. cit. The following quotations are from pp.77-78

63. In Jainism the rhinoceros was the emblem of the 11th *Tīrthankara Sreyāmsa.* The virtue of 'going alone as the rhinoceros(*khaggavisāṇaṃ va ekacce*) is praised also in the biography of *Mahāvirah* in *Kappa-suttaṁ* 118, and as a characteristic of a *muni* in general in *Suyyagada-suttaṁ*, II,2,70.

64. *L'Enseignement de Vimalakirti (Vimalakirtinirdesa), traduit et annoté par Etienne Lamotte. Biblioteque de Muséon, vol.51. Louvain, Publications Universitaires*, 1962. pp. 438-440.

65. WWR II, ch. XVII, p.169 in Payne's trans.

66. *The Complete Works of Swami Vivekananda,* Advaita Ashrama, Calcutta, 3rd. ed. 1959, Vol. VIII, p.254-5, "The Essence of Religion" (report of a lecture delivered in America).

67. *The Reconstruction of Religious Thought in Islam,* Lahore 1954, p.126-7

68. *The Will to Power,* Section 55.

69. See my articles "Buddhismus - Religion oder Philosophie?" in *60. Schopenhauer-Jahrbuch 1979* and "New Approaches to Buddhism - the Hard Way" in *Pali Buddhist Review,* London, Vol. 5, No. 3, 1980. (Pp.69-73)

70. The following quotation is from *Der Formalismus in der Ethik und die Materiale Wertethik,* Zweiter Teil, VI, B.2. P.494 in 4th ed., Bern 1954.

71. To this extent at least I agree with J. Krishnamurti's attitude: *Meditations* (Madras 1980, pp.6 and 45): " Meditation is hard work. It demands the highest form of discipline - not conformity, not imitation, not obedience - but a discipline which comes through constant awareness, not only of things about you outwardly, but also inwardly.... Without laying the foundation of a righteous life, meditation becomes an escape and therefore has no value whatsoever... to observe in such a way is a discipline, and that kind of discipline is fluid, free, not the discipline of conformity."

72. *Sein und Zeit,* Section 9. p.42 in 7th ed., 1953.

73. This problem and its analogy with the category designated under the same term "the ripening of fruit" by H. Bergson and M. Heidegger is the topic of my paper "Karma - The ripening Fruit" in the symposium *Kamma and its Fruit,* Kandy, B. P. S. 1975.

74. Cf. Krishnamurti, op.cit. pp.9 and 62: "This meditation cannot be learned from another... It is for you to learn all this by looking at yourself - no book, no teacher can teach you about this... But for that, there must be no fragmentation and therefore immense stability, swiftness, mobility."

75. Cf. Th. Stcherbatsky, *Buddhist Logic,* Vol. 2, pp. 101 and 11, ref. to *Dharmakīrti, Nyāya-bindu,* Ch. II, 45 (37, 15) and ch. III, 1 (41.3).

76. D. XVI, *Mahāyānaāa-parinibbana-suttaṁ*, ch. II, 25.

77. *Critique of Pure Reason* (transl. by N. Kemp Smith, London, Macmillan, 1950). A 568-569, B. 596-597.

78. *The Gospel of Sri Ramakrishna*, Madras, Mylapore, 1964, (4th ed.) p. 111.

79. Cf. K.C. Bhattacharyya, "The Jaina Theory of Anekanta", in his *Studies in Philosophy*, Vol. I, Calcutta, Progressive Publishers, 1956. 30, p.343.

80. Cf. Part I of this book, 1, text (6).

81. Cf. Part I of this book, text (12)

82. *The Complete Works of Swami Vivekananda*, Third edition, Calcutta, 1959, Vol. VIII, p. 92.

83. Max Weber, *Gesammelte Aufsatze zur Religionssoziologie*, II. Band, *Hinduismus und Buddhismus*. Tubingen 1921. pp.170-250. (Cf. a recent English translation.)

84. Characteristic for Buddho's ironical rebuke of brahmans are among other: M. 51, *Kandaraka-suttaṁ*, on the four types of men (the first, "torturer of himself" is the Jain ascetic, the third, "torturer of both himself and others" is the brahman performing sacrifices for a king and the king himself (cf. text (13) in PArt I above); D. 31, *Sigalovada suttaṁ* (the stupidity of literal understanding of ritualistic texts); D.4. *Sonadanda-suttaṁ* (on self-conceit of a mighty brahman); and on the whole last chapter, XXIV, of *Dhammapadam*, *Brahmana vaggo*.

85. The corresponding Jain rules (on *eṣaṇā* faults), that can be found in the *cheya-suttas* of the *śvetāmbara* canon , and are contained in *Nisīha-suyaṁ* (e.g. II 21, X 40-43, XII 1-6, 13, 15, 17, 20-28, XVI 29); in *Anagāra-dharmāmṛta* 7, 55; S. Dh. Deo, *Jaina Monastic Jurisprudence*, Poona 1960, and N.K. Prasad, *Studies in Buddhist and Jaina Monachism*, Muzaffarpur 1972.

86. Cf. NC 1, p. 22, and 3, p. 37, as referred to in *A Cultural Study of the Niśītha Cūrṇi* by Madhu Sen, P.V. Research Institute, Varanasi 1975, p. 242.

87. Cf. T.W. Rhys Davids, *Sacred Books of the Buddhists*, Part III, p. 198. London 1921.

88. Quoting this text in the Introduction to his translation of *Jaina Sutras*, p. XV, vol. II, H. Jacobi confirms that 'the Jaina counterpart of these tenets can be collected from the *Uttardhayayana XXIX*". Later Jain philosophers had to defend and to try to find rationally tenable psychological explanations of this difficult statement in their discussions with Buddhists. A survey of such discussions from the Jaina point of view is presented in the Ph. D. thesis of Pushpa Bothra , *The Jaina Theory of Perception*, Delhi, M. Banarsidas, 1976.

89. Quoted from Buddho's life-story in the Introduction to *Jātaka* Stories.

90. The subsequent texts are taken from H. Jacobi's translations of *Jaina Sutras*, vol. 22 and 45 of the *Sacred Books of the East Series*, second edition, M. Banarsidass, Delhi 1964. Discrepancies between translations from the Prakrit and Pali in analogous texts are partly due to my impossibility to consult original Prakrit editions.

91. For the Pali text and its earlier translation see Pali Text Society editions, London, 1957 and 1963.

92. Cf. The *Milindapañho*, PTS edition, London 1962, and the *Questions of King Milinda*, Vol. XXXVI, *The Sacred Books of the East*.

Part Two

Jhānam: The Abstract Art of Buddhist Contemplation

Introduction

The Pali word for mental absorption, *jhānam,* corresponds to the Sanskrit *dhyānam,* classified in *Patañjali's* Yoga-*sūtrāni* (II 29, III 2) as the seventh of eight basic "limbs" (*añgāni*) of the Yoga system of spiritual development (*bhāvāna*). "Contemplation" is an analogical term borrowed from medieval Christian mystical theology (Hugo of St. Victor). It is used in the title of the present survey with the intention of replacing the more popular but less adequate word "meditation". Both have the same Christian source, Contemplation, however, corresponds more adequately to the stages of verbal prayer and ruminative thought, whose proper place in the Buddhist system of *jhānam* we will subsequently discuss. The Chinese *ch'an,* Japanese *zen,* and Tibetan *dzyan* are phonetical adaptations of the basic Pali term *jhānam.* The widest term encompassing various aspects of so-called Buddhist meditation is *bhāvanā,* as expounded in the *sati-paṭṭhāna-suttāni,* or Buddho's discourses on the "stability of attention" or "mindfulness". The most comprehensive text concerning *bhāvanā* is in the *Dīgha-nikāyo* collection, discourse twenty-two, expanding on the cultivation or ennoblement of the human being. It is in Buddho's teaching on *gotra-bhū,* or "change of lineage", or in a stricter sense, a change of the animal species within the human genus. The pivotal point for the whole structure and procedure of *jhānam* is elicited in the following text of the *Saṁyutta-nikāyo* XXI 1, *Kolita-suttaṁ*

> "The noble silence (*ariyo tuṇhibhāvo*): It is called the noble silence. And what is the noble silence? My experience of it, friends, corresponded to the following (description): - In this state the *bhikkhu,* with the stilling of *logical and discursive (theoretical) thinking* (*vitakka-vicāro*), attains the *second jhānam*: the internal clearness, the one-pointedness of mind without logical and discursive thinking,

the alertness-and-ease (*pīti-sukkham*), - and abides therein. This is called the noble silence."

Since reference is made in this statement to the second *jhānam*, let us compare this attainment of concentration (*samādhi*) with the description of the first *jhānam* in its basic formulation. (Its position in the complete structure of four *rūpa-* ("formative") and the corresponding four *arūpa-*("formless") levels of *jhānam* will be explained subsequently.)

"Thus in complete isolation (*vivicca*) from sense-desires and from states which are not advantageous to his end, he attains the first *jhānam*, which, born of seclusion (*vivekajam*), (still) includes logical and discursive thinking, alertnesss-and-ease, and abides therein."

On this basic level, *jhānam, the abstract art of Buddhist contemplation,* is consequently both a *reduction* of mental states and the intention "to still logical and discursive thinking" (*vitakka-vicāro*). It is essential for our purpose to mark a distinction between two levels of theoretical thinking, *vitakko* and *vicāro*. The term, *vi-takko*, is derived from the Sanskrit *tarka*, which in Indian philosophy, is the widest general designation for logic. The meaning of *vicāro*, however, refers to the application of the logical functions. Buddhaghoso (the compiler of the Pali commentarial literature in the 5th century A.D.) left an extensive, coherent and well-documented differential analysis on the subject in his compendium of *The Buddhist Way of Purification* (*Visuddhi-maggo*, IV 88-92)[1]:

Vitakko : "Hitting upon is what is meant. It has the characteristic of directing the mind onto an object. Its function is to strike at and thresh - for the meditator is said, by virtue of it, to have the object struck at by *vitakko*, threshed by *vitakko*. It is manifested as the leading of the mind onto an object."

vicāro: "Continued sustainment is what is meant. It has the characteristic of continued pressure on (occupation with) the object. Its function is to keep mental states (occupied) with it. It is manifested as keeping consciousness anchored (on that object)."

"And though sometimes not separate, *vitakko* is the first impact of the mind in the sense that it is both gross and inceptive, like the striking of a bell. *Vicāro* is the act of keeping the mind anchored, in the sense that it is subtle with the *individual* essence of continued pressure, like the ringing of the bell. *Vitakko* intervenes, being the interference of consciousness at the time of first arousing (thought), like a bird's spreading out its wings when about to soar into the air, and like a bee's diving towards a lotus when it is minded to follow up the scent. The behaviour of *vicāro* is quiet, being the near non-interference of consciousness, like the bird's planing with outspread wings after soaring into the air, and like the bee's buzzing after it has dived towards the flower."

The first and even the second *jhānam* are stages of *isolation* (*viviccam*) or reduction of intellectual (logical annd discursive) processes and exclusion of their mental contents. The result of this *seclusion or detachment* (*viveko*) is the *absorption of the mind in one point* (*cittass' ekaggatā*). This attainment is characterized as the *noble silence*.

Long before Buddhaghoso, a few prominent authors of early Pali literature pointed out the importance of attaining to the "noble silence" (*ariyo tuñhibhāvo*) as the basic contemplative mood which leads beyond the incipient stages of the first two levels of *jhānam*. In *Milinda-pañho* (472), Nagaseno, the Buddhist teacher of the Greek king Menandros, emphasized the necessity of maintaining the noble silence as a *continuous mood* until the highest and ultimate attainment of spiritual liberation: "the noble silence should be understood as the fourth *jhānam*". The *Paṭisambhidā-maggo* (II,169) also refers to "the noble silence" as "a basic subject of contemplation" *mūla-kammaṭṭhānam;*[2]. The "abstract" character of this art of spiritual cultivation consists in the absence of any "concrete object" or idea to be elucidated and explicated, due to the reductive isolation (*viveko*) and to the exclusion of such contents from "emerging in the stream" of re-flectively introverted consciousness (*bhavaṅga-soto*). Here, the term 'abstract', as in modern figurative art, underlines the intention of abstracting the 'material' or "content-laden" representation of the un-reflected immediate naive "flux of experience". Thus the reductive process of the meditator's spiritual isolation on the "way of purification" (*visuddhi-maggo*) corresponds also to the method of transcendental introversion in modern European philosophy.

The 20th century post-Kantian transcendentalist philosophers, with their critical attitude, no longer consider logical deduction of categorial concepts from general premises of judgment[3] as the sole method of abstraction. They also consider the "phenomenological reduction" (*Epoché*) as a legitimate method. By promoting the development of logics of cultural sciences based on specific principles of 'individual universals' as postulated in Hegel's philosophy of culture, one can attain "the greatest possible *exclusion* of all greedy connative attitudes" which are found in the discipline of emotional and volitional cultivation, as well as in the spheres of morality, arts, religion.[4]

The particular metaphysical interests and artistic ideals of the meditator determine the aim of cultivation of a noble mind as well as that upon which one's alertness is attentively sharpened. Both in Hinduist and Christian religious cultures this ideal is determined by the figurative concreteness of imagination. Even Zen art can be considered in this connection as an alternative method to logical abstraction. It represents one of the historical variations of *jhānam* and fits within the broader frame of *philosophia perennis (sanātana-dharma)* in its more or less rational or irrational proclivities.

Against all such "natural" incentives to creativity, the final aim of Buddhist contemplation remains the attainment of a complete reduction of the "thirst- (or will-) to-live"[5] to the "zero point" of its "extinction without remainder" (*niravasesa-nibbānam*). Buddho has described this attainment as "nothingness (*suññatā*) which is the abode of the great man" (M. 151).

Later I shall try to elucidate further using analogous models closer to the western mentality, the differential aspects of motives, aims and methods of attainment here presented in a superficial comprehensive glance.

To start with, let us look at these two basic aspects of the reductive and isolating processes:

(a) The Phenomenological Reduction of Activity and Intentionality:

is the phenomenological reduction of the whole range of "formative" activity and intentionality (*rūpatvam* corresponding to German *Gestaltung* in modern philosophy and psychology) towards its "zero point" (in Pali: *suññam*, Sanskrit: *śūnyam*, Chinese: *wu*, Japanese: *mu*, Tibetan: *stong-pa-nyid)*[6].

This point of annulment - *śūnyatā* in its original meaning in Indian mathematics should not be mistaken for what is (so wrongly and tendentiously) called "annihilation" in the materialistic theory of "destruction" - *uccheda-vādo*, which existed both in the naive Biblical "creation-destruction" belief in the power of one absolutist God (and to which "modern" colonial exegetists also tried to reduce Buddhism along with the rest of Indian religions), and in much older atomistic theories of archaic science from pre-Sumerian origins. In India *śūnyatā* was broadly developed before the time of Buddho. We can find, in the oldest *upaniṣads*, often in a more extensive presentation, *exactly* the same variations of teachings on "the first element" (*arché*) as in Greek hylozoist philosophies. These appear also in the identical historical sequence (water, fire, air etc.), and most probably stem from common mythological backgrounds. Buddho rejected this whole materialistic cosmogony as destructive: *uccheda-vādo*; incompatible with the essential turning of his authentic theory of nothingness *suñña-vādo*. In Europe, under the influence of Hume's pseudo-empiricism, even Kant was reproached for being unable to eliminate such mythological influences from his critique of metaphysical ontology.[7]

The clearest formulation of Buddho's *ontological and not epistemological*, nihilism can be found in *Saṁyutta-nikāyo*, XXXV, 85:

> "The Venerable Anando said thus to the Exalted One:
>
> - 'The world in nothing' is the saying, Lord. Pray, Lord, how far does this saying go?
> -Because the world is nothing in itself and for itself (*suññam attena vā attatniyena vā*), Anando, therefore it is said that the world is nothing. And what, Anando, is nothing in itself and for itself? (The organs of) sight, hearing, smelling, tasting, touching, and the mind, their objects and the (corresponding types of intentional) consciousness are nothing in themselves and for themselves. That is why, Anando, it is said that the world is nothing."

In the Third Part of this book I shall try to show how in the later mahayanist idealism the double aspect of the same principle of *śūnya-vāda* was consequently elaborated into the theory of "double nullity", i.e. both of the world and of the "self" in it. Thus the original negation of the Self-substratum can be deduced as a logical corollary of the basic theory of nothingness, understood as the earliest and most radical *idealist ontology* in the world history of philosophy. (This will be confirmed also by the later development of Buddhist idealism as *vijñapti-mātra-vāda* or theory that "consciousness alone" exists. Its earlier formulation by Nagarjuna[8] was simply that "there is no Self (*ātmā*) and no Being (*sattvam*)".

(b) The existential seclusion in meditative isolation.

Buddho compared the method of such an attainment often described as the analytical "way of purification" through the progress of absorption - *jhānam* - to "crossing the stream" of existential attachment:

"Neither standing still, nor overstraining myself,
I crossed the stream.
If I stand still, I may sink down. By proper effort
I shall be brought across.
....
And thus at last
I crossed over the impact of lust in the world."

(Saṁyutta-nikāyo, I,1,1.)

Buddho's designation of this "stream" as *bhavanga-soto*, or articulation (*angaṁ*) of the existential (*bhavo*) flux (*soto*), comes closest to Bergson's *flux-du-vécu*[9] I have tried elsewhere[10] to show how closely, in the context of our modern philosophy, this analogy corresponds to W. James' interpretation of the "stream of consciousness" or "stream of thinking", which, "when scrutinized, reveals itself to consist chiefly of the stream of my breathing" (in his essay "Does 'Consciousness' Exist?"). Also in the chapter on Husserl we shall see how his method of *Epoché* is based on the essential insight into the same "stream of consciousness."

The approach to the problem of nothingness from this existential vantage point, or rather through nothingness, to the whole subject-matter of Buddhist meditation, reveals another specifically Buddhist outlook. Our initial definition of meditation as *bhāvanā* or cultivation raises a further question concerning the *object* on which this method of ennobling and purifying can and has to be applied: Is it the spiritual cultivation of our Soul or Self-substance that still can be maintained (and sublated) by some dialectical *tour de force*, notwithstanding the principle of "double nullity" as unambiguously stated already in the text of *Saṁyutta-nikāyo*

XXXV 85, quoted above? Certainly not. After considering the passages quoted up to this point, it appears that the only adequate conclusion is that the object and the purpose of Buddhist meditation is the cultivation of "noble silence" (*Ariyo tuñhibhāvo*) based on the consciousness of nullity and "nihilation" (to use the term adequately coined by Sartre in our specific meaning, diametrically opposed to the tendentious interpretation of the "annihilationist" materialism as indicated above). The whole dilemma has been summarized already by Nagarjuna at the outset of independent Buddhist philosophy:

> *"For whom nothingness is logical, all is logical.*
> *For whom nothingness is not logical, nothing is logical."*
> *(Madhyamaka-kārikā, XXIV, 14)*

Thus the attainment of nullity and of nihilation (as the "state of abiding") has two levels: first the initial effort of 'isolation' from *both* the 'self' and the 'world', and beyond that the cultivation of the capacity to maintain this attainment of the "level of pure nothingness" (*ākiññcañ'āyatanam*), "the abode of the great man", defined as the third level of 'formless' *jhānam*. In the concluding chapter of this book we shall present a closer analysis of its integral structure.

> "By a comprehensive knowledge both wisdom and liberation should be intuited." (*Majjhima-nikāyo,* discourse 149)

In the following chapters I shall try to present the apparent difficulty which the *motivation* of these two aspects - *phenomenological reduction and existential seclusion* - poses to the "meditating philosopher" (as described by Husserl in his Cartesian Meditations), not only at the time of Pyrrho and the Stoics, but even in our days, when applying the method of *Epoché*. A method that seems to re-emerge in each "axial" epoch of world-cultures from the depth of the *philosophia perennis* as the "eternal recurrence", ontologically based on, and transcendentally limited to, the anthropological *hypokeimenon* of the faculty of Reason.

Chapter One

The Indian Origin of Pyrrho's Epoché

One of the earliest contacts of a Greek philosopher with Indian *śramaṇā*, ascetics "striving towards the attainment of wisdom"[11] registered in the history of philosophy, was that of Pyrrho of Elis, who together with Anaxarhos, a follower of Demokritos, and with Onesikritos, a disciple of Diogenes, the famous Kynik, joined the scientific retinue of Alexander the Great's expedition to India. The basic characteristic of Pyrrho's philosophy was the attitude of *epoché*, or refraining from judgment and 'views' (Greek *doxa*, Sanskrit *dṛṣṭi*, Pali *diṭṭhi*). Pyrrho's principle "Not rather this than that" - *ouden māllon*-suggests the analogy with the Jain principle of *anekānta*, the "theory of indeterministic truth" or "toleration of many modes of truth", as defined by K.C. Bhattacharyya, the best known Indian philosopher in the twentieth century who founded his philosophical investigation on his study of "The Jaina Theory of Anekanta" ished in 1925[12].

Among several analogous aspects which we will discuss in this chapter, the basic tenet of Jain religious teaching - *ahiṁsā*, or nonviolence, should be considered as a prominent motive on both sides (although in later philosophical discussions it remained neglected, as we shall see later). There are good reasons to support the hypothesis that the "naked sages" (Greek *gymnosophists*) at Taksasila (Taxila), described in the reports of Alexander's expedition[13], were Jain *munis* ("silent sages") and not so much Buddhist *samaṇā* whose influence on Hellenistic culture prevailed later (particularly in Alexandria). Nevertheless, some analogies between Pyrrho's and Buddho's formulation of the same basic ideas may astonish the conversant reader at first glance. Therefore, first we will bring out these analogies. In keeping with his teaching of *epoché*, Pyrrho lived after his return from India as a "silent sage" (*muni*) practicing the virtues of *epoché*: *aphasia* (not talking), *ataraxia* (dispassion), *metriopatheia* (moderation), *apatheia* (non-suffering resulting from indifference to pleasure and pain)[14], *adiaphoria* (equanimity), *isostheneia* (equilibrium, cf. Pali *tatra-majjhat'upekkhā*, mainly with reference to judgment, in the sense closest to the Jain *anekānta-vāda*.)

Diogenes Laertius, the author of the first extensive and systematic "biographies of great philosophers" and historian of ancient philosophy, quotes Pyrrho's saying "refraining from judgment is followed by peace of mind like a shadow" (D.L. IX, 108). This could be understood almost as a quotation from the opening *gāthās* (stanzas) of the most popular Buddhist sayings, the *Dhamma-padaṁ*: "If with a clear mind one speaks or acts, happiness follows him like his never-departing shadow."

In his native town of Elis, Pyrrho was honored as the high priest, though he refrained from all public offices. Cicero praises him for high moral and ascetic virtues (*De finibus*, III, 4, 12), emphasizing also that his moral standards were higher than those of the Stoics (*Academica*, II, 12, 130). Diogenes Laertius (IX, 55, 49), comparing the import of the virtues of *adiaphoria* and *apatheia* in Pyrrho's theory of *epoché* with the position of the same values in the systems of Demokritos and Aristoteles, states that the latter did not develop a theory of *epoché*. For the system of Demokritos these values had no constitutive significance. In Aristotle's ethics the term *epoché* does not appear either. As to its importance for the post-Pyrrhonic philosophy, Diogenes Laertius was so much impressed by it that he took it for the widest basis of his classification of all systems of philosophy dividing it in two groups: *dogmatic* and *epehtic* or based on *epoché*; both terms - epehtic and *epoché* are derived from the Greek verb *epehein*, 'to refrain' from apodictic judgment. Also the later, most misused term 'skepticism', as we shall see later from its history, is of the same origin.[15] (Cf. D.L. I, 10, Intro.) Pyrrho's disciple Timon summarized his teacher's doctrine as follows:

> - He who wishes to live happily should apply three criteria in considering: first, the nature of the things in themselves[16], then the attitude that he ought to take towards them, and finally the consequences of such attitude. In themselves things do not differ from each other, they are equally unclear and uncertain. As for our sen-

sations and judgments, they do not confirm either truth or falsity. We therefore should not trust either our sensations or our reasoning, but should persist in not holding views *doxa*[17] nor commitments either for the one or for the other side. Whatever issue may be at stake, we should say that it has to be *neither affirmed, nor denied, nor both affirmed and denied, nor neither affirmed nor denied*. Taking this attitude we shall attain first to *aphasia* (silence, cf. Sk. *maunyam,* Pali *monam,* the attitude of the *muni*), and then to *ataraxia* (indifference, Pali *upekkhā*).

The underlined formulation corresponds *verbatim* to the basic rule of Buddhist logic, *catu-koṭikam - tetralemma,* applied by Buddho in the case of *avyākatāni,* or questions "not expounded" by him (comparable, as we shall see, to the antinomies formulated by Kant).

The formula has remained foreign to European logics from Aristotle's time to the present day.

The basic criteria of Pyrrho's method of *epoché* were formulated in a scheme of ten *tropes.* Diogenes Laertius discusses them in his report (IX, 79-88). We shall point out first their implicit analogy with Buddhist principles, and then consider the Jain alternative.

The first trope addresses the same problem as Buddho's First Noble Truth - the difference among living beings concerning joys and sorrows, harms and advantages (cf. *kusalā* and *akusalā dhammā*). The conclusion is that equal stimulations do not provoke equal representations in our minds. This inconsistency should induce us to refrain from apodictic judgments. *The second, third and fourth tropes* extend the same argumentation to the structure of bodies, sensations and feelings. They can be compared, in the same sequence, to the fifth, sixth and seventh *nidānam* or rings in the chain of interdependent causation in the Buddhist *paṭicca samuppādo (salāyatanam, phasso, vedanā).*

The fifth trope refers to ways of living as regulated by laws and beliefs. The "right way of living" is the topic of the fifth step on Buddho's Noble Eightfold Path.

Tropes six through nine deal in a broader sense with the objective nature of world-constituting *relations,* according to Pyrrho's principle "not rather this than that." This criterion, *"ouden māllon",* as mentioned above, could easily be interpreted as Pyrrho's formulation of the Jain principle of *anekānta.*

The tenth trope addresses the correlativity or mutual dependence of phenomena (Pali *dhammā*): light and heavy, strong and weak, bigger and smaller, higher and lower etc., or the interrelations between day and night, or anything brought into relation with our mind.

Thus Pyrrho's principle "not rather this than that" has been elicited in a scheme of ten tropes. Although there are these occasional points of comparative reference to Buddhism there is a closer correspondence with the Jain homology which comprises the entire structure of corresponding schemes on both sides. The Jain *anekānta-vāda* theory based on the analogous principle "not only one meaning", is explicated in two correlative structures of sevenfold (*sapta-bhañgī*) schemes: seven *nayā* or methodological criteria, and seven "modes of truth" (according to K.C. Bhattacharyya's terminology) of a 'theory of possibility' (*syād-vāda*).

The last three of the seven *nayā* and the last four terms of the *sapta-bhañgī* are modes of predication. In the first set they are designated as *śabda-nayā* and refer to etymological criteria for the use of 'names' or derivation of words. In the second set, the word *avyaktavyam* expresses the impossibility of either affirming or negating being (or non-being) in any categorical form of logical predication.

Such criteria of predication are only implied in Pyrrho's wider theory of relations (tropes 6-10), but on the Indian side, the analogy of the four *avyaktavyam* modes in the *sapta-bhañgī* scheme in Jain logic are noteworthy. Buddho applied the same principle avyakatam in his formula of *catu-koṭi* (tetralemma). In his logic, too, the formula pertains to *existential judgments*: "Neither being, nor non-being, nor both being and non-being, nor neither-being-nor-non-being" can be predicated in answering antinomical questions. In some other formulations these are astonishingly comparable to Kant's Antinomy of Pure Reason[18]. Some of Buddho's standardized sets of 4x4 topics are:

"Whether the world is eternal... Whether the world is infinite...Whether the soul is the same as the body, or distinct from it...Whether a man who has attained to the truth (*buddha tathāgato*) exists after death..."

A difference between the Jain and the Buddhist scheme appears in the first Jain mode and in the last Buddhist mode:

The first three *bhañgī* ('sections') of the Jain *syād-vāda* state simply that an object seen from a chosen standpoint (*syāt*) can be signified: (1) as existent, (2) as non-existent (i.e. regarded under the aspect of another object) and (3) as both existent and non-existent (the former seen under its own aspect and the latter under alien ones). The three corresponding formulae are: *syād asty eva, syān nāsti eva, syād astināsti ca*."[19]

Much more significant for our comparison with Pyrrhos's tropes are the first four *nayā*:

(1) *naigama-naya*, "the figurative standpoint" (or "conventional mode of contemplation")[20] "takes into account the *purpose or intention* of something which is not accomplished", or a "general *custom*, according to which the intention alone is referred to as the basis of an unaccomplished thing." It can be compared with Pyrrho's fifth trope on the relativity of social customs.

(2) *saṅgraha-naya*, "synthetic standpoint which comprehends several different modes under one common head through their belonging to the *same class*. For instance, existence (being), substance,...". This is the logical method of abstracting the *notion of genus*. It can be compared with Pyrrho's sixth trope concerning the relativity due to association of ideas ("mixtures and connections").

(3) *vyavahāra-naya*, "the analytic standpoint,... the division of objects comprehended by the synthetic viewpoint... up to the limit beyond which there can be no further division into sub-classes. This is the method of abstracting particular qualities of the *species*, interpreted as the *empirical standpoint*.[21] It can be compared with Pyrrho's seventh and eighth trope concerning "different aspects of a picture" due to the relativity of "relations in space... in quantity and quality."

(4) *ṛjusūtra-naya*, "the straight (direct) viewpoint... It confines itself to the present moment... as no *practical purpose* can be served by things past and things unborn." It is a theory of momentariness, corresponding to the Buddhist *kṣanika-vāda*. It can be compared with Pyrrho's ninth trope, concerning "duration of phenomena".

In the suggested comparison it appears that the Indian scheme is based on a much more explicitly elicited system of logic. Also the intention of the method is to serve a wider range of scientific investigation. This advantage should, however, be ascribed to a much later formulation and interpretation of the basic teaching.

Jain syād-vāda	**Buddho's catu-koṭi**
(4) *syād avaktavyam* *(it may be indetermined)*	....
(5) *syād asti avaktavyam* (it may be, but indetermined)	(1) *(avyākatam)* atthi (it is not declared:) 'it is'
(6) *syād nāsti avaktavyam* (it may not be, but indetermined)	(2) *(avyākatam) n'atthi* (it is not declared:) 'it is not'
(7) *syād asti nāsti avaktavym* *atthi ca n'atti ca* (it may both be and not be, but undetermined)	(3) *(avyākatam)* (it is not declared:) 'it both is and is not'
....	(4) *(avyākatam) n'ev'atthi na n'atthi* (it is not declared: 'it neither is nor is not'

Further speculation on this comparative subject - on a purely doxographic ground[22] - might raise the question, how far a prevalently *humanistic turning*, distinguishing Pyrrho's basic interest from the Jain epistemological inquiry, could have been influenced or suggested by his possible acquaintance with specific Buddhist trends. For our context it may suffice to underscore one basic difference of the Jain *anekānta-vāda* from both Buddhist (cf. Nagasena's *Milinda-pañhā*, about 2nd c. B.C.) and Pyrrho's "skepticism." In order to indicate the differential elements on the ideal point of intersection of the three trends in whose comparative study we are interested - the Jain, the Buddhist, and the Pyrrhonian - I wish to refer first to the concluding paragraph (30) of K.C. Bhattacharyya's essay on *The Jaina Theory of Anekanta*, mentioned at the beginning of the present chapter:

> "The Jaina theory elaborates a logic of indetermination not in reference to the will - but in reference to the knowing, though it is a pragmatist theory in some sense. As a realist, the Jaina holds that truth is not constituted by willing, though he admits that the knowledge of truth has a necessary reference to willing. His theory of indeterministic truth is not a form of skepticism. It represents, not doubt, but toleration of many modes of truth. The faith in one truth or even in a plurality of truths, each simply given as determinate, would be rejected by it as a species of intolerance."[23]

The principle of *anekānta* seems, however, to be closer to Pyrrho's *ouden mallon* than to the *catu-koṭi* criterion as Buddho applied it. This latter, as stated above, seems to be a reduction and readaptation of the *sapta-bhañgī* scheme, without the semantic reduplication, from an essentially different standpoint and for a specific methodological purpose pursued by Buddho (viz. in early Pali texts) by *strictly rational means.*

On the other hand, the Jain standpoint remains always realistic. It is never skeptic, not even in the primordial meaning implied in Pyrrho's method of *epoché*. The Jain epistemology serves the purpose of establishing a theory of *cosmological realism in ontology*. To that effect the *anekānta* "realism" can be envisaged as an endeavour to connect the prevalent criteria of truth into a coherent cosmology. For the same reason the semantic modes had acquired a prevalent importance in the methodology of the *naya* scheme. This aspect of a theory of truth had no more meaning for the Buddhist model. The *acosmic* attitude of Buddho was the most radical and consequent rejection of all cosmological and ontological standpoints in the history of philosophy up to our day[24]. His theory of nothingness (*suñña-vādo*), arose from a purely meditative *epoché*, concentrated on the reductive effort of the meditator to attain the level of both subjective (*ajjhattaṁ*) isolation "born of seclusion" (*vivekajam*), and objective (*bahiddhā*) abstraction from disturbing influences (*vivicca akusalehi dhammehi*). This level of nothingness (*ākiñcaññ'āyatanaṁ*) is described in the aspect of meditative experience. For such a theory of pure introversion there is no need of methodological dichotomy of insight and verbal expression as it was needed for the Jain *anekānta-vāda* which aimed at the analysis of a pluralistic world-structure. At the time of Pyrrho's acquaintance with the Indian alternatives of *epoché*, Nagarjuna was not yet born. The Buddhist theory of 'indeterministic truth' (as formulated in Buddho's antinomies concerning 'world-views' in general) from a nihilist standpoint (or standpoint of 'nihilation', to adopt the adequate expression coined by Sartre) was not yet elaborated in its dialectical aspects. Thus Pyrrho's theory of *epoché*, both in its historical provenance and systematic scheme, remains halfway between the cosmological interest of the Jains and its acosmic reversal by Buddho. The inquiry of comparative philosophy has brought us to the crossroad of three possible directions that may be followed by a meaningful interpretation of the basic problem of *anekānta-vāda*: The original Jain interpretation, its Buddhist alternative, and Pyrrho's intermediate position, unprotected against later 'sceptical' misunderstandings on an alien soil.

Fragments of a philosophical poem by Pyrrho's disciple Timon (in D. Laertius, IX, 65, and in Sextus Empiricus, *Adversus mathematicos*, XI, 20) contain the following rhetorical question of the disciple to the master:

> "I would like to know, O Pyrrho, how is it that you, being only a man, can have such a light and quiet life? How is it that you are able to guide men like a god who revolves the fiery circle of his sphere all around this earth, and makes it visible to our eyes?"

It was this man who by the "objective" history of philosophy was held responsible for what has been labeled "scepticism." Skepticism, in this historical meaning, was a product of a later development, at the beginning of the Christian era, which was due mainly to Sextus Empiricus and Aenesidenus, under obvious influence of the predominant trend in the later Platonic Academy. Cicero, in his critique of the Academic skepticism (Acad. 1, 12,44; II, 23,72ff) never mentions Pyrrho in this connection. For him, too, Pyrrho was above all a staunch opponent of the sophists. Even according to earlier testimony, he has to be compared instead to Socrates, though more "appeased and resigned. He has destroyed sophistry, and did not attempt to replace it."[25]

In Alexandria, at about the same time and in the same ambience of Hellenistic culture, when the 'skeptical' trend reached its culmination in the academic school of philosophy, in Alexandria Pyrrho's teaching and its representatives were identified with Buddhist *samaṇā* and made responsible for the same course of ideas.

It is interesting to read in the light of these historical circumstances the explanations of the *Buddha-dhammo* that Nagaseno tried to adapt to his Hellenistic interlocutor in the *Milinda-pañhā*. In the subsequent distortion of their misunderstood ideas under Christian and Moslem biases ultimately the Arabic term *sumanīya,* through the "heresy" of Indian *samaṇā,* became a synonym of "scepticism" as understood in the Latin Christian tradition.

Due to such an alien historical condition which provoked a fast degeneration of the original philosophy of *epoché* into "scepticism", it is understandable also that its modern revival could occur only in an indirect way without explicit reference to the forgotten Indo-Ionian depths of its origins. Thus *epoché* in its essential meaning reappears in the philosophy of Edmund Husserl as the pivotal point of his transcendental logic which, in the first half of the twentieth century was recognized as the most suitable and broadest methodological platform for the contemporary European philosophies beyond their differences in trends, individual views or thematic aspects for whose analysis it is applied.

The method of *epoché* in such application is designated as "phenomenological reduction" (to *eidetic,* intuitive, essences), "suspension", or "bracketing", or "switching off", of the "doxic" (dogmatic) character or of existential determination by "viewpoints", of phenomena as they appear to the immediate, theoretically unprejudiced and unbiased intuition in and for themselves. In the "back-stage" (as Nietzsche ridiculed the Kantian conception of "things") of phenomena as they *appear* (Greek *phainestai-phantasia*) there is no hidden "thing-in-itself". Though Husserl remained a consequent idealist in claiming that by his method of *epoché* only "the transcendent in the immanent" is attainable to the insight of our immediate experience, his basic principle, "Back to the things themselves!", has encouraged his followers and critics to transcend the *aporia* of idealism and realism as an artificial Kantian device, and thus to disclose new dimensions and approaches to philosophical problems in our existential immediacy. The ontology of *praxis* should not be mistaken or reduced to pragmatism. The specific interest in overcoming the difficulty of the Kantian heritage has been predominant in the philosophy of the twentieth century, diverting some early followers of Husserl's phenomenology (Max Scheler and the existentialists) to pathways almost devoid of the initial conception of *epoché*.

At a later stage of advanced critical pondering over the *value aspect of existence* the meditative inclination disclosed again a deeper import of *epoché*. This has been recognized most unequivocally in the later meditations of Heidegger, both distinguishing and reconnecting himself as "Heidegger II" to "Heidegger I[26]". In deepening his meditations on the "forgetfulness of Being" and on the essentially antiontological direction of "metaphysics, which as such in its proper intention is nihilism[27], Heidegger disclosed a new existential purport of *epoché* in the "withdrawal of Being" and its tendency of hiding in forgetfulness and nothingness. Thus the primary intention of *epoché* to serve as a method of disclosing the essence of Being (Heidegger's *aletheia*, also in his "phenomenological destruction of the history of ontology") has been extended to encompass at the same time the dialectical opposite of concealment in its meaningful withdrawal.

Without entering any further into such possibilities of extending the scope of the philosophy of *epoché* in its modern phenomenological context, I shall hint at a few specific fundamental positions laid down by Pyrrho which Husserl implicitly but essentially maintained.

The *antidogmatic standpoint* of Pyrrho's philosophy implies *epoché* as "refraining from judgment" for reasons which can be summarized broadly for the purpose of our analogy as follows (in the wording of Sextus Empiricus, *Pyrroneion hypotyposeon*):

(1) Within the purview of *view-points* the intention of the skeptic is to remain undisturbed (*ataraxia*) by their aporetic appearances (*phantasia*), since as soon as he begins to philosophize how to judge of them and to understand which are true and which are false, with a view to reach an undisturbed certainty, instead of that he will be caught in an equally strong contradiction, and being unable to solve it, he will apply *epoché* - refraining from judgment. (I, 12)

(2) The reason for such abstention is the failure to attain imperturbability (*ataraxia*) by a definite judgment in view of the *inadequacy of the appearance* on one hand *and the thought referring to it* on the other. (Ibid.)

(3) If therefore perceptions do not grasp *external things*, thought cannot comprehend them either. Refraining from *judgment on external things* should consequently also follow for this reason. (1, 14, II,6) Thus the theoretical faculty of reasoning reaches its high-

est critical attainment in abrogating itself. What was considered as the advantage of dialectics for speculative views and systems, appears now as a danger for the skeptical critique of thought, both in its theoretical and practical intentions. In this way objects are never contemplated as they are given without interference of intellectual views and theses in their contents. With the rejection of logical proofs the skeptical critique excludes at the same time the procedures of syllogism, induction and definition as *valid means of knowledge*. (II, 14- 16)

(4) Notwithstanding the correct statement that "we do not take part in the research of nature" (I, 9) - "those who assert that the Skeptics deny the world of phenomena, are not correctly informed on the proper meaning of our statements. When we are in doubt whether an object (in itself) is such as it appears, we still do recognize that it appears, and *we do not doubt of what appears*, but of the statements made about it." (I, 10) In other words, the principle of "refraining from judgment on external things" does not imply either a psychologisitic or subjectivistic idealism in the meaning analogous to that in which Husserl criticized the neo-Kantian idealism and established his "Principle of principles", as we shall see in the subsequent analogy.

(5) In Indian logics the critique of valid "means of knowledge" (*pramāṇaṁ*) is the epistemological precondition for the construction of any system of world-views (*darśanaṁ*, Greek *doxa*). The skeptic discussion of the problem of existence of God and of the possibility of its proof reminds us, also in this logical implication, of the prevalently non-monotheistic, henotheistic or pantheistic, and even atheistic (Jain and Buddhist) attitudes to this speculative problem in Indian philosophies. It may suffice for our purpose to compare it with Husserl's application of the same principle of *epoché* to the same problem.

(6) In order to conceive God it is requisite, in consideration of the statements of dogmatists, to refrain from the judgment that he either exists or does not exist... This unsolvable contradiction has brought us to the surmise that God's existence is not evident and that it requires proof... Since it is neither self-evident, nor can it be proved from anything else, the existence of God remains unattainable as a part of our knowledge. Hence we conclude that

those who with deep conviction affirm that god exists are unavoidably bound to fall into ungodliness.(III,3)

In the next chapter we will consider the analogy between the positive structural elements of archetypal models mentioned here and their modern revival in the philosophy of *epoché* based on Husserl's phenomenological transcendentalism. Here, we will briefly delineate differential elements to bring out some commonplace statements from the history of philosophy.

The refutation by the Skeptics of all theses and opinions (*doxa*, Sk. *dṛṣṭi*) in earlier cosmological philosophies on the first elements (*arché*) of Being, serves the purpose of establishing a diametrically different approach to the dialectical problems of philosophy, starting from the investigation of the structural formation of the faculty of reasoning. Anticipating an analogy with Husserl we can interpret his skeptical "principle of principles" as *epoché* applied to all differences of opinions or beliefs, bearing in mind that the skeptics do not assert specifics that could be used to refute different and opposite views.

Without denying the objective givenness of phenomenal appearance (as stated under (4) above), the Skeptics exclude only the presumption of valid inference from subjectively relative conceptions to the objectively established Being of that which appears, considering that inferential (deductive or inductive) reasoning cannot ascertain anything beyond that which appears to us subjectively.

The ideal of the Pyrrhonian *ethos of knowledge* required that man should be enabled to establish and to maintain the state of equilibrium in his reasoning (*isostheneia*, cf. *tatra-majjhatt'upekkhā* in Pali Buddhist contexts). *The logical function of negation* has to be considered as the methodological implement of this postulate. The aim of such reasoning was to demonstrate how all pre-epechtical philosophy was one-sided and dogmatic.

In these basic analogies, Pyrrho's ideas, quoted by Sextus Empiricus, correspond to the dialectical intentions of Nagarjuna in Buddhist philosophy (2nd c. A.D.). For, as a representative of this school of thought says,

> "the *mādyamika* has no counter-thesis to offer, because that would entail yet another position."[28]

Therefore he is unbeatable in discussion. In Nagarjuna's basic formulation:

- If an exposition takes recourse to nothing (*śūnyaṁ*), then all critique is out of place and entails a *petitio principii*."

(*Madhyamaka-kārikā* IV, 9)

Despite the fact that Husserl's logic represents a modern renewal of *epoché*, initially it did not include its central concept: both in its explicit final aim and its dialectical method which the skeptic philosophers adapted to serve their *ex-clusive* intention (particularly in its later polemical degradation - "Contra mathematicos"). In bringing out the following statements which are analogous to those quoted from Sextus Empiricus we should take them only as *prima facie* indications of possibilities for further critical studies.

(Ad 1) "The scientists speak of mathematics and of all what is eidetic as *skeptics*, but in their eidetical method they *proceed as dogmatics*. This was their fortune: The greatness of natural sciences arose from their daring rejection of the luxuriant skepticism which had invaded the Ancients, and from *renouncing* to overcome it... To the cycle of researches which can be properly designated as *dogmatic*, viz. *pre-philosophic*, pertain, among other sciences, all the natural sciences..., *sciences resulting from the dogmatic attitude* turned to things and not permitting to be disturbed by problems of epistemological or skeptical nature."[29]

For Husserl's "meditating Ego", on the contrary, applying "the universal *epoché*" is understood as "universal abstention from behavior natural to the experience-belief,... transfer of attention from the world given in experience to the experience itself, in which alone the world does possess sense and being for me".[30] Thus the intuited (eidetic) *essence* appears in Husserl's "neutrality modification of a doxic consciousness... as a pure *representation*", or "a neutrally modified perception upon the switching off of all transcendent"[31] constituents.

(Ad 2) While Descartes still took it for granted that "knowledge of reality and knowledge of causality are inseparable", for Husserl, on the contrary, reality has no being "in and for itself", it is what it is only in its categorical, causal, determination, while "causality, on prinicple, is relative". Neither causality nor the real in its causal implications can be simply "given" in any empirical texture.[32]

(Ad 3) "Processes of consciousness... have no ultimate elements and relationships fit for subsumption under the idea of objects determinable by fixed concepts... It would be hopeless to attempt to proceed here with such methods of concept and judgment formation as rare standard on the objective sciences."[33]

Phenomenology being *"a purely descriptive* discipline investigating the field of transcendental pure consciousness in *pure intuition*"[34] no mediate logical deduction is required within the limits of this scope, and consequently, no concepts and no judgments have to be formed. As Husserl often used to repeat, phenomenology does not establish theories.

(Ad 4) "A meditating philosopher... in a meditation of Cartesian type can neither have a use for, nor accept as given, any whatsoever scientific idea" for the simple reason that both life and positive science are naturally realistic, while the philosopher has to ask himself whether the very existence of the world is apodictically 'evident'... The philosopher who is in doubt of this realism and who practices *epoché* will, consequently, lose the world as real foundation of 'evidences' related thereto. Yet he will not lose, for that reason, all being and all 'evidence'. On the contrary, behind the being of the world the very being of the subject, his meditation...[35] Thus the universal *epoché* applied by "the transcendental-phenomenological reflection" aims at the suspension of "the being or non-being of the world" and "lifting us off from this ground"[36] Husserl's *Principle of Principles*[37]: "Every type of first hand intuiting forms is a legitimate source of authority; whatever presents itself in 'intuition' at first hand, in its bodily reality, so to say, is to be accepted simply as it presents itself to be, though within the limits within which it presents itself." Thus, complementary "to each region of object, there corresponds a basic type of primordial self-evidence (*eidos*)". - "Each regional ontology is constituted by a specific set of categories whose *a priori* and universal validity is not limited to the condition of being formal."

(Ad 5) "After abandoning the natural world, we strike in our course another transcendence, which... comes to knowledge in a highly mediated form, standing over against the transcendence of the world as if it were its polar opposite. We refer to the transcendence of God... We naturally extend the phenomenological reduction to this Absolute and to this transcendent. It should remain disconnected from our field of research..., so far as this is to be a field of pure consciousness... There no god can alter anything.[38]

Independent of Husserl, K.C. Bhattacharyya's contemporary interpretation of the Jain *anekānta-vāda* quoted at the beginning of this chapter also suggests a renewal of *epoché*. Linking the above points, this implication is evident in the following summary of K.C. Bhattacharyya's basic intention formulated by his closest friend D.M. Datta[39]:

> "The recognition of the indefinite would cure logic of the dogmatic tendency to treat the definite, the rational, the knowable as the sole content of thought, and would change its general outlook."

Bhattacharyya's own description of "different felt modes like knowing, feeling" - and other functions corresponding implicitly to the Cartesian *Cogito* as interpreted in the phenomenlogical analysis of Husserl's "Cartesian Meditations" - seem to correspond to Husserl's Principle of principles. Bhattacharyya's formulation of his basic principle was[40]:

> "Every system of philosophical thought or religion has its own logic and is bound up with one or other of the fundamental views of negation."

The advantage of this logic of the indefinite is that it "finds categories for widely different metaphysical notions of reality"[41], which are not reducible to common denominators.

Bhattacharyya's intention to elicit his conception of the indefinite as a "correction of dogmatic biases" is applied (in his critique of Hegel) also to the antinomy of "being and non-being":

> "In fact the opposition between the two definite contents of thought, being and non-being, cannot be understood at all without something which is neither and can yet make their relation possible... Recognition of the indefinite corrects this dogmatic bias of each, and yet gives to each a new light and reformed character."

The same criterion is consequently applied, here too, to the field of religious experience which "by its self-deepening gets opposed to or synthesized with other experiences.[42]

Chapter Two

Husserl: "The Meditating Philosopher"

At the outset of the following analysis it may be useful to show through one case of typical misunderstanding how faithfully Husserl followed the primal Greek intention of the complex and difficult theory of *epoché*.

Karl Jaspers, independently of Husserl's school, in his late but very significant work for the new trends of comparative philosophy, *The Great Philosophers*[43] insists on the essential difference between ancient and mystical "experiences in meditation" and modern methods of "suspension" (*epoché*) in transcendental analysis of the *"subject-object relationship"* such as expounded by Martin Heidegger, Husserl's most prominent disciple. The clearest formulation of the difference is given with reference to "Buddha's doctrine of redemption by insight: It "springs from experience in the transformation of consciousness and the stages of meditation". While modern "science and philosophical speculation remain within our given form of consciousness, ... this Indian philosophy may be said to take consciousness itself in hand, to raise it in higher forms by exercises in meditation."

It seems that Husserl, to whom the first part of this statement obviously alludes, must have been aware of the likelihood of such a misunderstanding so typical of modern science and the restrictions it imposes due to its prejudices. In the attempt to break this objectifying attitude of science and to eliminate it radically at least from the domain of philosophy, Husserl was most emphatic in the introduction to his main work[44] just about this difficulty of properly understanding the intention of his method of phenomenological reduction (*epoché*). It was meant to serve the purpose of a "science of phenomena which lies far removed form our ordinary thinking..., so extraordinarily difficult" to understand by reason of employing consciousness in a completely different dimension, in "a new way of looking at things, one that contrasts at every point with the *natural attitude* of experience and thought".

The "aristocratic" and even "ascetic" character of Husserl's "eidetic" method (or method of "seeing essences") has been exposed by his critics with a negative rather than a positive intention.[45]

The purpose of *epoché* in Husserl's philosophy is fundamentally different from the intentions of positive sciences which remain within the scope of their "natural attitude" necessarily "doxic" and "dogmatic". This attitude remains unchanged both in natural science (*Naturwissenschaften*) and in cultural, historical sciences or humanities (*Geisteswissenschaften*). The method of phenomenological reduction proposes, on the contrary, to disclose thematically a knowledge which is not based on such worldly ("mundane") principles. It "reveals... the dimension of the world's source" in the "stream of consciousness", as formulated by one of Husserl's earliest and closest collaborators.[46]

Thus phenomenology as "eidetic science of pure consciousness" is the immanent study of pure experience. In "bracketing" the transcendent world it does not negate, or even annihilate, its existential reality-dimension, it merely contemplates it from another perspective in changing, as it were, its (±) mathematical symbol[47]. The same meditative attitude of *epoché* is essential for a correct understanding of the idea of nothingness (*suññatā*), so central to Buddhist philosophies (as we shall see in the basic Buddhist text quoted in chapter IV) on nullity or nihilation (*Cula-suññatā-suttaṁ*). Husserl is aware of the fact that consciousness in general characteristically fluctuates in various dimensions, so that an exact conceptual fixation (*schema*) of any "eidetic concretes or of their immediate constituent moments" remains out of question. Phenomenology is the philosophical discipline dealing with our experience of the world in its vital fluctuation and with its intentional correlate *(noema)*.[48]

In the second Cartesian Meditation (20, end)[49] Husserl considers "the fact that the realm of phenomena of consciousness is so truly the realm of a Heraclitean flux. It would in fact be hopeless to attempt to proceed here with such methods of concept and judgment formation as are standard on objective sciences". For Husserl it is a priori evident that "processes of consciousness... have no ultimate elements and relationships fit for subsumption under the idea of objects determinable by fixed concepts." And yet, "in spite of that, the idea of an intentional analysis is still legitimate."

It seems that Nagaseno, the first Buddhist missionary who tried to explain the teaching of Buddho to a Greek interlocutor, Menandros (in *Milinda- panhā*, second century B.C.), attempted to express, on one point, the same initial difficulty as discussed by Husserl in the quoted context:

> "The difficult achievement, o king, accomplished by the Fortunate (Buddho) was to define incorporeal phenomena of *cognizance* (*cittam, noesis* in Husserl's analogy) and of its *modes* that may be *apparent on a single object*.[50]

We have reached the point from which, retrospectively, the misunderstanding with Jaspers, singled out at the beginning of this chapter, on "experiences in meditation" and stages of *epoché* can be further clarified by *defining Husserl's idea of "the meditating philosopher"* and comparing it with the scope of the Buddhist analogon of *epoché*.

(1) In the sequel of the text quoted in our preceding chapter (as 4, n. 35) Husserl explains how "with the universal *epoché* and the *transfer of attention* from the world given in experience to that experience itself, experience within which alone the world has a meaning and being for me", ... "the meditating philosopher" will attain "the transcendental experience". Thus "the Ego absorbed in phenomenological meditation is the *transcendental spectator of his own life and of his own being*, though this life and this being themselves are turned towards the world" - an attainment analogous to that of the first *jhānam* (with reference to the description of that state in the first chapter above).

Already in his first attempt to draft "the idea of phenomenology" (in a course of five lectures in 1907)[51], Husserl is concerned above all with the problem of possible isolation of a reduced "sphere of usable objects or of cognitions which present themselves as valid, and which can remain free of *the sign of epistemological* nullity", a sphere still "not reduced to zero". Thus "a sphere of absolutely immanent data" is obtained.

From Buddhaghoso's explanation of the *method of isolating the intended "sign" (nimittam) on the object of concentration (kamaṭṭhānam)* we can single out almost literal correspondence of some key-terms to Husserl's analogous designations. Thus *nimittam* is defined by Buddhaghoso as "a mere mode of appearance", "born only of perception"[52]. Husserl extends his explification of his "singular essences" of intuition (*eidos*) also to the "neutrality modification" or "a *neutrally modified perception*" upon the switching off of all transcendent constituents[53].

According to the commentary of Buddhaghoso's *Visuddhi-maggo,* what is thus switched off, neutralized or isolated from a given complex of experience are "*simple modes of interpreting* the kinds of materiality... that are interpreted in such and such a wise, for apart from that there is in the ultimate sense no such thing as a hand and so on"[54], i.e. "transcendent constituents of things". The procedure is exemplified in the same commentary with reference to the basic *suttaṁ*-text from *Udānam*, I, 10: "He stops at what is merely seen" - as follows:

> "As soon as the color basis has been apprehended by the consciousness of the cognitive series with eye-consciousness, he stops; he does not fancy any aspect of beauty etc. beyond that."

The following example from Husserl[55] may help us to get a comprehensive picture of the whole analogy:

> "Let us suppose that we are looking with pleasure in a garden at a blossoming apple tree, at the fresh young green of the lawn, and so forth. The perception and the pleasure that accompanies it is obviously not that which at the same time is perceived and gives pleasure. *From the natural standpoint* the apple tree is something that exists in the transcendent reality of space, and the perception as well as the pleasure a physical state which we enjoy as real human beings... Now in such conditions of experience, and in certain cases, it may be that the perception is a mere hallucination, and that the perceived, this apple tree that stands before us, does not exist in the 'real' objective world...Let us now pass over *to the phenomenlogical standpoint*. The transcendent world enters its 'bracket'... Together with the whole physical and psychical world the real subsistence of the objective relation between perception and perceived is suspended, and yet a relation between perception and perceived (as likewise between the

pleasure and that which pleases) is obviously left over, a relation which in the essential nature comes before us in pure immanence, purely, that is, on the ground of the phenomenologically reduced experience of perception and pleasure, as it fits *into the transcendental stream of experience*. This is the very situation we are now concerned with, the pure phenomenological situation."

(2) Further elucidation is required here to explain how far and in what sense the Buddhist method of isolating *nimittam*, or the eidetic (purely intuitive) 'sign' from the object of contemplation, can be considered as an *archaic analogue* to Husserl's description of the "pure phenomenological situation", in which, despite 'suspension' (*epoché*), though not 'annihilation' of its reality dimension (in the sense of the *uccheda-vādo*, rejected by Buddho), "a relation between perception and perceived... in its *essential nature* comes before us in *pure immanence* ...on the ground of the *phenomenological reduced experience*".

For Husserl philosophical phenomenology "is a *purely descriptive* discipline investigating the field of transcendental *pure* consciousness in pure intuition[56]. Within the limits of this scope no mediate logical deduction is required and consequently no concepts and no judgments have to be formed:

> "Like every other already-given science, logic is deprived of acceptance by the universal overthrow" in phenomenological investigation on this level[57].

In the words of the Buddhist commentary: "The seen shall be merely seen." Husserl often used to repeat to his students that phenomenology does not establish theories, or 'doctrines'. And his student Heidegger cautioned Sartre in their discussion about 'humanism' that "in the actual precarious situation of the world we need less philosophy and more mindfulness in thinking"[58].

(3) In the context of Husserl's description of the apple-tree the direction of his meditative proceeding towards "the transcendental stream of experience" is also indicated at the end of the quoted passage. The same direction is followed on the Buddhist side as well where "the stream of experience" is designated with the equivalent term *bhavāñga-soto* (as it was mentioned above, in ch. I, with reference to Bergson and W. James). It may appear easier at this point to understand from a new dimension both the diffi-

culty and the urgency of the turning against the stream in terms of Buddho's teaching about *gotra-bhū*, or "change of lineage". In Buddhaghoso's interpretation this problem is formulated as follows:

> "How is it that understanding of emergence and turning away from the external is change-of-lineage knowledge?... Change-of-lineage knowledge does not induce emergence from occurrence, *because it does not cut off origination, but it does induce emergence from the sign* ... Hence it is said: Understanding of emergence and turning away from the external is knowledge of change of lineage."[59]

The broader range of the existential meaning and intention for which this "turning away from the external" is designated here as "knowledge of change-of- lineage" is explicated in the sequel of the same text, which should be understood in the light of the following specification of *epoché* in Husserl's *First Cartesian Meditation* (Sect. 8, p. 60):

> "This universal depriving of acceptance, this 'inhibiting' or 'putting out of play' of all positions taken toward the already-given objective world and, in the first place, all existential positions (...), - or, as it is also called, this *'phenomenological epoché and parenthesizing'* of the objective world... does not leave us confronting nothing... and what I, the one who is meditating, acquire by it is my pure living, with all the pure subjective processes making this up..."

The specific aim of the Buddhist "turning away from the External" (corresponding to the capitalized "Objective" in Husserl's text) is elucidated in Buddhaghoso's commentary by the following statements, among others:

> "It overcomes arising, occurrence,... the sign of formations externally, thus it is change of lineage (V.M. XXIII 7).

> "It is the understanding of the turning away that is being effected, which turning away is emergence from the field of formations"[60] or reality-factors. The sign (*nimittam*) "is the sign of formations. This is a term for past, present and future formations". In another context "all signs mean the sign of materiality, sign or feeling, perception, (volitive) formations, and conscious-

> ness" (or the five *khandā*, constituents of psycho-physical reality). (V.M. XXI 34, and XXIII 13.)[61]

The arising of the sign of contemplation (*nimittam*) and its fixation in the ray of attention (*avadhāraṇam*) is an intentional act of *epoché*, which, expressed in Husserl's terminology, aims at the intuitive grasp of an 'eidetic singularity'. According to the *Visuddhi-maggo* commentary, "here the illumination is the revealing of the visible datum according to its *singular essence*, in other words the apprehending of it in evident perception". In another context: "The visibly given element itself is the illumination-element (or essence)... The sign of the beautiful is the beauty element and that does not exist apart from visible data and the like."[62]

Thus *nimittam* is described as the essential (*bhāvo*) sign emerging from the object of contemplation (*kammathānam* in a meaning analogous to Husserl's *noema*), illuminated by the ray of attention, intuited in a specific act of 'isolation' (*viviccam*), "born of seclusion" (*vivekajā*) or inhibition (*epoché*) of intellectual functions (*vitakka-vicāro*, cf. Husserl's *noesis*). This emergence of essence in the characteristic sign of the object of contemplation is the fruit of cultivation (*bhāvanā*): "The path is called emergence because it emerges externally from the objective basis interpreted as a sign" (*noema*) (V.M. XXI 83). In its broadest meaning the term *nimittam* comprises the 'characteristic sign' of any whatsoever object, "material and immaterial" *kammathānam* (V.M. XX 89), regardless of the meditator's intention either to exclude ('isolate' or 'inhibit') its penetration into the ken of his ray of attention, or to include, penetrate, and cultivate its essence for the purpose of *jhāna-bhāvanā*. Consequently the process of 'isolation' has for the Buddhist meditator both a noetic and a noematic intention" first, the noetic attitude of *epoché* to isolate the well focussed ken of attention, second, the noematic intention to mark off the isolated *nimittam*. The first, negative, intention is elucidated in the commentarial statement by Buddhaghoso (V.M. I 53-4):

> "So the meaning is this: 'On seeing a visible object with eye-consciousness - he apprehends neither the sign - nor the particulars'; e.g. he does not apprehend the sign of woman or man, or any sign that is a basis for defilement, such as the sign of beauty etc.; he stops at what is merely seen - he does not apprehend any

aspect classed as hand, feet, smile, laughter, talk, looking ahead, looking aside, etc., which has acquired the name 'particular'..."

On another occasion the words of Buddho are quoted as a standard test for the adequacy of noetic factors:

"Bhikkhus, there are three signs that should be given attention from time to time by a bhikkhu intent on higher consciousness: the sign of concentration..., the sign of exertion..., the sign of equanimity. (*Anguttara-nikāyo*, III)

The second, positive, meaning of purposive fixation on the lowest level of sense-experience is exemplified in the description of a physical object of contemplation (*kasiṇam*) and its preparation for that special purpose of exercise:

"For this it is said: 'One who is learning the earth-kasinam apprehends the sign in earth that is either made up or not made up, that is bounded, not unbounded, limited, not unlimited, with a periphery, not without a periphery, circumscribed, not uncircumscribed... He sees to it that the sign is well apprehended, well attended to, well defined'." (V.M. IV 22)[63]

"When, while he is developing it in this way, it comes into focus as he adverts with eyes shut exactly as it does with his eyes open, then the learning sign is said to have been produced... But it is *born only of perception* in one who has obtained concentration, being *a mere mode of appearance*." (V.M. IV 30-31)

Beyond this archetypal level in exercises of intuition of essences, emotional states of mind (cf. Husserl's "pleasure valuations") can, the same as intellectual intuitions, be singled out as *nimittam* in "immaterial objects of contemplation" as described by Buddhaghoso. Thus contemplating the 'sign of formations' of phenomenal existence (*saṅkhārā*; including emotions, perceptions, volition and consciousness, comparable to the range of Descartes' Cogito):

"The meditator sees only the death of formations when he brings them to mind as impermanent, and so the sign appears to him as a terror" (V.M. XXI 34).

By "overcoming the sign of formations externally" the existential feeling of "despair" has also to be overcome "for the purpose of attaining the signless region" (V.M. XXIII 7).

> When the meditator "brings them to mind as impermanent, formations appear as liable to destruction. When he brings them to mind as painful, formations appear as terror, when he brings them to mind as not-self, formations appear as null and void" (*Paṭisambhidā-maggo*, II 48).

On account of the heterogenous eidetic aim, Husserl's method of attaining "eidetic singularities" by *epoché* as a process of generalization remains completely separate from the process of logical formalization. It seems that Buddhaghoso envisages a similar aim of attaining eidetic singularities when he describes the higher levels of *nimittam* emerging from the "removal" of eidetic signs characteristic of the same objects (*kasiṇam*) on lower levels of sense perception. Ultimately "he adverts again and again to the sign of the space by the removal of the *kasiṇam*" (V.M. X9). In the next chapter we will discuss the structure of categorical regions reached by this reductive procedure in connection to Table 2. The following explanation is important from our comparative prospective:

> "He removes the *kasiṇam* (the object of sense-perception) by giving his attention to the space touched by it, as 'space'... When he is removing it, he neither folds it up like a mat nor withdraws it like a cake from a tin. It is simply that he does not advert to it or give attention to it or review it... It is simply that it is called 'removed' on account of his non attention to it, his attention being given to 'space, space' ... He cannot enter and dwell on that without completely surmounting perceptions of matter" (V.M. X 7, 8, 14).

Husserl and his followers (Heidegger in particular) often revert with emphasis to this phenomenologically important circumstance and principle of intuition. At the end of the First Cartesian Meditation Husserl says:

> "The following should be noted in this connection: Just as the reduced Ego is not a piece of the world, so, conversely, neither the world nor any worldly object is a piece of my Ego, to be found in my conscious life as a really inherent part of it, as a complex of data of sensation or a complex of acts."

In the same manner "the addition of, e.g., desire to some underlying presentation, is not the addition of something that exists independently".[64]

Heidegger, in his essay "On the Question of Being" (*Zur Seinsfrage*)[65], speaking of man's "forgetfulness of Being" considers also "various occurrences" where Being is imagined, so to say, as if it were the umbrella left somewhere behind by a philosophy professor out of forgetfulness.

Buddhaghoso (in V.M., XXII 113) enumerates "eighteen principal insights". Under No. 11 the ultimate reduction of "the sign through the contemplation of the signless" is referred to. In the same connection a text from *Majjhima-nikāyo* is quoted in the subsequent chapter (V.M., XXIII 12):

> "There are three conditions for the persistence of the signless mind- deliverance: they are the non-bringing to mind of all signs, the bringing to mind of the signless element, and the prior intention."

'Signless' describes the attainment of nullity (*suññatā*) or nothingness (*akiñcaññāyatanam*), as we will see in the next chapter. The distinction between 'signless' and 'null' (*suññam*) and the transition on to the next is explicitly stated as:

> "First, seeing all formations as limited and circumscribed, and the entering of consciousness into the signless element, second, ... into the desireless element, third, seeing all phenomena (*dhammā*) as alien, and entering of consciousness into the element of nullity." (V.M., XXI; 67)

(4) In the Fifth Cartesian Meditation Husserl uses the term 'purification'. Sounding so astonishingly similar to the Buddhist use of the term, a term so basic to the definition of Buddhist meditation (*Visuddhi-maggo* = "The Path of *Purification*", Buddhaghoso's manual of meditation), that we can use it to gain access to the next essential problem in our analogy:

> "If *ownness-purification* of the external world, the animate organism, and the psychophysical whole, has been effected, I have lost my natural sense as *Ego*, since every sense-relation to a possible Us or We remains excluded, and have lost likewise all my worldliness in the natural sense."[66]

All that remains is the *nimittam* or the essential 'sign' of the initial intentional relation.

> In "the life of consciousness conceived as the Heraclitean 'stream'... the general unity of the Ego is a unity of *synthesis in which the Ego becomes aware of itself as a unity*".[67]

In the Fourth Cartesian Meditation (§ 4) Husserl says that:

> "only through the phenomenology of genesis does the ego become understandable: *as a nexus, connected in the unity* of an all-embracing *genesis,* an infinite *nexus of synthetically congruous performances* - at levels, all of which fit the universal persisting form, *temporality*".

From a Buddhist standpoint, the terms I have underlined may appear as a rather scholastically pedantic translation of the basic terminology itself: *paṭicca-sam-* as 'nexus of synthetically congruous', *uppādo* as 'genesis', implying 'temporality' in 'congruous performances', rather than a free descriptive definition of the principle of *paṭicca-samuppādo* (usually translated as inter-dependent origination).

From such statements a Buddhist reader could easily deduce the analogy of the principle of *anattā* ('non-self', or negation of a permanent Ego-principle) as 'originated in dependence' on *aniccam* ('temporality'). This, however, would not be quite accurate. Husserl's attitude in this respect, if approached from a Buddhist standpoint, can be understood as a question which remained open for a considerable period of his phenomenological investigation. During this period he applied *epoché* to various levels of transcendental purification, thus developing different phases of a central conception. The prevalent tendency indicates a development from an initially negative toward an affirmative solution.

In the first volume of *Ideas..*[68], referring to his earlier investigations, Husserl says:

> "In the Logical Studies I, I took up on the question of the pure Ego a skeptical position which I have not been able to maintain..."

At the same time, however, he complains that his position on the ego has been misunderstood by the idealist metaphysical philosophers. It was always clear to him that in his philosophy "the psychological subjectivity loses just that which is something real in the world that lies before us". "The pure psychical being of the psychical life is regarded as a nature-resembling *flow of events* in a quasi-space of consciousness... in an experience that is continuous, and *held persistently together* through a thread of widespread unanimity." [69] The words I underlined correspond verbatim to Buddhaghoso's interpretation of *sam-ā-dhi* ("holding well together in itself", in Nanamoli's translation). Thus in both systems the world is a phenomenon of the well focussed "ray of attention".

In the *Formal and Transcendental Logic* Husserl reaffirms the initial phenomenological stance on the Ego in relation to *epoché*: If we persist, in applying reduction, to penetrate deeper into the primal dimension of our experience, and do not admit anything on the ground of belief in the existence of the world, then we shall have to exclude also our own personality as a psychological unity, since it is also a part of the spatio-temporal world.

In the First Cartesian Meditation, Section 10 is dedicated to "Descartes' failure to make the transcendental turn". Due to this failure he "mistook the Ego for a *substantia cogitans*, for a separate human *mens sive animus*". By this mistake Descartes became "the father of the absurd doctrine of transcendental realism".[70] Accepting it "as a matter of course that, with our apodictic pure Ego, we have rescued a little tag-end of the world, as the sole unquestionable part of it for the philosophizing Ego", Descartes took it for granted that "knowledge of reality and knowledge of causality are inseparable"[71] - a thesis strictly comparable to the one rejected by Buddho. Buddho clearly rejects the Vedantic doctrine of a Self-substance in the back-stage of "an all-embracing genesis" behind the phenomenal "infinite nexus of synthetically congruous performances" of *paṭicca-samuppādo*.

Max Scheler, clearly recognized from the very beginning of his phenomenological investigations the necessity of rejecting the idea of a soul as ontical entity, or "soul substance". This position he held despite his belief in the necessity of the idea of a personal God which he maintained in conformity with his Roman Catholic commitment; the initial "theistic" postulate in the "highest questions of metaphysics" he abandoned much later, when in *Die*

Stellung des Menschen im Kosmos (The Position of Man in the Universe", 1927) he gave an explicit account of his new cosmological and anthropological position. But already in his basic work on ethics[72] Scheler insists on the logical necessity to conceive God as the highest "idea of person" in which "there is no more I and no more having-a-soul (*Beseeltheit*)", since we cannot confront God "either with an outward world or with a You." Therefore,

> "Against erroneous attempts of a certain kind of philosophy to consider man as a species of nature endowed with specific faculties of speech, of morality, of reasoning, and even with a so-called immortal soul- substance," Scheler denies "explicitly any whatsoever significance of such attempts" in discussing the problem of "man's position in the All." "Since the concept of soul and the concept of body do not represent classes of absolute objects, the question about their possible interaction is also meaningless."

The whole problem appears to arise arbitrarily "out of its own", "as it was correctly observed already by Kant." Connections between psychical and physical events can be properly explained only as being effected by the integrating activity of a person. A person "'is' only as the concrete unity of acts accomplished by that person, and only in their actual accomplishment". A person is only an experienced (*er-lebt*) and "never a *lived* being and life". 'Person' "does not mean anything psychical at all," and the phenomenology of inner experiences should not any longer (at least since Kant) be misunderstood as 'psychology'. From the historical viewpoint of the Buddhist doctrine of personality (*puggala-paññatti*) all this sounds as an up to date confirmation of the thesis of 'momentariness' or temporality-activism (*khanika-vādo*) which excludes the soul-substance of a permanent self (or transcendent, divine Self). This is the Buddhist doctrine of *an-attā* (Sk. *nairātmyah*, no-self).

(5) In the next chapter basic Buddhist documentation leading to a *differential analysis* of the *ultimate aim of meditation* will be quoted. As a preliminary task one more restriction in the application of *epoché*, according to both methods, has to be singled out; it is the *principle of non-transcending* the limits of the 'purely cognizing' (*vijñapti mātratā*), 'descriptive' or 'registering' (*tad-ārammañam*)

function of the meditative consciousness, or the strictly *non-ecstatic* attitude of the meditating philosopher, which is also an ascetic virtue *par excellence*, excluding all indulgence in visions or occult phenomena, considered here as 'impediments' (*āvaraṇam*) on the ascetic way of purification (*visuddhi-maggo*). It is at the same time the principle of parsimony of the truth applied to the specific context of the *ethos* of knowledge for reasons of *apatheia* in the original meaning laid down in Pyrrho's tropes. Kant also pointed out in the "Preface to the Metaphysical Elements of Ethics" under the heading "Virtue necessarily presupposes Apathy (considered as Strength)"[73] the ethical aspect found in the original meaning of apatheia which is still pertinent to our modern phenomenological criticism:

> "This word (apathy) has come into bad repute, just as if it meant want of feeling, and therefore subjective indifference with respect to the objects of the elective will, it is supposed to be weakness. This misconception may be avoided by giving the name *moral apathy* to that want of emotion which is to be distinguished from indifference. In the former the feelings arising from sensible impressions lose their influence on the moral feeling... The true strength of virtue is the *mind at rest*, with a firm, deliberate resolution to bring its law into practice. This is the state of *health* in the moral life."

Husserl's philosophical inquiry as a whole ultimately aimed at establishing an apodictically evident criterion of distinction between "solipsistic and intersubjective experience." In the systematic plan of the *Ideas...* the inquiry into the problem of solipsism was foreseen as the central theme of the Second Book ("Phenomenological Analysis of Constitution") which, however, was edited and published only posthumously, apparently because of Husserl's dissatisfaction with his own earlier attempt. An essay of his monadological solution is contained in the Fifth additional Cartesian Meditation.

Husserl's transcendental idealism in treating the critical problem of the 'constitution' of the whole world will remain focussed on the problem of the actuality (*Wirklichkeit*) of the *alter-ego* in it, or of the solution of the problem of *solipsism*. This solution will necessarily be sought predominantly in the existential sphere of life. (This tendency will appear more and more explicitly among Husserl's followers, beginning with Scheler and Heidegger.) The problem of the reality of the "world-whole", "the one and the only universe", or "a unitary universe", is presented at the end of Section Fifteen in the Second Meditation as follows[74]:

> "We now understand that, by our universal *epoché* with respect to the *being or non-being of the world,* we have not simply lost the world for phenomenology, we retain it, after all, *qua cogitatum.* And not only with respect to the *particular* realities that are meant (and as they are meant) in some set or other of separate acts of consciousness - or, stated more distinctly: that are meant selectively. For indeed their particularity is particularity within a unitary *universe,* which, even when we are directed to and grasping the particular, goes on "appearing" unitarily. In other words, there is always co-awareness of it, in the unity of a consciousness that can itself become a *grasping consciousness,* and often enough does. This consciousness is awareness of the world-whole in its own peculiar form, that of spatio temporal endlessness. Throughout every change in consciousness the universe, changeable in its experienced (...) particulars, but still the one and only universe, remains as the existing background of our whole *natural life* ... Accordingly, not only in respect of particulars but also universally, the phenomenologically meditating Ego can become the *"non-participant onlooker"* at himself - including furthermore every objectivity that "is" for him, and as it is for him... Only by virtue of this *new attitude* do I see that all the world, and therefore whatever exists naturally, *exists for me only as accepted by me,* with the sense it has for me at the time - ... and I now accept it solely as that."

In the Buddhist *vijñapti-matratā* (or 'pure consciousness') idealism the essential difference from all this consists, as far as I can see it *prima facie,* only in the existential "measure" (*matratā*) and intentional direction of the criterion of "acceptance" as formulated by Husserl. And this difference is not just a vague (accidental) fact resulting from the heterogeneity of their historical situation. It is based on the explicit principle of the *acosmic turn* founded on the *ethos of knowledge.* This principle formulates the intention of Buddhist *epoché,* or *jhānam,* a system we will discuss in the following chapter.

Unfortunately, a dogmatic and doctrinary division line separates the universal *philosophia perennis* (Indian *sanātana-dharma*). On the Eurocentric side, those who are unable to visualize even the possibility of a meaningful and fruitful *tertium conparationis* between Buddho, Pyrrho, and Husserl might still find in Husserl's Cartesian Meditations an incentive to continue meditating on critical observations concerning the philosophy of science. This would be a means to span distances which are divided-and-united by spatio-temporal medians (in the sense of Husserl's logical terms synthesis and analysis)[75]:

(a) "... the Cartesian idea of a science (ultimately an all-embracing science) grounded on an absolute foundation... is none other than the idea that distantly furnishes guidance in all sciences and in their striving toward universality - ..."

(b) "First, anyone who seriously intends to become a philosopher must 'once in his life' *withdraw into himself* and attempt, *within himself, to overthrow and build anew* all the sciences that, up to then, he has been accepting. Philosophy - wisdom (*sagesse*) - is the philosopher's quite personal affair. It must arise as his wisdom, as his self-acquired knowledge tending toward universality, a knowledge for which he can answer from the beginning, and at each step, by virtue of his own absolute insight. If I have decided to live with this as my aim - the decision that alone can start me on the course of a philosophical development - I have thereby chosen *to begin in absolute poverty...*"

(c) "*A science whose peculiar nature is unprecedented* comes into our field of vision: a science of concrete transcendental subjectivity, as given in actual and possible transcendental experience, a science that forms the *extremest contrast to sciences in the hitherto accepted sense*, positive, *'Objective'* sciences... Now, however, we are envisaging a science that is so to speak, absolutely subjective, whose thematic object exists *whether or not the world exists.*"

Ad. (b) cf. in their wider aspects and contexts the following few statements on which Buddho often insisted and reverted:

"The teaching of the Buddho (*Bhagavatā dhammo*)... is to be comprehended by the wise, *each for himself* (*paccattaṁ veditabbo viññ'ūhī*)."

" - It is proper for you, Kalamas, to doubt, to be uncertain, uncertainty has arisen in you about what is doubtful. Do not go upon what has been acquired by repeated hearing, nor upon tradition, nor upon rumor, nor upon what is in the scriptures (*piṭakaṁ*, term referring typically to the 'collections' of Buddho's own talks),... nor upon a bias toward a notion that has been pondered over... Only when you yourself know and see: 'These things are not blamable...', enter on and abide in them."

(*Anguttara-nikāyo,* III. 65, Mahavaggo)

"The thicket of views, the wilderness of views, the vacillation of views, the fetter of views... by which the untaught ordinary man is bound" - refers to world-views (*diṭṭhi,* Sk. *dṛṣṭi,* Greek *doxa*) classified in the first long talk (*Dīgha-nikāyo* 1) on "The Net of Brahma" into sixty two divisions whose sub-sections correspond to Kant's four antinomies of the pure reason: limits of time and space, causality and immortality of the soul. The conclusion derived from this analysis is:

"Whatever recluses or brahmans assert various conceptual theorems referring to the past and the future - all are trapped in this net with its sixty-two divisions."

After the present survey was written, I read Prof. Debabrata Sinha's article, *Theory and practice in Indian thought: Husserl's observations,* in "Philosophy East and West", July 1971. It is based on an unpublished manuscript of Husserl (MS B 121, Husserl-Archiv, University of Cologne). Though Husserl's acquaintance with Indian philosophy seems to have remained superficial, his second-hand information included, maybe as its basic source, H. Oldenberg's book on the Buddho. One quotation from the MS. (p. 49) and Sinha's further reference to the same subject of central importance seem to confirm above all Husserl's awareness of the fact that the primeval meditative attitude of the Indian philosophic thinking is characterized, beyond all distinctions and trends, by the fundamental importance of an authentic method of *epoché*. Here is the German text and Sinha's free interpretation:

Husserl: Aber selbst da ist doch fur die Inder das Denken der Erlosungslehre *nicht* in seiner Form (und Logik sozusagen) *von dem natürlichen Denken unterschieden*, sonder durch seine Konsequenz, seine Vorurteilslosigheit, seine Entschlossenheit in der *Ausschaltung des natürlichen Lebensinteresses,* und der interesselosen Bewertung desselben und Auspragung der Wertungen in Wissensurteilen.

Sinha: As Husserl states, Indian thinking proceeds to liberation, to bliss through "unreserved knowledge" (*Seeligkeit durch ruchsichtslose Erkenntniss*)... He significantly adds that the Indian pattern of thinking about the theory of liberation in its essential form and logic is *not distinguished from natural thinking*. What distinguishes it from the latter are its consistency, its freedom from prejudgment, its *switching off (Ausschaltung) of the natural interest of life*, and the disinterested valuing of the same.

(Statements relevant for topics discussed in the present paper especially in ch. II. are underlined by the author.)

Chapter Three

The Reductive Structures of Jhānam

Pali texts, in formulating *jhānam*, distinguish two sets of four stages which were later coordinated, in *abhidhammo* literature, and presented under the following two headings:

(a) *rūpajjhānā*: The "formative" components of the reductive process, analogous to Husserl's "intentional subjective process" on the noetic side of the act of *epoché*.

(b) *arūpajjhānā*: Their reduction to the "formless" (*arūpam*) 'null-point' (*suññam*) of 'objectifying' concretion in the transcendental 'stream of consciousness' (*bhavañga-soto*). The noematic contents of the acts find their categorial counterpart in the structure of *arūpajjhāanā*.

The text of the *Cuḷa-suññata-suttaṁ* (at the end of this chapter) can serve also as an example of how the basic four-member sets of *rūpa-* and *arūpa-jhānā* can be, and often are, included in other variants of extended structures of contemplative practice. Such examples show that these two basic structures should not be considered as necessarily conjoint into an inseparable hierarchical whole. A systematic study of such extensions in different concrete situations has not yet been done, as far as I know, and cannot be undertaken in the present survey.

(a) Rūpajjhānā

The standard formulation of the first two *jhānā* has been cited at the beginning of chapter I, and analysed in its first part, referring to the initial reduction of its intellectual (*vitakka-vicāro*) component. The emotional side of the noematic act (qualified e.g. as 'pleasure valuation', 'dread', or simple 'existential care') will be further explained later in the discussion of the completed scheme of both sets and their interrelations.

The formulation of the remaining third and fourth stages of reduction is cited here from the *Sāmañña-phala-suttaṁ* (D.2) [76] which contains the most extensive description of this structure (though here it is not quoted in its entirety.):

(3) "Then further, with the fading away of alertness as well, he remains in equanimity, mindful and fully aware, he feels with his body that ease which the noble ones talk of when they say: "He who hasequanimity and is mindful dwells at ease". So he attains the *third jhānam*, and abides therein. He suffuses, permeates, fills andpervades *his very body with ease devoid of alertness*, so that no spotin his whole body remains untouched therewith..."

(4) "Then further, with the abandoning of ease and anguish, and with theprevious disappearance of elation and depression, he attains the *fourth jhānam*, without anguish and without ease, but only with purity of mindfulness due to equanimity, and abides therein. And he sits there so suffusing *even his body* with his cleansed and purified mind that no spot in his whole body remains untouched therewith..."

b) Arūpajjhānā

The following basic structure of *rūpajjhānā*, is found in M. 113, S. 36, 19, and in several other texts. An independent structure is contained in D. 16 (*Mahā-parinibbāna-suttantam*, Ch. III, 33).

"Then further, with the complete overcoming of form-perceptions, withthe disappearance of perceptions of resistance, with non-attention to perceptions of variety, (aware of) *infinite space*, he attains the (categorial) region of infinite space, and abides therein.

Then further, by completely overcoming the region of infinite space,(aware of) *infinite consciousness*, he attains to the (categorial) region of infinite consciousnesss, and abides therein.

> Then further, by completely overcoming the region of infinite consciousnẹss, (aware that) there is nothing, he attains the (categorial) region of *nothingness*, and abides therein.
>
> Then further, by completely overcoming the region of nothingness, he attains to the region of *neither-perception-nor-non-perception*, and-abides therein."

In *Table I*, the formula of the *rūpajjhānā* is schematized in a set of three series of constituent phenomena. In the first column the characteristics of the *cognizing faculties* (corresponding to the noetic region of Husserl's *cogito*) are progressively reduced. In the second column the parallel phenomena of *attentiveness* proceed in an opposite direction, since they are strengthened by the reduction of the scope of *cogito*. In the third column, phenomena of *concentration* are correlative to those of attentiveness, and follow the same course. While the phenomena of attentiveness are described in their negative noetic correlation to those in the first column, phenomena of concentration (determined by the *contents* of the contemplated object) denote a positive noematic intentness.

TABLE 1

Reduction of cognizing faculties (noetic aspect)	Strengthening of attentiveness	Intentness concentrated on the object *(noematic aspect)*
FIRST JHANAM		
Formation of logical concepts - *vitakko*	Reduction of emotional and volitive adherence (*vivicc'eva kāmehi...*)	Isolation *viveko* ("The meaning is: disappearance of hindrances")[77]
Discursive thinking - *vicāro* Alertness - *pīti* Ease -*sukham*		Tightness of structural fixture
Reduction of cognizing faculties (noetic aspect)	Strengthenining of attentiveness	Intentness concentrated on the object (noematic aspect)
SECOND JHANAM		
Alertness - *pīti* Ease - *sukham*	Reduction of intellectual attitudes (*sampasādanam*)	One-pointed concentration *-samādhija-ekodibhāvo*
THIRD JHANAM		
Ease - *sukham*	Equanimity - (*upekhako satimā...*)	"Equanimity about formations-equanim ity about insight"[78]
FOURTH JHANAM		
Equanimity - *upekhā*	Purity of attention (*sati-pārisuddhi*)	Liberation of mind *ceto-vimutti* Reduction of intentionality to the pure flux of consciousness (*bhavanga-soto*)

Notes to Table I

The first and the second *jhānam* are stages of progressive elimination of intellectual (logical and discursive) processes. The intention (obvious at least on this level) is not to attain some kind of "empty consciousness". Therefore, in practical exercises, the mind has to remain concentrated (bound to "the post of attention") on the simplest and smallest possible sign (*nimittam*) of pure *sense-experience* (like color *kasiṇam*, or breathing, or touch). In modern (especially Burmese) methods of *sati-paṭṭhanam* it has been particularly emphasized (in a recent discussion on these psychological misunderstnadings) that it is *not* necessarily the *process of breathing*, but only the actual slight sensation of touch on some specific point of the "breath- body" which characterizes the ideal one-pointedness in focussing the ray of attention. Touch is the most primitive sense-perception, as it is remotest from the self-centered intellectual conceptualization which one aims at excluding in the *jhānam* exercise.

Following the reduction of the intellectual function, which is here characterized by its two basic aspects *vitakka-vicāro*, their positive emotional counterpart, whose two basic grades are characterized in our texts as *pīti-sukham*, has to be reduced too. My translation of this compound with 'alertness-and-ease' requires interpretative justification. The commentarial and lexicographic interpretation of *pīti* follows the intentional direction of 'joy' to 'zest' to 'interest.[79] *Sukham*, in its basic and widest meaning, is 'happiness'. In our terminological context it is usually interpreted as 'ease'. In translating *pīti* with 'alertness', I wished to bring out a subtle tension emerging in the act of experiencing the difference in degree between *ıiti* and *sukham*. The importance of this distinction will be realized only with reference to the correlative double meaning of *upekhā* on the last two levels of *jhānam*.

One is confronted by an intellectual reduction in which the first two stages of *jhānam* form an integral unit of experience whose initial and final terms can be distinguished only in their logical differentiation while the actual experience remains an indivisible continuum. The third and fourth *jhānam* are again integrated as one specific unit or level of experience, characterized, in this case, by a formally identical term, *upekhā*, equanimity. A brief analysis of this term in its contextual meaning is necessary in order to show that our classsification of the term *upekhā* in the column of the third *jhānam*, and in the first column of the fourth *jhānam* is not arbitrary. In the third *jhānam* a state of equilibrated attentiveness is maintained, and a positive feeling of ease is still felt as a relief from the burden of active interests and intentions preoccupying the mind at the initial stages of its "right effort" (*sama-vāyamo*). It is the feeling of *catharsis* (purification, *visuddhi*) very well known in European philosophy since Aristotle and re-evoked in a modern version in Schopenhauer's theory on the liberating effect of art. Schopenhauer was aware also of its metaphysical deeper Buddhist analogy[80]. Thus the feeling of ease appears as the immediate psychological effect of the realization of inner poise. Only in the fourth *jhānam* the equanimity of *upekhā* becomes a total and stabilized state of mind, an effortless and emotionless state of purity.

The 'cultivation' (*bhāvanā*) of consciousness in the attainment of one-pointed concentration of the ray of attention by reducing its 'formative' (noetic) intentions on the way of *rūpajjhānā*, will result, on each level, in the corresponding reduction of contents (noema) intended by each peculiar function of *cogito* in its specific categorial region (*āyatanam*). Thus, in corresponding with the "intentional subjective process" on the noetic (*rūpajhānā*) side, there is a parallel structure of chatagorial regions on the side of noematic contents of the same process. The latter is schematized in the quaternary structure of *arūpajhānā*. The analogy of the term *rūpam* (understood as the act of 'forming') to the noetic intention of Husserl's *cogito* needs no further explanation. The designation of the noematic aspect of *cogitatum* as the attainment of *a-rūpam*, i.e. the 'form-less' "realm of a Heraclitean flux", presupposes a comprehensive insight into the accomplished process of reduction of essential signs (*nimittam*) to their ultimate categorial regions (*ayatanam*). It is from this widest vantage ground (*bhūmi*) that the noematic counterparts of the noetic functions are reduced to the corresponding four levels of *arūpajjhānā*.

In Table II, the four stages of *rūpajjhānā* (1-4) have been abstracted from the complex aspects of their structural analysis on Table I. Categorial regions (*āyatanam*) of the *arūpam* counterpart (5-8) are evident in their simple Pali formulation.

TABLE II Rūpajjhān (1-4)	 Arūpajjhān (5-8)
(1) *vitakka-vicāro* (initial stage of intellectual activity- *cogito*)	(5) *ākāsānañcāyatanam* (region of infinite space)
(2) *avitakka-avicāro* (suspension of intellectual activity)	(6) *viññāṇañcāyatanam* (region of infinite consciousness)
(3) *upekhako satimā (sukham)* (intent on inner equilibrium)	(7) *ākiñcaññāyatanam* (region of nothingness)
(4) *sati-pārisuddhi upekhā* (equanimity of pure attention)	(8) *neva-sañña-nāsaññāyatanam* (region of neither-perception-nor-non-perception).

Notes to Table II

The natural attitude characteristic of the non phenomenologically-reduced mind (*cogito*) consists of apprehending the world in modes of its givenness, and assimilating it intellectually. It uses its world in this process as "food" (*ahāro*), as it is interpreted in a striking coincidence of terms by Buddho and Nietzsche[81]. The "coarse" material world is first given to the *cogito* (mind) in its space dimensions. Even time is spacialized[82]. The infinity of the world is the infinity of mind's "hunger" and "thirst" (*taṇhā*), or of the "Self-creating" "will to power". Thus *vitakka-vicāro* is "co-primeval", reciprocal and mutually conditioned, with the unlimited horizon of space (*ākāsānañcāyatanam*).

The suspension (*epoché*) of *vitakka-vicāro* means therefore at the same time the reduction of the contents (*noema*) of world-consciousness (*viññāṇam*) to empty categorial forms of the cognizing consciousness. Infinity of space is strictly coextensive with the infinity of mind (*viññāṇañcāyatanam*). The reduction of the outward (*bāhiram*) to the inward dimension (*ajjhatam*) is well known to modern phenomenological philosophy as introversion of spatial to temporal consciousness, whose infinity ultimately merges in our experience of a pure flux of the existential stream (*bhavañga-soto*).

Reduction of the categorial (structural) consciousness to the pure stream (transcendental in Husserl's interpretation) could, in terms of our contemporary philosophy, be called its "nihilation" (cf. Sartre), or, "nullification" in the strict meaning of the Pali equivalent *suññatā* (*śūnyatā* in Sanskrit Buddhism). Thus the attainment of the 'pure stream of consciousness' coincides with the awareness of 'nothingness' (*ākiñcaññāyatanam*). This equilibrating act of outward and inward purification of consciousness is an experience of difficult floating without 'support' (*ālambanam*) by any reality belief on a stream, vividly described by all those who have reached it or even attempted to approach it, be it in the "ancient East" or in the "modern West" (since W. James and H. Bergson). It is the experience of the world as samadhi, or "keeping tightly together" within the focus of the ray of attention.

Such equilibrium still requires a tremendous effort of awareness. If successfully maintained, it will naturally result in a poised attitude of relaxed attention (*sati-paṭṭhānam*) where both perception and non-perception will have fulfilled their purpose and lost significance in a purely intensive experience - and this is 'equanimity' in its second essential meaning, *upekhā* as *apatheia*: *neva-saññā-nāsaññāyatanam*[83].

Buddhaghoso's explanations of the *arūpajjhānā* bring out the basic elements of these essential experiences in their human immediacy. A film of historical opacity is laid upon their original meaning by the petrifying commentarial tendency toward theological mythologization of such "exceptional states" of mind (in which still today some traditionalist western interpreters prefer to see "celestial" or "godly" "realms" rather than meaningful dimensionns of actual experience, normally attainable for a cultivated mind).

It has been observed that the term *arūpajjhānā* appears only in the *abhidhammo* systemization of the basic *sutta-piṭakam* texts. In these latter texts often only the first (*rūpa-*) *jhānam* scheme is quoted. In other cases an eight *jhānam* scheme is given as a whole (sometimes even extended beyond the fourth arupam grade). In a few texts the *arūpam* group is included in differently extended structures without any reference to the basic *rūpam* correlate.

The fact that already the earliest *abhidhammo* systematization had separated these two groups indicates the difference in their structural character. The distinction can be explained by the analogy of the two groups to the noetic and noematic structure of the cognizing mind (*cogito and cogitatum*) in modern terms, as we have seen.

If these two groups of reductive processes, differentiated by their respective intentions, are classified in a successive rather than a parallel order, then one should consider the following two points. First, the order of enumeration does not necessarily reflect the order of structural integration of classified elements. Secondly, even in abstracting from such naive simplifications and interpretions of complexes of actual experience, the subsequent location of the second group, and also the considerably greater importance given to the first in basic texts (where the *arūpam* group is often omitted) has its good reasons in the structure of the experience itself. Furthermore, the proper constitutional understanding of the experience can be realized only by adequate insight into the actual process of epoche. The noetic act-capacities of the cognizing mind, serving as a tool of actual noematic (content's) reduction, must first be compared to the specific task of "cultivationg the fields" (*āyatanaṁ*) of "transcendence in the immanence" (in Husserl's terms). Otherwise, commentarial formalization and verbalization of such 'tool and field elements' cannot bring us further than it ultimately did in its historical relapse into the utterly un-buddhistic "realms of formless gods", held up to derision by such genuine practitioners as was the Tibetan yogi-poet Milarepa:

> *Alas, these heavenly births*
> *have neither sense nor value.*
> *When they think vicious thoughts*
> *they start to fall again,*
> *As to the reason for their fall*
> *scholars with empty words*
> *have dried their mouths in explanation.*[84]

In the *Introductory Discourse on Nullity, (Cuḷa-suññata-suttaṁ,* M.121) the progressive isolation and suspencion of "marks and particulars" in "restraining the senses" (including the "mind at ease organ", *mano-indriyam*) is explained through concrete examples of training in the *jhānam* method, whose purpose is to reduce progressively the eidetic preception (*saññā*) of clearly selected and properly focussed 'marks' (*nimittam*) to the 'zero point' (*suññatā*) in the transcendentally purified 'stream of experience' (*bhavañga-soto*). The specific importance of this *suttam* on contemplation consists also in the advantage it offers for the study of mutual relation between two basic terms of the Buddhist theory of 'nothingness' (*ākiñcaññ'āyatanam*) and 'nullity', (as *suññatā* is rendered in the following illustrative exposition) on their proper significance for a contemplative approach ro the problem of human existance.

In the following condensation of the *suttam* I wish to demonstrate the authenticity of our archaic prototype of 'essence insight', or *eidos*,through the process of its suspensive isolation *viveko, epoché*. The significant moments in the development of this aspect of *bhāvanā* will be marked out in order to exemplify the meaning of 'eidetic singularities' and of other characteristic elements referred to in the course of this survey.

> "..... without giving attention to the perception of village, without giving attention to the perception of man, the *bhikkhu*'s attention is concerned exclusively with the perception of forest. By this perception of forest his mind is penetrated, clarified, stabilized and released. He realizes thus: 'Whatever cares (*darathā*) the perception of a village may provoke, such cares are not now present in me. Care is restricted exclusively to the perception of forest.' He realizes in his perception there is nothing of village or of man, and that there is only the perception of forest which has not been annulled. So he discerns what is not there as null. But of what there remains he realizes that it is still present. This, Anando, is his access to the actual undisturbed and pure experience of nullity."

In the same manner the meditator proceeds to the suspension of the awareness of forest, so that there remains only the awareness of "earth" in its purely eidetic, perceptual comprehensiveness, peculiar to the kasinam contemplation :

> "Just as though a bull's hide were freed from folds by stretching it with a hundred pegs, so too, without giving attention to all the ridges and plains on this earth, the *bhikkhu* gives attention exclusively to the perception of earth...."

On the following steps of extending annulment, the stages of the four *arūpajjhānā* are gradually suspended. Thus the regions (*āyatanam*) of "the infiniteness of space" and of "the infiniteness of consciousness" are progressively annulled, and then even the region of "nothingness" (*ākiñcaññ-āyatanam*), and ultimately the awareness of "neither-perceiving-nor-non- perceiving".

> Further, Anando, without giving attention to the perception of nothingness, without giving attention to the awareness of neither-perceiving-nor-non-perceiving, the *bhikkhu*'s attention is concerned exclusively with the signless concentration of mind. His mind is penetrated, clarified, stabilized and released by the signless concentraraion of mind. He realizes thus: "This signless concentration of mind has been carefully established and pondered over. Yet, whatever has been established and pondered over is impermanent and liable to stopping." When he knows and sees thus his mind is released from the influence of sensual desire as well as from influences of being and ignorance. Such is the knowledge of release in the released... He realizes that cares provoked by the influence of sensual desire as well as by influence of being and of ignorance are no more there. Care is restricted exclusively to this body endowed with six sense-faculties motivated by life... So he realizes what is not there as null. But of what there remains he realized that it is still present. - This, Anando, is his access to the actual undisturbed and pure experience of nullity.

Thus by the method of *epoché*, in meditative isolation, also the existential problem of nothingness is solved in a consciousness of 'nullity' or 'nihilation', which, however, is bereft of its basic existential realization "of what there remains" even when "care" is reduced "exclusively to this body".

Appamaññā
The four "immeasurable virtues"

Parallel to the basic four *(rūpa-) jhānā* there is a more popular and extensive quaternary structure guiding the meditator through a gradation of purely moral virtues to the same ultimate attainment of *upekkhā* as the final deliverance from suffering (*apatheia*). The correct Pali term for this is *appamaññā* (Sk. *apramānyā*) - the four "immeasurable" or "boundless" virtues"[85]:

mettā (Sk. *maitrī*) - friendliness
(usually translated as "loving kindness")
karunā- pity, compassion

muditā- joyful empathy ("soft-heartedness")
upekkhā- (Sk. *upekṣā* - equanimity)

The more popular term for the same structure is *brahma-vihārā* or "dwelling places (heavens) of the Brahma gods", or "divine abodes" in general. This name, also repeated often in Buddho's discourses[86], confirms the extension of this practice far beyond its Buddhist application. Along with a reference to *jhānam* (Sanskrit *dhyānam*) Patanjali's *Yoga-sūtrāni* also contains a reference to this quaternary gradation of virtues, designated by the same terms in I, 33, as "the cultivation of mental purity" (*bhāvanāta' citta-prasādanam*).

A remarkable similarity has been disclosed also in comparative studies of Sufism as well where[87]

1. *Muaththar* corresponds to *maitrī*. "It is the empathy, described by Rumi as "the love of God growing in your heart, enabling the devotee to feel the bestowing of grace".
2. *Karāmat*, corresponding to *karuñā*; "magnanimosity felt through the bestowing of grace."
3. *Maḥabba* corresponds to *muditā*: "the selfless pure love which 'bubbles' in the heart burning all feeling of fear or misgiving".
4. *Tawakkul* corresponds to *upekṣā*; "an equanimity where mind can be stilled". Characterizing the popularity of this meditation,

Pali texts on the subject are prevalent in the most popular collection of *Añguttara-nikāyo*[88]. The following standard formulation is quoted from Buddho's conversation with the young brahman Subho Todeyyaputto:

- Master Gotamo, I have heard it said that the ascetic Gotamo teaches the path to the retinue of Brahma. It would be good if Master Gotamo would teach me this path. - Then, young man, listen and attend carefully to what I shall say. - Even so, sir, - replied the young Subho Todeyyaputto. The Blessed One said this: - And what is the path to the retinue of Brahma? Here a bhikkhu abides with his mind embued with friendliness (*mettā*) pervading one quarter of the world, likewise the second, likewise the third, likewise the fourth, and so above, below, and across, everywhere identifying himself with all he is pervading the whole world with mind embued with friendliness, wide, exalted, measureless, free from hate and ill-will. And when by his mind released through friendliness he has attained this level of development, no activity restricted by limited measure-

> ment is found there, none persists there. Just as a vigorous trumpeter could easily make himself heard in the four directions, so too when the mind released through friendliness has attained this level of development, no activity restricted by limited measurement is found there, none persists there. - This, young man, is the path to the retinue of Brahma. And thus he continues to pervade the whole world with mind embued with pity..., with joyful empathy..., and with equanimity, wide, exalted, measureless, free from hate and ill-will..."

The simile of pervading the universe with rays of spiritual enlightenment may evoke a stronger impression than the trumpetering going on in the various religious temples even today, albeit with less and less conviction. The rays of spiritual illumination are still imagined to reach us from elsewhere, reminding us, at best, of children playing with mock electric torches.

In a commentary of Patanjali's Yoga-sutrani, recently discovered in Madras and attributed by several Indian, European and Japanese scholars to Sankarah[89], *sūtraṁ* I,33, is interpreted as:

> "... meditation on friendliness towards the happy, compassion for the suffering, goodwill towards the virtuous, and disinterest in the sinful".

These limits, especially for the last and highest virtue of *upekkhā*, are acceptable for me, too, as the most reasonable aspect of the whole structure discussed in this chapter.

Designated in Pali and in Sanskrit contexts as *brahma-vihārā* - the four "boundless states" or "divine abodes" are described as moods of *sublime virtues*. These pervasive emotional attainments on the subjective side of mindfulness correspond to *rational purification* (inhibition by *epoché*) as effects in "pilgrim's progress" on the way of the four *jhānas*. The following table shows the close and necessary correlation of these *appamaññā* cittam to the *rūpa* and *arūpa-jhānas*.

TABLE III

<table>
<tr><th>rūpa-jhānam</th><th>arūpa-jhanaṁ</th><th>appamaññā cittam</th></tr>
<tr><td>(1) sa-vitakkaṁ sa-vicāraṁ
applying conceptual and discursive thinking</td><td>(5) ākāsāñ-cayatanaṁ
encompassing the sphere of objective world in space</td><td>(1) mettā
friendliness, empathy</td></tr>
<tr><td>(2) a-vitakkaṁ a-vicāraṁ
detachment from conceptual and discursive thinking</td><td>(6) viññāṇañ-cāyatanaṁ
refraining to the subjective counterpart (paṭibimbaṁ) and constitution in the stream of consciousness (saṁsāro)</td><td>(2) karunā
compassion</td></tr>
<tr><td>(3) pīti-sukhaṁ
ease and joy</td><td>(7) ākiñcann-āyatanaṁ
sphere of nothingness</td><td>(3) muditā
gladness, sympathethic, easeful joy</td></tr>
<tr><td colspan="3">-Suffering (dukkhaṁ) being dependent on impermanence (aniccaṁ) of the being-in-itself (anattā) - according to the ti-lakkhanaṁ complex constitution of phenomenal existence - "the total overcoming of the spheres of boundless space... and boundless consciousness, with the realization 'Nothing is there'..." results in the peculiar experience of release.</td></tr>
<tr><td>(4) upekkhā
equanimity</td><td>(8) neva-sanna-n'āsaññ-āyatanaṁ
the sphere of neither-perception nor-non-perception</td><td>(4) upekkhā
equanimity indifference (Greek apatheia, ataraxia isostheneia)</td></tr>
</table>

Chapter Four

The Way of Training the Mind

> *"If you silence yourself as a gong that is broken,*
> *you have already attained nibbanam,*
> *since there is no aggressiveness in you."*
> *(Dhamma-padaṁ, 134)*

1. Introduction

The way from solitude to silence, leading to the ascetic purity of a hermit's contemplative life (as I have chosen it), is the way of "taming the mind". I shall try to show at the end of this chapter how misleading, and even dangerous, it may be to identify *moral* purification with any "technique". What does it mean to be alone, to be silent? How and why should "the right effort" (*sammā-vāyāmo*), the sixth step on Buddho's "eightfold path to the cessation of suffering", the decisive step for concentrative absorption (*sati-samādhi-jhānam*), be undertaken?

Solitariness precedes silence. To "go to the end of the world" (as I have tried to do) does not yet mean to remain alone:

> "I do not say, brahmans, that by such journeys the end of the world may be known, seen, reached; yet I declare that without reaching the end of the world there is no ending of suffering. These five strands of sense-desire are called the world in the doctrine of the Noble One: shapes noticed by the eye, sounds noticed by the ear, scents noticed by the nose, tastes noticed by the tongue, touches noticed by the skin. Now consider the monk who in complete isolation from sense-desires and from states which are not advantageous to his end... attains the four stages of formative and of formless absorptions (*rūpa-and arūpa-jhānā*). In each of these cases he is said to have come

to the world's end and to abide there. And yet some say of him... and I, too, say of him that he is still world-bound, still not gone out from the world... Only that monk who in the ending of perception and feeling sees by wisdom that the corruptive influences are completely destroyed, is said to have come to the world's end..., to have passed through the worlds entanglement."

(*Añguttara-nikāyo*, IX,4,38)

Anando questions:

"Could there be, lord, for a monk, such an attainment of concentration wherein he will not be conscious of earth in earth, nor of water in water, nor of fire in fire, nor of air in air, nor will he be conscious of the sphere of infinity of space, nor of the sphere of infinity of consciousness in the sphere of infinity of consciousness, nor of the sphere of nothingness in the sphere of nothingness, nor of the sphere of neither-perception-nor-non-perception, nor will he be conscious of this world in this world, nor of the world beyond in the world beyond - and yet he will be conscious?"

Buddho gives an affirmative answer to his question:

"In this state, Anando, a monk is thus conscious: - This is peace, this is the best, namely the calming down of all formations, relinquishment of all substrata, destruction of craving, detachment, cessation, extinction (*nibbānam*). It is thus, Anando, that there could be for a monk such an attainment of concentration..."

(*Añguttara-nikāyo*,X,1,6)

This is the state of mind attained in the progress of absorption (jhanam) described more extensively in *Cū*a-suññata-suttaṁ* as discussed at the end of the previous chapter on the reductive structure of *jhānam*.

Without such prerequisite "an untrained man who has gone to the forest or the root of a tree or a lonely dwelling-place, lives with a mind obsessed by desire and lust, overwhelmed by desire and lust, and he does not know the way out of desire and lust when they arise. Keeping desire and lust within him he muses (*jhāyati*), he is bemused, he is immused, he is de-mused."[90]

(*Añguttara-nikāyo*, XI,1,10)

"To go to the forest or to a lonely dwelling-place are things hard to bear. Who should say: 'Though I have not won concentration of mind, yet I wish to go to the forest or to a lonely dwelling-place, of him it is to be expected that either he will sink to the bottom or float on the surface... Why so? - The smallness of his person finds no footing in deep water..." (Id.X,10,99)

Thus, living as a hermit does not necessarily mean "living alone", as Buddho emphasizes in another place.

How should the way of going to the "world's end" and of transcending its aim (*param-attho*) be conceived and undertaken? The method of practical training and conduct designated by Buddho as "the cultivation of four right efforts" (*cattāro sammappadhānā*) corresponds to the sixth stage of the eightfold path: *sammā vāyāmo*. To some extent these methods of precaution against neurotic complexes and crises could be compared with that of modern psychoanalytical treatment. Yet, *psychoanalytical tabus* are not only ignored beyond the strictly ascetic limits of mental training, but are insistently rejected as dangerous. The psychoanalytical principle of non-repression of libidinous instincts and impulses stands in integral contradiction to the *ethos of knowledge* maintained by all teachings of asceticism. Above all it stands against the ethics of non- violence (*ahiṁsā*). The apologetics of asceticism may find nowadays its strongest argument in the politically unrefrainable outbursts of anarchistic violence of the young generation educated under the influences of psychoanalytical "humanism".

Karl Jaspers, the author of an extensive "General Psychopathology", considers psychoanalytical "cures" as demonic interference with human freedom. It is "a modern form of superstition" which, both as "a world-view and quack-medicine is tampering with the freedom of man as its alleged research-object".

"The man disappears when, under the pretension of being understood or made understandable in a totality, he becomes the research-object of race-theory, psychoanalysis, or Marxism". "Attitudes appearing grandiose in words behind which the inferiority of life was hidden, were unmasked by psychanalysis", but this "psychotherapeutic movement expanded later into a confused world-view, and its partial truth sprung up in confrontation with an untruthful generation and remained dependant on it."

Thus "the mission of man's being disappears from the pictures of man's ideal."[91]

Pali texts on "the right efforts" (*sammappadhānā*):

"My disciples, cultivate four right efforts:

A monk brings forth his will, exerts himself, stirs up energy, strains his mind and endeavors that evil and unwholesome states of mind that have not arisen within him may not arise;

-....that evil and unwholesome states of mind that have arisen within him may be eliminated;

-....that wholesome states of mind which have not arisen may arise;
-....that wholesome states of mind which have arisen may persist undisturbed, that they may be further cultivated and fully developed. In this way my disciples live in the attainment of perfection in superior knowledge."

(*Majjhima-nikāyo* 77)[92]

If all these psychological methods of avoidance cannot help, then:

"Even though a monk's mind is intent on these (wholesome) thoughts and mental tendencies, there arise evil and unwholesome thoughts provoked by bad impulses, hate and delusion, then he should with teeth set upon teeth, tongue pressed against the palate, restrain, subdue, burn away his thoughts by his mind, so that they be eliminated and dispersed. When they have been abandoned, the introverted mind will be stabilized, settled and concentrated on one point."

(*Majjhima-nikāyo* 20)

Another important text, explaining the four methods of padhana in details, is the discourse IV, 14 of *Añguttara-nikāyo*:

"These four efforts are: the effort of restraining (*saṁvaro*), the effort of abandoning (*pahānam*), the effort of developing (*bhāvāna*), and the effort of protecting (*anurakkhanam*). - And what is the effort of restraining? - Perceiving a form with the eye... hearing a sound with the ear, feeling an odor with the nose, a taste with the tongue, a touch with the body, cognizing a mental phenomena (*dhammo*), the monk neither grasps its characteristic feature (*nimittam*) nor its details, but he strives to ward off the motive through which evil and unwholesome states might influence him, such as greed and sorrow, if he remained with unguarded senses; and he watches over his senses and restrains them. This is called the effort of restraining.

- And what is the effort of abandoning? - The monk does not retain any thought of sensual lust, but abandons it, dispels is, gets rid of it, causes it to disappear. And even so he overcomes thoughts of hate and violence. This is called the effort of abandoning.

- And what is the effort of developing? - The monk develops mindfulness as the factor of awakening wisdom, bent on solitude, dispassionateness, cessation, relinquishing. He develops the investigation of the law (*dhamma-vicayo*), energy, joy, tranquility, concentration (*samādhi*) and equanimity (*upekhā*) as the factors of awakening wisdom (*bojjhañgam*). This is called the effort of developing. - And what is the effort of protecting? - The monk keeps firmly established an impressive mark of concentration, such as the clear perception (*saññā*) of a skeleton, of a corpse infested by worms, of a corpse blue-black in color, of a festering corpse, of a corpse riddled with holes, of a corpse swollen up. This is called the effort of developing."

The progress of introversion in meditative absorption necessarily runs parallel to a progressing and *successful escape* from the world. Thus escape constitutes a basic virtue of all religious efforts to break down the *idola fori.* Already the first step of the noble eightfold path of Buddho, "right views" (*sammā diṭṭhi*), should have prevented prejudices in this respect and immunized us against them. The process of ennobling (*ariya-maggo*) can proceed successfully only in a creative atmosphere of protective mood. This has been comparably described in poetical terms of the following two texts:

"Just as the great ocean gradually slopes and inclines and shelves without any sudden drop, so too in this dhamma-discipline there is gradual training and work and practice; there is no abrupt penetration of knowledge." (*Udānam* V,5)

"Like the moon passing by, bhikkhus, keep remote your body, keep remote your mind, from dwelling-places of family... as if a man would look into a dilapidated well, or in the precipice of a mountain, or at the difficult passage of a river..." (*Saṁyutta-nikāyo* XVI,3)

2. Training the mind - Personal Experience

The actual progress on the way of ennobling the mind can be described only in strictly personal terms of individual experience in meditation. The value of such experiences "for others" (a method of thinking explicitly different from the method of thinking "for oneself" or the original revealing thinking ({cf. Heidegger's *alethea}*, according to Indian logics) can be considered analogous to "individual universals" understood in terms of a strictly descriptive phenomenological method.[93] Therefore the only possible way to approximately compare such individual universals is through statements formulated in the first person singular, within the scope and limits of one's own horizon. I shall try to do this starting from the inspiring analogy of the last quoted metaphor.

In keeping with the traditionally established third stage of a brahman's life, *vānaprastha*, retreating to ascetic life in a forest hermitage, *tapovanaṁ*, I retired in 1966 at the age of fifty, to the Island Hermitage in the backwaters of the Sinhalese seashore. The age for a *vānaprastha*'s retreat from the householder's duties of a brahman priest had to be fixed beyond the ripening stage of youth when no sacrificial and mantric tricks would be strong enough to cheat the sex of a chaste student of theology (*brahmacāri*); a rule of precaution unfortunately neglected by many Buddhists.

In my early introspective efforts I first endeavored to establish a better order by cleaning the overcrowded mind and redistributing *its reduced contents in harmony* with breathing in a less stuffy atmosphere of a clarified natural ambience.

A casual observation made by William James puzzled me at first and then remained a recurrent theme over which I pondered for several years as its meaning became clearer, it gradually penetrated beyond its initial range. In his essay *"Does Consciousness Exist?"*[94] W. James describes the "stream of consciousness" or "stream of thinking" in terms closely corresponding to the Buddhist theory of *bhavañga-soto* (articulation - *añgam* - of the existential *bhavo* - flux - *soto*), upon which is based the negation of a permanent "self", a bearer of a static faculty of consciousness. Analyzing the "stream of thought" James observed in a parenthesis that it, "when scrutinized, reveals itself to consist chiefly of the stream of my breathing". "... this succession of an emptiness and fullness... in small enough pulses" constitutes "the conscious self of the moment" as "the instant field of the present". In the Buddhist analogue the task of "right effort" in meditation consists in reducing the scope of attention (*sati*) to the "one-pointedness" of the mental process of thinking (*cittam*). This "thought-moment" corresponds to the "instant field of the present" in James' formulation. In pursuance of the same intention Buddho used to repeat the following advice to interlocutors:

> "Let us leave alone the past and the future. I shall teach you the general law (*dhammo*)." (*M. 79*)
>
> "Let not a man trace back a past or wonder what the future holds. Instead, with insight let him see each thing presently arisen." (*M.10*)
>
> "Bhikkhus, when one's turban or head is ablaze, what is to be done? Lord, when one's turban or head is ablaze, in order to extinguish it one must put forth utmost will, effort, endeavor, exertion, courage, mindfulness and attention. Well, Bhikkhus, letting alone paying no heed to the blazing turban or head, for the adequate comprehension of the four noble truths..." the same exertion of effort is necessary.
>
> (*Saṁyutta-nikāyo*, LIII, 34)

The chapter on old age in the *Dhammapadam (XI, 146)* begins with an existential question on the same depth:

> "Why is there laughter, why is there joy while this world is always burning? Why do you not see a light, you who are shrouded in darkness (ignorance)?"

The initial task of my exercises in meditation was, within the limits of the first *jhānam*, to coordinate the ṣtream of thinking with the stream of breathing in order to inhibit the mind's rapid flow. Much later Samkara helped me describe more explicitly this first effort. In his sub-commentary to Patanjali's *Yoga sūtram* I, 13,[95] referring to the steadiness (*abhyāsa*) of this effort, Samkara says:

> "The steadiness which is the cause of the inhibition of the mind is the result of effort, and the effort which is its cause is practice. The *tranquil flow* as it were of a stream free from mud is a transformation into a pure form of a *mind without mental processes*, which have been inhibited."

It is a good habit, if understood properly, in all religions to begin meditation by creating the atmosphere of quietness and detachment by transforming the subject of a heart-raising prayer or *mantram* to the higher level of steady contemplation. In terms of *Yoga-sūtrāni* this initial aim is designated as *saṃprajñāta-samādhi,* concentration "accompanied by reasoning, reflection, bliss and sense of individuality". (Y.s. I. 17)

While on the Island Hermitage as I stay on the shore in the thin morning mist usually in an imaginary mood rather than in bodily *āsanam,* streams of thought and streams of breathing coincided with the hardly perceptible narrow streaks of water currents on the quiet opaque surface.

Buddho described clean and transparent Himalayan lakes as a simile of the meditative attainment of "concentrated mind, made pure, translucent, dispassionate, devoid of defilements, supple, ready to act, steady and imperturbable... as if in a mountain fastness there were a pool of water, clear, transparent, undisturbed; and a man, standing on the bank, and with eyes to see should perceive the oysters and the shells, the gravel and the pebbles and the shoals of fish, as they move about or lie within it..." (D.2)

In my early equatorial ambience the backwater, although with no outgrowth on its brackish surface, still remains dark and not translucent, with muddy grounds swallowing the exuberance of rotting leaves. Yet, Shri Ramakrishna said after the marriage of his dearest young disciple Rakhal: "He lives with his family, no doubt, but he knows what it means... he has realized that all these are illusory and impermanent. Rakhal will never be attached to the world. He is like a mud-fish. The fish lives in the mud, but there is not the slightest trace of mud on its body."[96]

Early in the morning streaks of thin mist move across the lake sanctuary barely perceptible on the surface of the quiet water, where shoals of fish gather at noon quietly expecting their share of our alms food. The situation reminds a beginning meditator of Buddho's simile of the next step in the second *jhānam*:

> "O maharajah, it is just as if there were a deep pool, with water welling up into it from a spring beneath, and with no inlet from the east or west, from the north or south, and the god should not from time to time send down showers of rain upon it. Still the current of cool waters rising up from that spring would pervade, fill, permeate, and suffuse the pool with cool waters..." (*D.* 2)

On stagnant waters recollections of shrill sounds and colors appear more quiet as they fade into the imperceptible than in the penultimate chapter of H. Hesse's "Siddhartha" where:

"the river was laughing clearly and merrily at the old ferryman" and "Siddhartha stood still; he bent over the water in order to hear better. He saw his face reflected in the quietly moving water, and there was something in this reflection that reminded him of something he had forgotten, and when he reflected on it, he remembered... Everything that was not suffered to the end and finally concluded, recurred, and the same sorrows were undergone... Siddhartha climbed into the boat again and rowed back to the hut... The wound still smarted; he still rebelled against his fate... Siddhartha listened. He was now listening intently, completely absorbed, quite empty, taking in everything. He felt that he had now completely learned the art of listening... He could no longer distinguish the different voices - the merry voice from the weeping voice, the childish voice from the manly voice... all of them together was the stream of events, the music of life..."

In my "Letters from the Island Hermitage" (written in my Yugoslav mother- tongue) I also described a strange boat that enticed and stimulated my imagination. Made from the motor hood of a Japanese aircraft, most probably shot down during the war, it belonged to the oldest servant Dasa, and was nicknamed Punchi-kochi, or "small train". Smoking his cheroots, Dasa used it to cross the lake from his home on the shore early in the morning and late in the evening, but also in the afternoon with the mail bag. For that official function he was authorized to wear an authentic colonial post-man's sombrero. Ten years later, in 1976, when I returned from the mountains for my maha-thero's funeral, the first thing I noticed near the small jetty was this boat, pierced with a few big holes, and hanging on a tree. One time, either too late in the evening, or too early in the morning, Dasa, entangled in the meshes of underwater creepers, or struck in the mangrove, drowned. At that time the analogy with Hesse's old ferryman Vasudeva in "Siddhartha", though probably not completely forgotten, had fallen far behind the ken of my actual exuberant memories. About fifteen years before arriving at the Hermitage I had read this story in Rome, in Italian translation, walking along the shores of waters still turbulent from the upheaval of European landslides provoked by the war. At the time of my imaginary paddling in Dasa's "Punchi-kochi" all such potential haphazard recollections were supposed in best faith to rot on the bottom of dark waters in the jungle, and to disappear there. But of course this could never completely happen at will. Recently, I was rereading the same book in

Bombay, waiting in the "Centaur" for my flight. I was intentionally looking again for more forgotten analogies previously mentioned. The difference in levels of experiencing is what attracted my attention during this second reading, about thirty five years later.

The ineradicable remainder of nomadic instincts in the Sinhalese people disqualifies them, to a considerable extent, from the long lasting patient meditative sitting in a Chinese-like pedantic style, a style still strongly developed and cultivated among sturdy Burmese athletic hermits who founded this order. This quiet model of cool meditation might be better suited to the nordic temper among Indo-European Aryans, but it appears to fit best the physically resistent structure of some Mongols, particularly the remainders of the Japanese samurai zen aristocracy. Early on, the tropical hermitages and meditation monasteries of South East Asia developed a peculiar style of "meditation in walking" limited to the so called *cañkamo* (or *cañkamanaṁ*) corridor.

Archeological excavations of monasteries in the old Buddhist university of Nalanda and in some other medieval rock-temples in India, can still be visited. Here there are short dark corridors that are not much longer than ten paces used for walking meditation and are cut separately behind each cell. I will describe my experience with a similar method of meditation, preserved in old forest hermitages in Sri Lanka.

The Island Hermitage and many other places, even in "meditation centers" recently imported from Burma now use modernized mass-media methods and have introduced abridged courses lasting only a few weeks (in Burma visitors for such purposes can obtain only one week's visa). For such purposes, the standardized style of *kuṭis* (hermits' huts) includes a narrow open veranda at the entrance, a little longer than the one-room. It made rather a scandalous effect among Buddhist recluses when I dared confess at the beginning of my career among them, still as an "untaught novice", that I did not believe much in this method (of running down the bowling-alley as I called it). I was always ready to apologize by adding that I still had rather a multipurpose use of it. Furthermore, the method had been sanctioned by the oldest commentaries of the *vinayo* code of monastic discipline.

After nearly one hour of quiet meditative sitting (*āsanam*) in contemplative exercise and concentration on breathing, I like to maintain the contemplative mood in an intermediate state of attentive expanding of the field of vision by walking as slowly and as carefully as possible.

It begins with sharpened image of the micro-world of colors, and also of sounds, that surround the ground of each step, when carefully treading in open space, on a narrow path. The slower the horizon extends laterally, the better for enlarging this initial microscopic vision. On the Island there were specks of water glittering in sunshine. They penetrated through dense foliage of high trees and the floral jungle vegetation growing in their shade. At the end of my short and narrow path a small Ashoka tree, always in red bloom, protruding gaily, twinkled signaling the nearing end of my blind alley.

This is how the world unfolds always anew from focal points of surprising beauty springing up at each step from leaves falling and still slightly moving and rustling on my path. It was this marvel that made me stop almost at each cautious step before letting the foot hesitantly fall, to avoid rushing the crisp constellation of instantaneous beauty brought from various directions by the breeze toward, if not against, the inborn brutality of my feet.

As the morning hours advanced, the glittering jungle-stars from the glowing lake attracted me more and more to the brittle bridges of mangrove on the shaky extension of the shore. This dematerializing extension of the walk along a way which vanished under my feet became more and more daring. It resembled the danger of imaginary travel in the "puchi-coachi" shell as mirage silhouettes from the forest emerged more sharply against the background of the apparently withdrawing shore. These were my fellow-travellers, most of whom I had met more or less casually in the course of the last few years during my errings across India, after the process of uprooting and the decision to escape the native ground on the "wild west" neared its geographical end by being submerged in the big ocean near Cape Comorin and re-emerging on the other shore of the narrow strait crossed once upon a time by the heroic monkey army in *The Rāmāyanam*.

Among the first fellow travellers who re-emerged from the recollection of the tragic Himalayan descent was the Dalai Lama. I had visited him a year earlier in 1965. Now for some time, until his bodily presence began to fade away, the Dalai Lama happened to appear as the merriest intruder from the kingdom of shadows into my contemplative prudence. Also, there were others whose synchronizing movement along the life-stream of *saṁsāro* I tried to avoid through the "technique" of mental exercises in correcting the inquisitive escapes of attention. The Dalai Lama would appear like some other spectators of my imaginary navigation looking from the shore almost encouragingly at my inept paddling - a sturdy boy with a hearty loud laughter. In serious philosophical discussions, which at that time were his favorite hobby, (if I may put it so in reference to His Holiness), unexpected outbursts of this healthy laughter were often felt as a perplexing shock, though I never felt either resentful or discouraged from continuing to talk about topics which despite their seriousness could provoke such explosions of his laughter, never a sarcastic sneer, never a polite hesitancy, sometimes, maybe, just the side - effect of an innocent casual encounter, in a hurry, of East with West.

Another faithful fellow traveller, hesitantly lagging behind in deeper shadow was my Jain niece Aruna. My first contact with her at an Indian university had been the first spontaneous meeting with the Jain community evoking for us both a dim recollection of a distant past and the effort to recognize the location of the ancestral origin wherefrom my Jain *gotra* appeared to have never absented itself very far and long, or else, a fantastic motivation of Platonic love for minors.

Several other less incisive acquaintances, almost all passers-by from a recently abandoned past, used to return for a short time as such superficial disturbances typical of the repudiated model of social calls. Just as in the real past when I had lived among them, I mainly applied the method of patience to get rid of them, letting them proceed, pass by and disappear in the imaginary world of shades. This was in keeping with the second of Buddho's four directions of "right efforts", the discreet intention of harmless avoiding.

With time I have learned more and more convincingly through experience that both the beauty and the fruitfulness of this path of purification avers itself only in slow and cautious treading on it; and the rhythm of steps creates, almost by itself, devotional emotions of loving kindness (*mettā*) and, *consequently*, of *ahiṁsā* (not hurting). This is how I might understand the "meditation in walking", outside, or at least alongside, the dark or bright corridors of *cañkamo*. Beyond any comparison with the described experiences, the instruction on meditation in walking found later in commentarial literature appeared completely different.

In Pali literature there are very few exegetical works of essential philosophical importance. The last and most voluminous work representing the highest standard of scholastic erudition was Buddhaghoso's *Visuddhi-maggo, The Path of Purification.*[97] In the fifth century A.D. he came to Sri Lanka from Southern India and wrote down the final commentarial version of Pali texts extant at that time and written already much earlier in various editions. *Visuddhi-maggo* was Buddhaghoso's own compendium intended also to prove the high standard of his scholarship.

As already stated "the path of purification" is the oldest definition of cathartic and atheist religions which existed both in Indian as well as Arabian and Iranian domains long before the Aryan invasions. Characterized as a wider form of Jainism, this religion belonged to a much higher spiritual and *consequently* also material world civilization whose common cultural features and heritage have been studied only very superficially in modern times.

In context of Buddhaghoso's compendium the term *visuddhi maggo* designates a manual of *bhāvanā* or cultivation of contemplative mind in all essential aspects of meditative practice. It is presented systematically in a gradual sequence classical for the Buddhist tradition.

This "description of concentration" begins with "taking a meditation subject" beginning with "earth" as *kasiṇam* or object of concentration on the lowest level of four material elements according to the universal archaic philosophy of nature: earth, water, fire, air. (Part II, ch. 4-5)

The analysis of "meditation in walking" is explained in the last (third) part of the treatise (ch. 20) due to the complexity of the "fifth stage of purification." In this stage the "comprehension of the material" aggregates begins with "the material septad" as the preliminary qualification for crossing over to "the immaterial septad" within "the 18 principal insights". Not entering into the complexity of the whole system, a few fragments from paragraphs referring to the analysis of the process of walking (ch.XX, 60-68) may suggest *prima facie* some segments of the picture. Here I would like to single out *exempli gratia* the incommensurable *difference in depths* that may help direct a beginner's initial stand.

The exercise of analyzing each "footstep into six parts" has a completely different meaning and intention than the realistic and passive observation from outside which I described above. Therefore it is worthwhile to notice the general difference in all such exercises between extrovert (*bahiddhā*) contemplation and introvert (*ajjhattam*) analysis. This distinction, often in a simpler form, recurs in many other exercises. Therefore it would be wrong to conclude that what I was doing as a beginner was all wrong, and only the following canonical instruction right:

> "Next he divides a single footstep into six parts as 'lifting up', 'shifting forward', 'shifting sideways', 'lowering down', 'placing down', and 'fixing down'... Herein, in the lifting up two elements, the earth element and the water element, are subordinate and sluggish while the other two (fire and air) are predominant and strong. Likewise in the shifting forward and shifting sideways. In the lowering down two elements, the fire element and the air element, are subordinate and sluggish while the other two (earth and water) are predominant and strong. Likewise in the placing down and fixing down... He attributes the three characteristics (impermanence, suffering and no 'self' being or soul) to materiality, according to 'disappearance of what grows old in each stage' by means of these six parts into which he has thus divided it. How? He considers thus: The elements and the kinds of derived materiality (in the act of vitalization - *jīvit-indriyam*, élan vital)[98] occurring in the lifting up all cease there without reaching the shifting forward; therefore they are impermanent, painful, not self. Likewise those occurring in the shifting forward... the shifting sideways... the lowering down... the placing down; those occurring in the placing down cease there without reaching the fixing down; thus formations keep breaking up, like sesamum seeds put into a hot pan; wherever they arise, there they cease, stage by stage, section by section, term by term, each without reaching the next part. Therefore they are impermanent, painful, not self."

Such is "the meditator's attribution of these three characteristics according to disappearance of what grows old in each stage" of each single step and its meditative reduction to nothing (*ākiñcaññam*).

Thus the whole practice of "meditation in walking" should serve the aim of attaining insight into the first of the three basic characteristics (*ti- lakkhaṇam*) of existence - *aniccam* or impermanence of all constituents (*saṅkhāro*) of the flux of life (*bhavaṅga-soto*)[99]

In considering this normal and natural sharpening of senses by the quieting effect of careful attention we underscore the deadliness and suicidal nature of poisonous and overexciting drugs for the psycho-physical organism. In order to achieve what can be attained we must soothe both the body and the mind through the utmost ascetic purity and not through "technical" artifice.

3. Visuddhi Maggo

Another text from the same classical meditation manual, *Visud-dhi-maggo,* fascinated me especially with the aesthetic mood its reading evoked soon after a spontaneous experience that I wish to describe. This basic teaching of concentration contained in Ch. 4 of Part II, on "Purification of Consciousness", concerns the "Description of Concentration" on "the earth *kasiṇam*" as the focussing point (*nimit-tam*) of pure sight:

> "One who is learning the earth *kasiṇam* apprehends the sign in earth that is either made up or not made up, that is bounded not unbounded, limited not unlimited, with a periphery not without a periphery, circumscribed not uncircumscribed, either the size of a bushel or the size of a saucer...
>
> He anchors his mind to that object, thinking: "Surely in this way I shall be freed from repeated aging and death." Secluded from sense desires... he enters upon and dwells in the first *jhānam*..."
>
> "... when a man has had no such previous practice, he should make a *kasiṇam,* guarding against the four faults... and not overlooking any of the directions for the meditation subject learnt from the teacher. Now the four faults of the earth *kasiṇam* are due to the intrusion of blue, yellow, red or white. So instead of using clay of such colors he should make it not in the middle of the monastery in a place where novices, etc., are about but on the confines of the monastery in a screened place, either under an overhanging rock or in a leaf hut... So a disk a span and four fingers across should be made with the quite pure dawn-colored clay... Then he should sweep the place out and have a bath. On his return he should sit himself on a well-covered seat with legs a span and four inches high, prepared in a place that is two and half cubits from the *kasiṇam* disk. For the *kasiṇam* does not appear plainly to him who sits further off than this; and if he sits nearer than that, faults in the *kasiṇam* appear. If he sits higher up, he has to look at it with his neck bent; and if he sits lower down, his knees ache... So he should develop it by appre-hending the sign (*nimittam*), keeping his eyes open moderately, as if he were seeing the reflection of his face on the surface of a looking-

glass... If he opens them too little, the disk is not obvious enough, his mind becomes drowsy, which also prevents the sign becoming apparent to him... While not ignoring the color, attention should be given by setting the mind on a "name" as the most outstanding mental datum. It can be called by any one he likes among the names for earth, such as 'earth' (*paṭhavī*), 'the great one' (*mahī*), 'the friendly one' (*medinī*), 'ground' (*bhūmi*)... etc., whichever suits his manner of perception..."

My first spontaneous experience with meditative concentration on the "element" earth reminds me now more of the second stage of extending the experience of nothingness described in *Cu*a-suññata-suttam* (M. 121), quoted at the end of the preceding chapter, where the meditator proceeded to the inhibition of the awareness of "forest", so that there remained only the awareness of "earth" in its perceptual comprehensiveness "without giving attention to the ridges and hollows, the river ravines..."

In 1965 I visited on a hill above Kandy an old primitive Sinhalese hermit who lived in a cave. At one end under the rock which protruded as a roof above the cave he had screened his meditation room with worn out tawny cloaks while the front side was left open. There was a bench carved out of the earth. He spread a mat and offered me his meditation seat for a test. I sat there cross-legged for about one hour, intent on the already known subject of earth-*kasiṇam*, feeling comfortably enclosed in the orange-brown Lankan clay whose open surface ahead, stretching toward the valley appeared more intensely visible from the perspective of the quiet delimited corner. The world spreading out in its normal light and shade confronted me. The farthest and broadest end of my perspective seemed an endless homogenous mud-material out of which there might, if not refrained, emerge shapes of the whole world and of all "beings breathing in it". At the margins of that dynamic vision there was a vague reminder of the *sāṁkhya* teaching of *sat-kārya-vāda*:

"There exist only things in modelled and not-modelled states, while their production and destruction are only appearances of shaping. Thus the pot, or anything else, existed earlier in an unshaped state in earth or in some other material. Later it was shaped into a visible thing, existing until it got broken. After that it continues to exist again in its unshaped state."[100]

Later the old hermit gave me a simple and useful explanation of the feeling of physical and mental lightness (*lahutā*) experienced by the meditator in the moment when he is taken up by the "wheel of law" (*dhamma-cakkam*) into the liberating stream of righteousness. He invited me to come again.

The earth-kasinam exercise has never lost attraction for me, but the aim of its application has continued to change its meaning. Living for one year (1968) in a hermitage much deeper in the jungle I tried to adopt the very primitive traditional means of this type of meditation, perhaps the only one which has never died out in this country. Yet, very unlike the poetic description quoted from *Visuddhi-maggo, kasiṇam* plates are now clumsily crafted by village carpenters who cut round segments of tree trunks and smear them, in the case of earth-*kasiṇam,* with a sort of red-brown shoe-polish. Being allergic to all shades of red (instead of light dove-blue or mother-of-pearl bright gray) I could not work on it and preferred the pure yellow color *kasiṇam.* The advantage of pure color models is that they reduce the subject of concentration to the purely abstract art of contemplating just "yellow", "yellow" without interference, or even the slightest admixture of imaginative "visualization" of such attributes as "the great one", "the friendly one" etc. (in the case of "earth"). This is the *first essential difference of the Buddhist from the Hinduized yogah meditation* which aims at hallucinatory creation of "divine" visions. The aim of abstract contemplation of pure elementary sense-data in their primitive givenness, purified from all overtones of intellectual or emotional backgrounds, is the only way of establishing the pre-condition of all forms of meditative concentration - *the one-pointedness* of mind, or, in psychological terms, *the non-splitting state of consciousness.* This essential principle of one-pointedness (*ekāgra*) is underscored also in *Patañjala-yoga*[101]. Most often this point of equanimity (*upekkhā,* Sk. *upekṣā,* Greek *apatheia,* in the meaning of equilibrium - *isostheneia* of the Greek sages, corresponding to the Pali *tatra-majjhatt'upekkhā*)[102] has to be sought and found in the sensation of touch of the breath on a specific ganglionic center, corresponding to the *cakras,* on the spinal cord of the autonomous nervous system, *kuṇḍalinī,* according to the Indian physiology (as explicated in the sequel).[103]

Returning to my individual case, it was upon coordination of these two functions - the one-pointed concentration of the yellow of the *kasiṇam* and the equilibration of breath - that an initial failure became evident. It was not possible to inhibit the splitting of consciousness since I was already too far trained in the concentration on breathing. So, in my basic exercises I had to return to the pure concentration on breathing (*ānāpāna-sati*, the Buddhist version of *prāṇāyama* in *yoga*). Another useful application of the kasinam disc in a subordinated function began forming itself in psychophysiological spontaneity. It became necessary to develop awareness of its structural background through an analysis based (at least in my individual case) on a sufficient knowledge of physiological psychology (at least practical and visual).

4. "The Rope of Mindfulness"

"Or alternatively, this *mindfulness of breathing* as a meditation subject - which is foremost among the various meditation subjects of all *buddhā, pacceka-buddhā and buddhā's* disciples as a basis for attaining distinction and abiding in bliss here and now - is not easy to develop without leaving the neighborhood of villages, which resound with the noises of women, men, elephants, horses etc., noise being a thorn to *jhānam* (see A.v, 135), whereas in the forest away from a village a meditator can at his ease set about discerning this meditation subject and achieve the fourth *jhānam* in mindfulness of breathing... that is why the Blessed One said 'gone to the forest'... in pointing out a favorable abode for him.... For this bhikkhu's mind has long been dissipated among visible data etc., as its object, and it dies not want to mount the object of concentration through mindfulness of breathing; it runs off the track like the chariot harnessed to a wild ox. Now suppose a cow herd wanted to tame a wild calf that had been reared on a wild cow's milk, he would take it away from the cow and tie it up apart with a rope to a stout post dug into the ground; then the calf might dash to and fro, but being unable to get away, it would eventually sit down or lie down by the post; so too, when a bhikkhu wants to tame his own mind which has long been spoilt by being reared on visible data... as object for its food and drink, he should take it from visible data... and bring it into the forest or to the root of a tree or to an empty place and tie it up there to the post of in-breaths and out-breaths with the rope of mindfulness. And so his mind may then dash to and fro when it no longer gets the objects it was formerly used to, but being unable to break the rope of mindfulness and get away, it sits down, lies down, by that object under the influence of access and absorption."[104]

"The rope of mindfulness" needed in order to tie one's own unbridled animal nature to the post of concentration (*nimittam*) is "warped and woven" (as the tissue of the world is described by the philosopher Gargi Vacaknavi in *Bṛhad-āraṇyaka-upaniṣad*, III, 8) with several strings (*guṇam*, meaning also virtues). It has to be strong enough so that a beginner can succeed in the principal exercise and gradually consolidate with accessory means over all other sense-organs (in my case in the slow and patient course of years). The steadier the ken (*nimittam*) of central absorption, the less disturbing and noticeable becomes the feeling of those accessory means of control. Here it may be useful to note that Buddho distinguishes six sense-organs that have to be kept under constant control of alert consciousness (the sixth is the inner organ of mental coordination, *mano indriyam*). As Ramana Maharshi (1879-1950) said: "At the beginning all is difficult. Later on nothing is difficult." Yet, this too, should not be taken lightly by an optimistic beginner.

The simile of the quail (M. 66)

> "Udayi, just as a quail, a little bird, because it is caught in a trap of creepers, comes to slaughter there or to captivity or dying, so that, Udayi, if any one should say: 'That quail, a little bird, because it is caught in a trap of creepers comes to slaughter there or to captivity or dying; yet for it this is a bond of no strength, a weak bond that rots away, a pithless bond' would anyone speaking thus be speaking rightly?"
>
> "No, sir. That quail, a little bird, because it is caught in a trap of creepers comes to dying..., since for it this is a strong bond, a bond that does not rot away, a thick log of wood." "Even so, Udayi, some foolish persons here, on being told by me, 'Give this up', speak thus: 'But what of this trifling insignificant matter? This recluse (Buddho) is hair-splitting' and they do not give up and they cause dissatisfaction to be nursed against me and against those bhikkhus who desire the training. This is for them, Udayi, a strong bond, a stout bond, a bond that does not rot away, a thick log of wood... But some young men of good family here, on being told by me, 'Give this up',... give it up and they do not cause dissatisfaction to be nursed against me or against those bhikkhus who desire training. These, giving that up, are unconcerned, unruffled... This for them is a weak bond, a bond of no strength, a bond that rots away, a pithless bond... It is like a king's bull-elephant whose tusks are as long as a plough-pole,

who is massive, finely bred, whose home is the battle-field, and who, if bound with a stout leather bond, having easily twisted his body, having burst those bonds tearing them asunder, goes away as he pleases..."

Several discourses and basic commentarial works under the heading of *upakkilesa* deal with the inner disturbances of the meditator's mind at the beginning of his effort to establish the equilibrium of right concentration. The most impressing discourse on this subject, (referring also to parapsychological experiences) is the *Upakkilesa-suttaṁ* (M. 128):

"...But have you, Anuruddhas, while living thus diligent, ardent, resolute, attained superhuman states, the excellent knowledge-and-insight befitting the Aryans, an abiding in comfort?"

"As to this, sir, we, while living diligent, ardent, resolute, and abiding in comfort, perceive the light-manifestation (*obhāso*), as well as the appearance of shapes. But soon the light-manifestation vanishes for us, as well as the appearance of shapes; and we do not understand the reason (*nimittaṁ*)." "But the reason should be understood by you, Anuruddhas!" "The unsteadiness of concentration can be due to distraction, lack of proper attention, sloth, and torpor, consternation, excitement, lust (*libido, duṭṭhullam*), too much energy, too feeble energy, yearning, perception of diversity, the state of being too intent on material shapes; these are defilements of the mind (*cittassa upakkilesā*)."

Here it is necessary to note that my intention from the very beginning was not to attain such "superhuman, truly noble states of knowledge and insight" characteristic of clairvoyance as described in this text, but rather to first reach a subjective state of appeasing (*samatho*) the unbridled mental chaos by purifying inner intellectual, sentimental and moral motives and incentives. Premature clairvoyant appearances are known to cause inner disturbances to concentration, as will be seen in the following analysis of the *upakkilesā*. A similar intention may have motivated the early exegetic analysts who had a tendency toward logical abstraction as apparent in Buddhaghoso's *Visuddhi-maggo*. The decadence of the practice degenerated into a tendency to reduce the whole method and aim of meditative ennoblement of mind (*bhāvanā*) to the abstraction of a "bare insight" (*sukkha-vipassanā*, etymologically more correctly "dry insight"), psychologically mistaken for an *alternative* to *samatho* or inner peace of mind. As in the previously described case of commentarial dissection of *rūpajjhānā* from *arūpajjhānā*, there was subordination instead of coordination of the noematic correlate of the latter to the noetic structure of the former. Here too the whole preliminary but essential part of *jhānam* and *samādhi* attainments were not psychologically coordinated but logically subordinated as a lower, and *therefore* negligible and unnecessary counterpart of the ultimate aim of "pure (dry) insight".[105]

I cannot expand on the reason for my disagreement with this logical simplification which is gaining momentum today in the superficial technicalized "shortcuts to Nirvana". The value judgment on my initial purpose, *samatho*, may suffice as justification of the course taken here. In *Visuddhi-maggo XX, 105f*, "the imperfections of insight" are listed and explained as follows:

> "When he is a beginner of insight, with this tender insight ten imperfections arise in him. For imperfections of insight do not arise either in a noble disciple who has reached the penetration, or in persons erring in virtue, neglectful of their meditation subject and idlers. They arise only in a freeman who keeps to the right course, devotes himself continuously (to his meditation subject) and is a beginner of insight.
>
> These ten imperfections are; (1) lustre, (2) knowledge, (3) rapture, (4) tranquility, (5) happiness, (6) resolution, (7) exertion, (8) assurance, (9) equanimity, and (10) attachment.
>
> For it is said: 'When a man is bringing (formations) to mind as impermanent, lustre arises in him... The distraction due to that is agitation... and the course of his insight is interrupted. He drops his own meditation subject and sits just enjoying the lustre. Likewise when his is bringing formations to mind as impermanent, knowledge arises in him... rapture... tranquility... happiness... resolution... exertion... assurance... equanimity... attachment arises in him... The distraction due to that is agitation...'."

A contemporary teacher of the Burmese method of "bare insight" (*sukkha- vipassanā*, mentioned above), Mahasi Sayadaw,[106] explains a commentarially extended list of the same "corruptions of insight" including the following remarks:

> "Further, strong *faith* pertaining to insight arises in him... There arises in him the wish to proclaim Buddho's teaching, joyous confidence in the virtues of those engaged in meditation, the desire to

advise dear friends and relatives to practice meditation, grateful remembrance of the help received from his meditation master etc... There arises also *rapture* in its five grades... When purification of mind is gained, that rapture begins to appear by causing 'goose-flesh', tremor in the limbs etc., and now it produces a sublime feeling of happiness and exhilaration, filling the whole body with an exceedingly sweet and subtle thrill. Under its influence, he feels as if the whole body had risen up and remained in the air without touching the ground, or as if it were seated on an air cushion, or as if it were floating up and down...

There arises further a subtle *attachment* of a calm nature that enjoys the insight graced with the 'brilliant light' and the other qualities here described. The meditator, however, is not able to discern it as a corruption but believed it to be just the very bliss of meditation... Now the meditator believes: 'Surely I must have attained to the supermundane path and fruition. Now I have finished the task of meditation.' This is mistaking what is not the path for the path, and it is a corruption of insight..."

Such misunderstandings typical to the superficial occultism and commercialized "Yoga" schools of competing great *gurus*, teaching how to fly free of charge and to read other people's hidden thoughts, confirm nevertheless a series of unavoidable epiphenomena which accompany any serious and successful course of disciplined spiritual training, and pose as such a serious problem of psychophysiological and moral investigation.

As we shall see, these phenomena appear normally as effects of conscious and methodical development of the latent capacities of the autonomous nervous system, located in the ganglionic centers along the spinal cord. Studies in comparative physiology have clearly established the analogy with the traditional Indian system of *kuṇḍalini-yoga*, described and applied in treatises subsequent to the basic *Yoga-sūtrāni* formulated by Patanjali (about the second century B.C.). He still did not speak explicitly about the system of *kuṇḍalinī* and the *cakras* along its tract, and still less about the *āsanam* or *yoga*-postures of the later meaningful and valuable system of physical exercises.

On the European side, Schopenhauer was among the first authors who interpreted, in a lengthy essay the *"Spirit Seeing and Everything Connected Therewith"*, parapsychological phenomena from their location, not in the central, but in the autonomous nervous system, although he most probably did not know much about the Indian correlate to the same tract.

To sum up the essential problem concerning the old and recently revived dogmatic misunderstanding among Buddhist schools on the relation of the *samatha-bhāvāna*, the appeasement of the normally turbulent mind, and the effect of its soothing on the purification of insight, *vipassanā*, in pure intuition (whose analogy with Bergson's theory of intuition and *"torsion"* could be extended farther than even guessed at first glance) - the following basic text from Buddho's *Sāmañña-phala-suttam* (D.2) may still offer an argument eloquent enough from the standpoint maintained in this presentation:

> "Just as a woman or a man, or a smart boy or girl, looking at the image of his own face in a *clean* and brilliant mirror or in a basin or *clear* water, if it had a mole on it, would know that it had, and if not, would know that it had not,... so the bhikkhu in his mind, concentrated, *purified*, translucent, blameless, *free of moral obstruction*, supple, ready to act, firm and imperturbable, directs and bends down his mind to that knowledge which penetrates the heart..."

In many Zen and Tibetan temples the symbol of a mirror is placed in the center of the altar reminding the devotee that only an unruffled quiet mind can mirror the image of things and beings "as they truly are" (*yathā-bhūtam*), and that the element of peace and tranquility cannot be organically and even ethically disjoined from the correctness of clear insight. That is why the sequence of spiritual development in all basic texts, including the *Visuddhi-maggo*, follows the same order: *sīlaṁ, saṁādhi, paññā* - virtue, concentration, wisdom.

5. The mindfulness of breathing: ānāpāna-sati

> "Thus developed, bhikkus, thus repeatedly practiced, the concentration on the mindfulness of breathing is of great fruit, of great benefit. Before my awakening, while I was still a *bodhisatto*, I too, dwelt much in this way of life. Dwelling much in this way of life, neither my body nor my eyes became tired, and through not clinging my mind was freed from defilements." *S. LIV, 8* "This concentration on the mindfulness of breathing, bhikkhus, developed and repeatedly practiced, is both peaceful and sublime, unadulterated and of happy life; it causes to vanish at once and suppresses evil and unbeneficial thoughts as soon as they arise. Just

as in the last month of the hot season the dirt and dust blow about, and then, out of season, a great rain-cloud causes them to vanish at once and suppresses them; so, indeed, bhikkhus, the concentration on the mindfulness of breathing... is peaceful and sublime..." *S. LIV.* "The mindfulness of breathing... perfects the four foundations of mindfulness; the four foundations of mindfulness, developed and repeatedly practiced, perfect the seven factors of awakening; the seven factors of awakening..., perfect clear-vision and deliverance. - And how developed, how repeatedly practiced, is the mindfulness of breathing of great fruit, of great benefit? - Here, bhikkus, a bhikkhu, gone to the forest, or to the root of a tree, or to an empty place, sits down; having folded his legs crosswise, set his body erect, established mindfulness in front of him, ever mindful he breathes in, mindful he breathes out." *M. 118*

In the continuation of the same text (and in several other texts on *ānāpāna-sati*) the subjects of contemplation follow the sequence of the four foundations of mindfulness (described in *satipaṭṭhāna* suttas, D. 22 and M. 10): the contemplation of body, feeling, mind and mind-objects or phenomena (*dhammā-anupassanā*). The standard formulation of the *four tetrads*, contain 16 subjects of possible contemplation to be developed gradually, beginning with "the body *in* the body, the feelings *in* the feelings, the mind *in* the mind, the phenomena *in* the phenomena". The stress is on *non transcending* into the spheres of "super-mundane" (*locuttarā*) mystical or occult visions, but on looking at objects of actual outer and inner experiences as they actually are given (*yathā-bhūtam*) in normal and normally sharpened consciousness concentrated in one point (*ekaggo*) in the selected ken. It is formulated as follows[107]:

(1) *Contemplation of the body:*

"Breathing in long, he knows, I breathe in long; or breathing out long, he knows, I breathe out long. - Breathing in short, he knows, I breathe in short; or breathing out short, he knows, I breathe out short. - Experiencing the whole body (of breath) I shall breathe in, thus he trains himself; experiencing the whole body I shall breathe out, thus he trains himself. - Calming the bodily-formation, I shall breathe in, thus he trains himself; calming the bodily-formation, I shall breathe out, thus he trains himself."

(2) *Contemplation of feeling:*

"Experiencing rapture (*pīti*), I shall breathe in, thus he trains himself; experiencing rapture I shall breathe out, thus he trains himself. - Experiencing bliss (*sukham*), I shall breathe in ...out. - Experiencing the mental-formation (*citta-samkhāro*), I shall breathe in ...out. Calming the mental formation I shall breathe in ...out."

(3) *Contemplation of mind (cittam)*:

"Experiencing the mind, I shall breathe in ... out. - Gladdening the mind, I shall breathe in... out. - Concentrating the mind, I shall breathe in... out. - Liberating the mind, I shall breathe in... out."

(4) *Contemplation of mental objects (dhammā)*:

"Contemplating impermanence, I shall breathe in... out. - Contemplating the absence of passion, I shall breathe in... out. - Contemplating cessation, I shall breathe in... out. - Contemplating relinquishment, I shall breathe in... out."

This broadest frame shows that the mindfulness of breathing can be limited, on the basic level, to the contemplation of itself as the "respiration-body" (a term appearing first in the commentarial analysis). But already at the concluding stage of the first tetrad, "calming the bodily formation", and then in experiencing and calming down emotions and mental states and their intellectual contents (*dhammā* as objects of reflection), the respiration- mindfulness can be attuned to states, or even objects, of contemplation blending gradually into complexes of a higher order. We have to assume *prima facie* that such progressively widening complexes will not, or rather should not, disturb the one-pointedness and split the highest point reached at any stage of concentration, but rather accomplish their gradual sublimation.

According to the commentary on the last stage of the first tetrad ("calming the bodily formation") in *Visuddhi-maggo*,[108]

"Here, the tranquilizing of the preceding by way of the subsequent is to be understood according to the method stated above. Thus should *grossness and subtlety*, as well as calming, be understood here."

In *Paṭisambhida-maggo* this is further explained with the simile of the gong[109]:

> "Just as when a metal gong is struck; at first gross sounds occur, and ... the sign of the gross sounds have ceased, then afterwards faint sounds occur, and the sign of the faint sounds is well grasped...; and when the faint sounds have ceased then afterwards consciousness proceeds because of having the sign of the faint sounds as object; so indeed, at first gross in-breaths and out-breaths occur and their sign is well grasped..."

In the commentarial literature the dying out of direct experience has caused, in this case too, the typical misinterpretation of living psychological practice. In the semantic exegesis of the school of logical vivisection (*vibhajja-vādo*) the formalized practice was subdivided into three phases of awareness logically bereft of the function of creative blending into a synthetic whole. This was in general the most typical shortcoming of the whole *abhidhammo* scholasticism in its effort to reconvert the new Buddhist process-thinking into the old grooves of the atomic mechanism of substance-thinking. The paradox of this scholasticism culminated in the lack of its grasping power to conceive the fundamental criterion of the Buddhist metaphysics of knowledge. This deficiency was revealed in the later criticism of *abhidhammo* noetics by Nagarjuna and the later *vijñapti-mātrā* gnoseological idealism. But its principle had been very clearly formulated in its various aspects by Buddho himself. The statement at the end of *Kevaddha-suttantaṁ* (D. XI) can be taken as its basic and most explicit formulation:

> "- Where do earth, water, fire, and wind no footing find...? - With the cessation of consciousness (*viññāṇam*) they, too, loose their footing."

This is the metaphysical premise of *Buddhist phenomenism* for which the problem of substance became insoluble. The reason behind its criterion can be understood even better today in the post-Kantian period than it could be in the whole period of Indian scholasticism in the first millennium of our era.

In *Paṭisambhida-maggo*, an early commentarial work on *Abhidhamma-piṭakaṁ*, the analysis of in- and out-breaths (*ānāpānam*) insists on the statement that "Sign, in-, and out-breaths are not object of a single consciousness." Speaking of a "connection which is the uninterrupted following of the in- and out-breaths with mindfulness", so that it flows like oil poured from a bottle, Buddhaghoso (referring to

Patisambhida) explains this "distribution of breath in particles" and says that connection (*anubandhanā*) can *not* be maintained "by following the beginning, middle, and end."

> "Of the breath issuing out, the navel is the beginning, the heart the middle, the nose-tip the end... And the mind of one who follows the breathing (through these three places) is confused by agitation and vacillation, according to the *Paṭisambhidā*: 'In one whose consciousness is distracted internally by following with mindfulness the beginning, middle, and end of the in-breath, both body and mind are disturbed, unsettled and unsteady.' - So when he gives his attention to it by connection, he should do so not by the beginning, middle and end, but rather by contact and by fixing."[110]

This analytical precaution against "distribution in particles" has brought forth in the later stages of stagnation the 'nose-tip' dogma. Its meticulous formulation quoted by Nanamoli from *Vimutti-maggo*, is a treatise shorter but analogous to the later *Visuddhi-maggo*, which, as we shall see in the sequel, still maintains (at least in part) a more reasonable attitude on such dogmatized points[111]:

> "Here, he trains himself in breathing in (and out), means mindfulness is fixed *at the nose-tip* or the upper lip... The *yogī* attends to the incoming (and outgoing) breath there. He coincides the contact of the incoming and outgoing breath through mindfulness which is fixed at the nose-tip or on the upper lip... He does not consider the breath when it has gone inside nor when it has gone outside (?!) ... If, when the breath comes in or goes out, the *yogī* considers it within or without, his mind will be distracted. If his mind is distracted, his body and mind will waver and tremble. These are the disadvantages... Thus countless impediments arise because the points of contact of the incoming and the outgoing breath are countless."

Buddhaghoso, in the following consideration, seems, however, to come closer to a psycho-physiologically comparable criterion of focussing the ken of attention in the process of expanding and retreating breath[112]:

> "To one bhikkhu the beginning of the in-breath body or the out-breath body, distributed in particles, is plain, but not the middle or the end; he is only able to discern the beginning and has difficulty with the middle and the end. To another the middle is plain, not the beginning or the end; he is only able to discern the middle and has

difficulty with the beginning and the end. To another the end is plain, not the beginning or the middle... To yet another all stages are plain; he is able to discern them all and has no difficulty with any of them. Pointing out that one should be like the last mentioned bhikkhu, he said, 'He trains thus: 'I shall breath in... shall breathe out experiencing the whole body" (of breath).

In the subsequent text[113] Buddhaghoso gives such a clear and convincing explanation of the whole process through the simile of a lame man that even the followers of the nose-tip doctrine feel they must and can adapt it to their interpretation:

"Here is the simile of the man who cannot walk: Just as a man unable to walk, who is rocking a swing for the amusement of his children and their mother, sits at the foot of the swing-post and *sees both ends* and the middle of the swing plank successively coming and going, yet does not move from his place in order to see both ends and the middle, so too, when a bhikkhu places himself with mindfulness, as it were, at the foot of the post for anchoring (mindfulness) and rocks the swing of the in-breaths and out-breaths; he sits down *with mindfulness on the sign* at that same place, and *follows* with mindfulness the beginning, middle and end of the in-breaths and out-breaths *at the place touched by them* as they come and go. Keeping his mind fixed there, he then sees them without moving from his place in order to see them."

But where is the place touched by them? This question, crucial for all dogmatists, remains open still today and is dependent upon personal capacities for such exercises.

Once I was in correspondence with a young tennis champion interested in the modern sport of meditation and gifted for it, the talent for his sport obviously requiring a strong capacity for instant-concentration on each one-pointed "now" of the flying ball. But this analytical precision in splitting a movement into its instant-points was realized by him too, introspectively, as a shortcoming in meditative absorption. Here the strength of his attention was not properly tuned to the refraining meditative mood. I could point out as the classical model applicable to his case Buddho's instruction to Sono the lute player, in *Vīṇopamā-suttam* (A.VI,55)

" -Sono, were you once a good lute (*vīṇā*) player as a layman?

- Yes, sir.

- When the strings of your lute were too taut, did your lute sound well and respond well then?
- No, sir.
- When the strings of your lute were too slack, did your lute sound well and respond well then?
- No, sir.
- When the strings of your lute were neither too taut nor too slack and were evenly tuned, did your lute sound well and respond well then?
- Yes, sir.
- So too, Sono, overstriving leads to agitation, and understriving leads to slackness. Therefore resolve upon *evenness of energy,* acquire evenness of the spiritual faculties, and take that as your sign."

In my sportsman's case I preferred to modernize the commentary, adding a more extensive and up to date critical analysis of the meditative type of attention, which I found in J. Krishnamurti's criticism of our contemporary culture:[114]

> " When you make an effort to pay attention, you are really resisting something - the desire to look out of the window and so on. Part of your energy has already gone in resistance. You build a wall around your mind to make it concentrate... But I think there is a different kind of attention, a state of mind which is not exclusive, which does not shut out anything; and because there is no resistance, the mind is capable of much greater attention. But attention without resistance does not mean the attention of absorption... Whereas, if you are aware of every movement of the mind from moment to moment, then there is no such thing as distraction at any time and the energy of the mind is not wasted in resisting something... That is why it is very important to have space in the mind. If the mind is *not overcrowded, not ceaselessly occupied,* then it can listen to that dog barking, to the sound of the train crossing the distant bridge, and also be fully aware of what is being said by the person talking here. Then *the mind is a living thing, it is not dead.*"

The concluding statement, which I have underlined, seems to be the clue to most dialectically sophisticated arguments discussed among the *takkī vīmaṁsī* logical analysts of exegetical "words that kill" the living experience.

The dogmatism of nose-tip concentration became dialectically connected with the heresy of belly-breathing, under the influence of the later development of the physiological system of *kuṇḍḍlinī* yoga which orthodox Buddhism ignored. In practice the experience of meditation has confirmed the rule of physiology that it is better not to purposely overload the lower (ganglia, *cakram*) centers of the *kuṇḍalini* tract in the lower region of the solar plexus, below the navel in the "breath body". This irritates very easily the sexual instincts whose sublimation became typical of the *bhakti cults* in later hinduism and tantrism. The better tendency is to raise the "sign of attention" to the "lunar region" in the head which helps to exclude mental associations with the instinctive functions of the lower body. But modern occultism has also attempted to mechanize the realization of this moral experience. A theosophist commenting on a late Sinhalese Buddhist "Manual of a Mystic", which had degenerated to a totally formalized prayer book with "wax taper exercises", remarks (with reference to C.W. Leadbeater's *The Inner Life*[115]:

> "It will be noted that the Buddhist method (here) does not seek to arouse the centers below the navel, a process attended with great danger."

Today, this danger is more clearly visible than ever.

On the other hand, the question already posed in the early Buddhist "commentarial developments" of meditational practices is the following: By which tools and devices of vívisection could we possibly exclude and eliminate these lower parts of the organic integrity of our "breath body"?

According to Buddho's "Great discourse on setting-up the mindfulness" (D. XXII), there is only "one way leading to the purification of beings" (*ekāyano maggo sattānam visuddhiyā*). It is the way of *ascetic purification* of the whole psycho-physiological organism by *moral virtue* (*sīlam*) whose consummation constitutes the preliminary requisite for concentrative absorption or *samādhi*.

This alone could have been the serious implicit reason for setting the nose-tip theory against the heresy of belly-breathing. But in practical application there immediately appears the difficulty of its physiological sustainment. If such focussing of attention were similar to the focussing of a camera, as complicated as the *statics* of its mechanism may be, there would arise no more problems. But already the old commentaries, if read carefully, clearly show that it is not so. In explaining the "sign" (*nimittam*) on which the mindfulness of breathing has to be focussed, as Buddhaghoso says in *Visuddhi- maggo* (VIII, 206):

> "When his gross in-breaths and out-breaths have ceased, his consciousness occurs with the sign of the subtle in-breaths and outbreaths as its object. And when that has ceased, it goes on occurring with the successively subtler signs as its object." (Here follows the simile of the gong, quoted above.)

In the older model of the same commentarial structure, *Vimutti-maggo,*[116] a more extended specification of "signs" on which mindfulness can be focussed is described:

> "If the yogi develops the sign and increases it through repeated practice, increases it at the nose-tip, between the eye-brows, on the forehead or *establishes it in several places,* he feels as if his head were filled with air. Through increasing in this way, his whole body is charged with bliss. This is called perfection."

But in more recent years, Nanamoli found in *Visuddhi-maggo* a remark critical of the earlier advice. It corresponds better to *praṇāyāma* in the yoga-system:

> "He who increases the respiration sign only increases the accumulation of wind and it is limited in locality."

The first tetrad of exercises in breathing, as described in the *Anāpāna-sati-suttam,* begins with mindful regulation of long and short breathing. This corresponds to the initial *prāṇāyāma* exercises in yoga. Yet, since the Buddhist method is not based explicitly on the *kuṇḍalinī* physiology, it excludes all artificial regulations, such as *recaka, pūraka,* and the corresponding *mudrās* for closing one nostril while breathing (naturally corresponding to the *cakraṁ* in which find their support) have to be "registered" by attentive awareness of the meditator just as they appear in their natural sequence, and not artificially chosen or arranged. This is described in a suggestive simile in *Visuddhi-maggo,* VIII,[117]:

> "Suppose a man stands still after running, or descending from a hill, or putting down a big load from his head, then his in-breaths and out- breaths are gross, his nostrils become inadequate, and he keeps on breathing in and out through his mouth. But when he has rid

himself of his fatigue and has bathed and drunk and put a wet cloth on his hearth, and is lying in the cool shade, then his in-breaths and out- breaths eventually occur so subtly that he has to investigate whether they exist or not; so too, in the case of the meditating bhikkhu, when the in-breaths and out-breaths are still and occur so subtly that he has to investigate whether they exist or not."

Thus the ideal effect is not the deepening of breath, but rather refinement tending toward suspension. Such attenuation in the course of contemplative absorption will normally bring the beginner to a liminal point of vanishing experience on which he will feel the natural reaction of an existential shock and fear imminent dissolution threatening his body and his mind. This specific kind of existential anxiety has been observed and described by several teachers of "insight meditation". Among recent reports on such "experiments with meditation" an extensive analysis can be found in the second part of Mahasi Sayadaw's *Insight Meditation*[118]:

"When he can contemplate well in such a spread-out manner, even if he does not notice an object with vigour, he knows that what he hears fades away, what he sees dissolves in broken parts, with no continuation between them. This is seeing things as they really are. Some meditators do not see clearly what is happening because the vanishing is so swift that they feel their eye-sight is getting poorer, or they are giddy. It is not so. They are simply lacking the power of cognition to notice what happens before and after, with the result that they do not see the features or forms. At such a time they should relax and stop contemplating. Besides, in the midst of contemplations, the meditator is likely to have an awareness of fearfulness... Then the meditator sees nothing to depend on and becomes as it were weakened in mind as well as in body. He is seized with dejection... However, if he fails to contemplate for some time, then grief will assert itself and fear will overpower him. This kind of fear is not associated with insight..."

When such epiphenomena of resistance of the existential will are overcome and brought under control, a deeper substratum of equanimity (reminding of the Stoic *hypokeimenon*) *upekkhā* (*apatheia*) is reached:

" ...the three characteristics of life (impermanence, suffering {anguish} and no-self or soul) will be fully comprehended and then no heed being given to them, equanimity will be gained. When the 'knowledge of equanimity about formations' becomes mature, the mind will be very clear and able to notice the formations very lucidly."

In the *Visuddhi-maggo* these typical characteristics accompanying the progress of the mindfulness of breathing are mentioned in simpler statements and different connections, e.g. (V.M. VIII, 208, 224):

"While other subjects of meditation become clearer at each higher stage, this one does not. But for him who is developing it, it becomes more subtle at each higher stage. Also it comes to the point at which it is not manifested. But when it is not manifested thus, the bhikkhu should not rise from his seat and go away. What should be done? ...By just sitting as he was, it should be reinstated from the point (where it was formerly established.) "When all formations have appeared as terror owing to the terror of the contemplation of their incessant dissolution, he becomes dispassionate towards them, his greed for them fades away..."

In comparison with the depth of this specific dimension of existential anxiety, the spontaneous outbreak of such subjectively motivated anguish, caused by the realization of the imminent threat by destructive consequences of the annihilationist *uccheda-vādo*,[119] can be considered as the primary intellectual substructure of the same emotional effect provoked in the normal surface-consciousness. Buddho's standard description of its effects on several occasions was:

"...He then hears the Perfect One expounding the teaching for the removal of all grounds for 'views', of all prejudices, obsessions, dogmas and biases, for stilling of all processes, for the relinquishment of all substrata of existence, for the extirpation of craving, for dispassion, cessation, extinction. He then thinks, 'I shall be annihilated, I shall be destroyed. No longer shall I exist!' Hence he grieves, is depressed and laments; beating his breast, he weeps, and dejection befalls him. Thus, bhikkus, is there anxiety about realities." (*Alagaddūpama-suttaṁ*, M.22)

Considering the remedy offered by the reductive method of *jhānam* in the teaching of progressive attainment of equanimity as a means of control[120], it is stated in *Saṁyutta-nikāyo*,(XXXVI, 11):

"I have seen that the ceasing of activities is gradual. When one attains the first *jhānam*, speech has ceased. When one has attained the second *jhānam*, initial and sustained thought (*vitakka-vicāro*) has ceased. When one has attained the fourth *jhānam*, inbreathing and outbreathing has ceased." Consequently: "Noise is a thorn to the first *jhānam*. Thinking and exploring are a thorn to the second *jhānam*. Rapture is a thorn to the third *jhānam*. Inbreaths and outbreaths are a thorn to the fourth *jhānam*." (A.X, 72)

In *Visuddhi-maggo* (VIII, 189) "the stages of giving attention to the meditation subject consisting in mindfulness of breathing" are: (1) counting, (2) connection, (3) contact, (4) fixing, (5) observing, (6) turning away, (7) purification, and (8) the looking back on these.

Counting the in-breaths and out-breaths "he should not stop short of five nor go beyond ten... For when the meditation subject is connected with counting, it is with the help of that very counting that the mind becomes one-pointed, just as a boat in a swift current is steadied with the help of a rudder. When he counts quickly, the meditation subject becomes apparent to him as an uninterrupted process " (Id. 193) "Counting, by cutting off thoughts which cling to external things, serves the purpose of establishing mindfulness in the in- and out-breathings as object" (195). "Having given attention to it by counting, he should now do so by means of connection. Connection is the uninterrupted following of the in- and out-breaths with mindfulness..." Connection is simply "carrying on". "So when he gives attention to it by connection, he should do so not by the beginning, middle and end, but rather by contact and by fixing. There is, in fact, no attention to be given to it by contact separate from fixing as there is by counting separate from connection." (196-8)

Instead of going farther in the commentarial vivisection of these experiential complexities, I shall try first to describe their connection and their expansion in my own slow progress of exercises, and then to explain them according to implicit physiological criteria.

Stages (5) to (8) (not contained in the earlier *Vimutti-maggo*) form a separate group of reflections that in the contemplative mind and mood should always follow the strict part of immediate exercise. Their rational meaning is self-explanatory.

Judging from my own practice of nearly twenty years of recluse life, I still consider the sequence of the first four stages to be essential for gradually expanding my experience in each single exercise. The superficial neglect of the very first step of "counting", also characterizing several other misunderstandings of elementary principles, results in the neglect of the harmonious structure of the whole *arc de voûte* which must be sustained from beginning to end of the typical curve of all psycho-physiological experiences following Weber's law of retardation - regulating the basic function of attention:[121]

> Unlike the primitive method of "counting sheep" against insomnia, or the gapless linking of reiterative slogans on Coue's method of autosuggestion, the purpose of contemplative *expanding* of blank emptiness is attainable only in gaps of breathlessness on the highest peaks of concentration in *samādhi*, where even the consciousness of breathing becomes a "thorn". A Burmese teacher of meditation[122] has described it with a simple analogy:
>
> > "Whenever something is done with great attention, the breath is naturally held back. For example putting a thread through a needle... In like manner hold the breath as long as the meditator can *normally* hold it."

It may be curious to note that Buddho referred to the same old saying of "counting the cows of others" with the emphasis on heedfulness (*appamādo*) in *Dhammapadaṁ 19*:

> "... the heedless man is like a cow-herd who counts other's kine; he has no share in the blessings of a recluse."

A mindful artist of the abstract art of contemplation can be compared with a virtuoso in piano playing whose symphonic performance depends on the harmony of a number of movements determined by a selected key, or *rāga* in Indian music, rather than on playing a score by rote. The essential point of this analogy is that the meditator on the described stage of transition from "counting" to "connection" and "contact" (comparable to "staccato" and "legato" in music) will be as little concentrated on, or even conscious of, counting in numbers as the virtuoso in the harmonious sequence of movements composing the melody he plays. The same is characteristic also of the dynamic structure of the whole. Although unforeseen, the temporal span of its regular curve does not normally extend much beyond the measure of one *muhūrta*, corresponding to forty-eight minutes, according to a Jain text, where I found an explanation regarding it also as a cosmological measure.

Since the measuring (or "counting") of movements corresponds to the "tempo" in musical composition, the temporal span of the curve of psycho- physiological retardation can be asymmetrically expanded or shortened either at the initial ascending stage, or in the span of the highest region of concentration attainable in *samādhi*, or even at the concluding, usually steeper side of the *finale* of one exercise. Due to this extensibility of the biologically variable duration of one *muhūrta*, the average of the larger unit of my exercises may vary, dependent on the meditative mood, between 50 and 70 minutes. Contrary to my expectations when I came here as an ambitious beginner, this basic measure did not continue to extend progressively throughout the subsequent years in its quantitative dimension, but only in the qualitative reliability. I might measure my progress according to the standard formulated by Buddho and confirmed by his disciples:

> "Now, if I so desire, in complete isolation from sense-desires and from states which are not advantageous to this end, I can enter upon the first (second, and the progressive) *jhānam* and abide therein." (S. XLI, 7,8, *Nigaṇṭha-suttaṁ*)

In Lao-tsu's biography it is mentioned that he would sometimes retreat into a state of absorption and remain "lying like a log" for several days. It occurred sometimes to Socrates, too, to remain in the middle of his way immovable for a long time, even the whole night, absorbed in his thoughts, standing in a position that might remind us of the Jain *utsarga*, typical also for the archaic art of sculpture in Egypt and of countries of the Ancient East, including the provenance of early Greek civilization. In the Jain texts the *utsarga* posture and its meaning are described and explained as a "part of daily routine of a monk"[123]:

> "Along with mental control, control over body was also essential. For that *kāyotsarga* was practiced... A number of rules pertaining to the performance of *kāyotsarga* are found. Standing with movement of the body or with a blank mind or with support of something or with movement of eyes or eyebrows or with change in calm facial expression was not allowed. Thus the practice of *kāyotsarga* tended to lead to the mental concentration and control over physical movements."

It is not difficult to associate this state of rapture (expressed also in the mild smile of the stiff Greek archaic sculptures) with the Buddhist theory of close gapless "connecting" and "fixing" of concentrative (*samādhi*) stages and rapturous states from one *muhūrtha* to the next in imperceivably slow "pulses" of stabilized attention.

In the text quoted earlier from A.X, 1, 6 (see "The way of training the mind" -1) Buddo, requested by Anando, confirmed the possibility of "such an attainment of concentration wherein a *bhikkhu* will not be conscious of earth in earth... nor of this world in this world... and yet he will be conscious..."

*Cu*a-suññata-suttaṁ*, M. 121, quoted as a model of "the reductive structures of *jhānam*" (in Part II, ch. 4), refers to the possibility of training in gradual phases towards the attainment of the ultimate limit of intentionally submerging consciousness.

Changes in posture and intensity without interrupting the depth of concentration are well known phenomenal appearances of *samādhi*. About the middle of the 20th century one of the most carefully studied cases of this type was Ramana Maharshi (died in 1950). At the age of 17 he escaped to the sanctuary of *Tiruvaṇṇāmalai* in Tamil Nadu. There, in "the great temple... he shifted himself to obscure corners, and even to an underground vault known as *Pātā*a-liñgam.* Undisturbed he used to spend several days in deep absorption. Without moving he sat in *samādhi*, not being aware of even the bites of vermin and pests... At long last he was removed from the pit by devotees without his being aware of it and deposited in the vicinity of a shrine... The Svami himself never spoke. Not that he took any vow of silence; he had no inclination to talk..."[124] emerging from his *samādhi* he sometimes found himself in different corners where he had shifted unconsciously. In such movements he hardly took any food from the near-by places of temple-oblations of ghee and coconut water.

In my own practice, limited to the basic aim of developing the purely mental discipline of equilibrating and maintaining the state of "appeasement of the faculties of sense" (*sant-indriyo* as defined in Sn. 144) in inner silence - the ideal attainment of the second *jhānam*, the function of "counting" in its described context is essential. While establishing the concentration on the in- and out-breathing, the concord of metrical components might be compared with the construction of phrases in grammatical exercises when learning foreign languages. Buddho compared the whole art of disciplining the mind with the craft of a fletcher:

"Just as a fletcher makes straight his arrow, the wise man makes straight his trembling, unsteady thought which is difficult to guard and difficult to restrain." (Dhp. 33)

My respiration is slow by nature, and the retentive capacity of my memory weak; therefore I have tuned the measure of my exercises to the rhythm of five in- and out-breaths. Just as in the grammatical translation of sentences, the first rule is precision. To that effect I apply two criteria:

(a) Units which are not correct, i.e. not uniform and accompanied by *unsplit attention*, are not recognized. I was able to sharpen and straighten this criterion only in the course of time. But even then it often occurs that the strength of attentiveness continues to increase and clarify in the course of each single metrical unit. Statical constants are biologically impossible.

(b) In favorable cases I apply the second criterion extending the duration of the same unit ("fixing" without reconnection or *anubandhanam*) for one half (7 instead of 5) or even a double measure. This may depend on the intensity of attention. Noticing such variations of biological tension need not, and even should not, include the verbalized intention of registering (*tad-ārammaṇa-cittam*). It is a generally recognized rule for practical exercises that all attempts at *verbalization* should remain inhibited and avoided as "thorns to the second *jhānam*".

"Counting" becomes impossible, even in the described indirect and implicit form already at the margin of the physiologically highest attainment of spontaneous temporary cessation of breathing, (different from its stoppage by purposeful attention (as attention to ...). When the breath becomes unnoticeable in the nostrils, attention may be attracted sometimes to the pulsation of the heart. More often it remains concentrated in the "breath- body" on physiologically determined points of the respiratory organism or on the after-image of respiration.

It seems to me essential, at least from the strictly phenomenological point of observation, to consider "after-images" not only as phenomena of the sensation of sight, but potentially of all sense organs. In the "description of concentration", in chapters III-IV of *Visuddhi-maggo*, ten objects (*kasiṇam*) described as means of absorption refer to four constitutive elements of the phenomenal world (earth, water, fire and air), to four pure colors, and to two constituents of transcendental *esthesis* (light and space). Their shape for the purpose of contemplation can be adapted (though it is not necessary) to the classical form of a *maṇḍalam,* circle or disc. In the description of fire *kasiṇam,* the meditator is advised that "he should not review the *color* as blue or yellow, etc., or give attention to its characteristics as heat, etc." In the next example of "air *kasiṇam*" the instruction in "apprehending its sign in air" refers at the end of its description to the possibility that

> "he can establish mindfulness where the wind strikes a part of his body after entering by a window opening or by a crack in a wall... Here the learning sign appears to move like the swirl of hot steam on rice gruel just withdrawn from an oven. The counterpart sign is quiet and motionless."

Thus the "after-image of respiration" arises from the gradual stilling of movement of the diaphragm, which in these intervals changes the pattern of its rhythmic measure, but it may also remain refrained in the lungs where the after- image of the discontinued breathing is still felt as the "dead sea" after the moving force of wind has abated. If the strength of attention remains undisturbed thereby, even such epiphenomena may die away (in my case for about one minute) and then slowly reappear following the same pattern in which their movement had been temporarily discontinued.

The change of intensity and frequency does not necessarily alter the pattern of breathing. The regular patterns of normal breathing spread from a supporting point in the more or less relaxed midriff towards diffused levels in the lateral parts of lungs. This regulates the variable dependence of the breath on the depth of breathing. A consciously felt need to change the pattern is often due to disharmony between the respiratory and the digestive functions. Such disturbances can be reduced by adaptation to an easier diffused foothold of breath in higher lateral levels of the lungs. Raising that level to the heart (plexus solaris) and farther towards the head occurs in functional connection with the increasing stiffening not only of the lower parts of respiratory but also of digestive organs; this becomes visible on the surface of abdomen (not necessarily in the form artificially provoked in *haṭha-yoga* by *nauli*). The quickness and slowness of breath are not necessarily conditioned by its intensity as in cases where such effects are provoked by brisk walk or some other kind of organic excitement - or the opposite effects of relaxation. In the conditions of my experiments the low breath can be very intensive in respiration with the top of lungs while concentrating on the throat center (*viśuddhi-cakram* with its 16 petals, "probably the pharyngeal plexus of the sympathetic... said to be the lotus of purification").[125] By raising the center of attention to *ajñā-cakram*, "which is situated between the two eyebrows,... the plexus of command", the intensity is immediately reduced. The stiffening of the supporting point of breath above the level of midriff by gradual raising of the breath-level to the area of heart or throat increases the effort to extend the keeping up of the breath on these levels, and also of its gradual lowering. This, too, should be accomplished by gradual exercise.

6. The Physiological System Of Kuṇḍalini

In the Indian philosophy of religion the term *kuṇḍalini* is associated with the system of *yoga* in its later development. In the original version of *Yoga-sūtrāni* by Patanjali there is no mention of *kuṇḍalini*[126], or "the coiled up" energy in the autonomic nervous system, which is described by Dr. Rele[127] as "the ventricular cavity in the brain" and "the passage to that cavity" which "is the narrow space at the lower end of the fourth ventricle in the brain with the channel in the spinal cord (*suśumṇa-nādā*) and the subarachnoid space (*ākāśa*). The dormant kundalini thus guards against the three important openings in the cerebro-spinal nervous system." The dictionary meaning of the word is "coiling (as a serpent)" (Apte). It corresponds in the Graeco-Roman mythology to the insignia of Aesculapius, the god of health, a staff intertwined with two serpents. In the detailed description of Indian anatomy it corresponds to the autonomic nervous system of European science, extending along the spinal cord and the ganglia centers designated and described in its Indian analogy as *cakraṁ*. The central column of the *kuṇḍālinī* nervous system is called *Meru-daṇḍa*, or the staff of mount Meru, the Himalayan axis of the world. It contains the *suśumṇa-nāḍi* from the left side of whose basis twines the *idā-nāḍi* which ends in the right nostril, while the *pingala-nāḍi* starts from the right side and ends in the left nostril. These *nāḍis* "correspond to the gangliated cords of the sympathetic system, which are situated on either side of the spinal column."[128]

> "It is also through this *suśumṇa-nāḍi* that we obtain knowledge of our relations with the external world. But a knowledge of the self and a control of the vital organs can only be achieved by consciously controlling *idā* and *pingalā naāḍis* which form a connecting link between the prevertebral plexuses (*cakras*) of the sympathetic system and spinal cord (*suśumṇa-nāḍi*). All these plexuses, in order to excite *suśumṇa-nāḍi* by their connection with it, must work through the *kuṇḍali-cakraṃ*. In fact, what the brain or medulla is to the central nervous system, *kuṇḍali-cakraṃ* to the sympathetic system. Normally, the central nervous system is well developed as regards its response to external stimuli while the sympathetic nervous system lies dormant. When the latter is made active by *prāṇāyama* (control of breathing)... a person develops the power to do certain things which are beyond the scope of an ordinary individual."

Schopenhauer, in his lengthy *"Essay on Spirit Seeing and Everything Connected Therewith"*[129], based his explanation of the whole range of parapsychological phenomena on the basis of autonomic functions of the same system

> "under the guidance and control of the plastic nervous system and thus of all the large ganglia in the whole length of the trunk which are connected with one another by leading nerve-cords and constitute the *great sympathetic nerve* or *inner* nerve center. This is completely separated and isolated from the *outer* nerve focus, the brain, which is exclusively concerned with the direction of *external* relations..."

Although Schopenhauer was a good knower and lifelong devoted reader of the *upaniṣads*, he never quotes them in this connection. It is hardly believable that he might have made any use of the fragmentary information on the autonomous nervous system, its leading nerve-cords" and "inner nerve-center... isolated from the outer nerve focus...", which, in the upanishadic references, corresponding to *nāḍi* and *hitā*.

One of the two longest and oldest, best known upanishadic texts, the *Chāndogya-upaniṣad*, in Part VIII section 6 deals with the system and structure of *nāḍi* - the three principal arteries (or channels) of the heart, " *suśumṇa-*, *idā-*, and *piñgala-nāḍi*:[130]

(1) "They consist of a fine substance which is tawny (*piñgalasy' aṇimnas*), white, blue, yellow and red. Verily, the sun yonder is tawny (*piñgala*), he is white, he is blue, he is yellow, he is red.

(2) Even as a great extending highway runs between two villages, this one and that yonder, even so these rays of the sun go to both these worlds, this one and that yonder. They start from the yonder sun and enter into these arteries. They start from these arteries and enter into the yonder sun.

(3) And when one is thus sound asleep, composed, serene, so that he knows no dream, then he has entered into these channels; even so no evil touches him for then he has obtained the light of the sun...

(4) But when he thus departs from this body, then he goes upward by these very rays or he goes up with the thought of *aum*. As his mind is failing, he goes to the sun. That, verily, is the gateway of the world, an entering in for the knowers, a shutting out for the non- knowers.

(5) On that there is this verse: A hundred and one are the arteries of the heart (*hṛidyasya nāḍya*). One of them leads up to the crown of the head. Going upward through that, one becomes immortal. The others serve for going in various other directions." (IV, 17-19)

In *Kauṣītaki-upaniṣad*, which is also considered as one of the five older, prebuddhist texts, *idā-nāḍi* and *piñgala-nāḍi*, though not mentioned under these names, appear to be identified as the person (*puruṣa*) who is in the right eye", on whom the teacher Belakih "meditates as the self of speech" and "the person who is in the left eye" on whom he meditates "as the self of truth, the self of lightning, the self of light"...

"The two then came upon a person asleep, then Ajatasatru called him - You great one clad in white raiment, King Somah. -But he just lay silent. Thereupon he pushed him with a stick. He got up at once. To him, then, Ajatasatru said: Where, in this case, o Balaki, has this person lain, what has become of him here, from where has he returned here, as I asked, are the channels (*nāḍi*) of a person called *hitā*, extending from heart to the surrounding body (*pericardium*). As minute as a hair divided a thousandfold, they consist of a thin essence (fluid) white, black, yellow and red. In these one remains while asleep he sees no dream whatsoever."

Dogmatic discussions on the transcendental nature and provenance of the *kuṇḍalinī* force (*śakti*) and its faculties (*indriyam*) in its cosmic relations can be mentioned here only as a subject of secondary importance to our descriptive phenomenological approach. Thus, according to J. Woodroffe, the highest authority in studies of Tantrism in the 20th century particularly in India:[131]

> "The Supreme, therefore, descends through its manifestations from the subtle to the gross as the six *Devas* (senses) and *śaktis* (faculties) in their six abodes in the world-axis, and as the six centers in the world-axis, and as the six centers in the body-axis or spinal column."

In his Foreword to Dr. Rele's book Woodroffe takes a critical stance to pure physiology on which Rele's analysis is based, though he does not want "to say that the Author's theory is without value", yet:[132]

> "His view is an original one, namely that Kundalini is the right Vagus Nerve. As to this I would say that Kundalini herself cannot be that and for this reason. She is the Grand Potential. As such she cannot, in my view, be identified with any of the products which she becomes. Kundalini, in my opinion, is a gross form of Shakti... She is then not, in my view, a nerve or any other physical substance or mental faculty but the Ground Substance of both..."

Apart from such religious-metaphysical reservations, modern authors, both Indian and European, agree that

> "*idā* and *piñgalā* correspond to the gangliated cords of the sympathetic system, which are situated on either side of the spinal column. At the cephalic end, each sympathetic trunk passes into the cranial cavity, arborises with its fellows of the other side and forms a plexus. Through this plexus the sympathetic trunks gain complex relations with the spinal cord (*suśumṇā-nāḍi*) where it joins the brain... This *nāḍi,* as it ascends and reaches the level of *kañṭṭa* (region of the larynx), divides into an anterior and a posterior part. The anterior portion goes toward the *ajñā-cakram,* the plexus of command, which is situated between the two eye-brows and joins the *brahma-rañdhram* which is supposed to be a cavity in the brain from which the yogi liberates his soul. It is this posterior portion that is to be developed by a student of yogic science. This description of the *suśumṇā-nāḍi* concurs quite accurately with that of the spinal cord. It seems that the ancients had a knowledge of the function of the two parts of the spinal cord, the anterior and the posterior... The yogi is told to develop the posterior portion of the *nāḍi,* which governs all sensations and supplies all the vital organs of the body, a portion which normally is not under our control. Of all the ten *nāḍis* these

three are the principal, and of the three *suśumṇā* is the most important..."[133]

"*Kuṇḍalinī* corresponds to the right *vagus* nerve... Our present knowledge of anatomy tells us that of the two *vagi* the left *vagus* is not so plentifully supplied with efferent fibers as the right and plays only a very minor part in the formation of the solar plexus and of plexuses situated below it, while the right vagus nerve, through its hypogastric branch, gains a direct connection with the solar plexus and the plexuses situated below it. The stimulation of the right vagus nerve at its central connection can control the activities of all six plexuses of the sympathetic system as it contains the most important part of the para-sympathetic portion of the autonomic nervous system."[134] *(See the table on the next page).*

Rudolph Steiner has carefully explained on the higher para-psychological and moral level the essential importance of distinguishing the genetic development of the posterior and anterior portions of ganglionic chords (*naḍi*) of the autonomous nervous system and the plexuses (cakram) of nerves arborising on their trunk. He limits his description to the biologically archetypal functions of the *cakram* or "lotuses and their petals"[135] I am not sure whether his distinction of upper and lower halves of each *cakram* coincides with Rele's genetic considerations especially in his underscoring of the cultivation of both the conscious and the subconscious. The crucial problem of psychoanalysis cannot therefore be discussed in this context[136] Our discussion will be limited to a broad survey of Steiner's approach to the prevalently *moral aspect of this parapsychological problem,* an approach compatible with my own.

Table 1			
cakram numerical and geometrical symbol, color	anatomic location	*tattvam* matter and sense function	archetypal symbols
1. mūlādhāra 4 petals square crimson	pelvic plexus	Earth-solidity smell	Indrah (Zeus) elephant
2. svādiṣṭhānaṃm 6 petals circle vermilion	hypogastric plexus	Water-fluidity taste	Varunah (Uranus) crocodile
3. maṇipūraṃ 10 petals triangle dark "like heavyladen raincloud"	plexus of coeliac axis solar complex	Fire "lustrous as a gem" (*maṇni*) sight	*Agni* ram
4. anāhataṃ 12 petals hexagon vermilion	cardiac plexus heart	Air touch	Vāyuh (Wind) antelope syllable *om*
5. viśuddha 16 petals circle purple	pharyngeal plexus throat	ether (*ākāśa*) hearing	Siva-Gauri white elephant
6. ājñ 2 petals white	naso-ciliary extension of the cavernous plexus between eye-brows, the plexus of command, the inner self (*antar-ātmā*)	mind (mana) breathing	Swan (*haṁsa*)
7. sahasrara	1000 petals, The White Lotus		*Brahma-loka* macrocosmos

In Steiner's presentation the order of *cakrams* follows a direction inverse to that of typical Indian standards. He starts from *ājñā*, the plexus of command, the seat of rational consciousness and inner mental self in the head. He then descends down to the fifth and sixth *cakram* (*svādiṣṭhanaṃ* and *mūlādhārah*) in the lower, abdominal part of the body: *cakrams* of sensual instincts which should be developed last as control-organs in order to establish a rational equilibrium among sensuality, passions, and ideas. This is the explicit guide-line of the *ethos of knowledge* by which the renaissance of our spiritual culture should be informed and guided. By the term of *renaissance* I wish to single out the basic conception of Steiner's genetics: spiritual education and revival of the whole *kuṇḍalinī* tract should begin, in his system, from the central *cakrams* located in the throat and in the heart (*viśuddhaṃ* and *anāhataṃ*).

Viśuddhaṃ, the sixteen-petalled lotus located in the region of throat, is the most important basic center for the spiritual irradiation of *nāḍis* because the development of its faculties depends on the strengthening of virtues identical with those of Buddho's eightfold path of spiritual liberation. This identity is recognized explicitly by Steiner in a footnote (though rather reluctantly on account of his euro-centrism).

> "Students will recognize in the conditions attached to the development of the sixteen-petalled lotus the instructions given by the Buddha to his disciples for the *Path*. Yet there is no question here of teaching Buddhism, but of describing conditions governing development which are the natural outcome of spiritual science. The fact that these conditions correspond with certain teachings of the Buddha is no reason for not finding them true in themselves."

Steiner explains the genetic development of this lotus, and also of *anāhataṁ*, the next and nearest in importance for developing a higher level of consciousness above the lower half of these lotuses (or *cakrams*), as follows:

> The lower "eight of the sixteen petals of this lotus flower were developed in a remote past, and these will reappear of themselves in the course of esoteric development. All the effort and attention of the student must be devoted to the remaining eight. Faulty training may easily result in the re-appearance of the earlier petals alone, while the new petals remain stunted. This will ensue especially if too little logical, rational thinking is employed in the training. It is

of supreme importance that the student should be a rational and clear thinking person..."

For our Buddhist analogy it is important to note Buddho's insistence on the first step of the *same* eightfold path - *sammā-diṭṭhi,* correct view, and the basic characteristic of the *first jhānam - savitakka savicāro,* logical and discursive thinking.

"The twelve-petalled lotus situated in the region of the heart is developed in a similar way. Half its petals, too, were already existent and in active use in a remote stage of human evolution. Hence these six petals need not now be especially developed in esoteric training; they appear of themselves and begin to revolve when the student sets to work on the other six. Here again he learns to promote this development by consciously controlling and directing certain inner activities in a special way." "The distorted development of a lotus flower results not only in illusions and fantastic conceptions, should a certain degree of clairvoyance be acquired, but also in errors and instability in ordinary life. Such a development may be the cause of timidity, envy, vanity, haughtiness, willfulness and so in a person who hitherto was free from these defects."

In protest against materialistic mass-media aiming at the destruction of their own apocalyptic world, "psychedelic" characters have been ruined by drug addiction, a type of spiritual suicide. All this, however, seems to have resulted from the repression of the upsurging natural need for religion.

It is sometimes asked why there is need for such meticulous care over each single "petal", over their sequence in the budding "flowers" in the making and opening of their faces to the rising sun. In answering this question, Steiner made a quick reference to one Buddhist model of classification, a model central to the Buddhist conception as well as to Steiner's. He opened me to a clearer insight and easier orientation in the numerological schematism of the Buddhist *abhidhammo* (= *peri phainomena*) - a method of "gradual" (*aṅguttarā*) and organically "intertwined" (*saṁyuttā*) subjects. Steiner explicitly recognized that the eight petals of the sixteen-petalled lotus, which have to be cultivated with fully rational conscious intention, are virtues and spiritual faculties identical to those of the gradual development on Buddho's eightfold path.

Steiner's presentation of the progress on the path of spiritual culture, following the track of physiological development of latent potentials of *kuṇḍālinī* energies (*śakti*) along the autonomic nervous system, starts from the sixteen-petalled lotus, corresponding to the pharyngeal plexus in the throat, the purifying focus (*viśuddhi-cakraṃ*) of mental capacities. From there Steiner follows the spreading of the same vital energy to the twelve-petalled lotus in the sphere of the heart. In Steiner's formulation, "this kind of perceptions can be approximately characterized by designating it as the warmth and the coolness of the soul".

From there he proceeds further to the description of the ten-petalled lotus in the sphere of the solar plexus (around the navel), radiating power of attention.

The lowest center described by Steiner is the six-petalled lotus (*svādiṣṭhānaṃ*) which, when properly and most cautiously and maturely developed, after some progress has been attained in the development and moral understanding of functions concentrated in the higher centers, serves to establish and maintain the equilibrium of impulses of "sensuality, passions and ideas".

It is only in the following section of the same chapter that Steiner reverts to the two-petalled *ājñā*, the traditional "plexus of command" of man's "inner-self" (*antar-ātmā*) "between eye-brows" where all lower control points of specific psycho-physical faculties are ultimately condensed and focussed. This is the spring-board wherefrom the skillful jump to spiritual liberation should be ventured to reunite, at the end of an accomplished cultivation of harmony, the well balanced microcosmic whole with its macrocosmic matrix. It is the deepest act of concentration (*yoniso manasikāram*) which opens, according to the brahmanic archetypology, the *brahma-randhra-cakram*, the opening of "the crown of the head", the aureole, the thousand-petalled white lotus, *sahasrāram*, to "the World of Truth" (*satya-loka*).

In elaborate treatises on the anatomy of *kuṇḍalinī*, *maṇipura-cakram* in the solar plexus is described as the "direct extension upwards" of the subjacent *kuṇḍali-cakram*. "It is called the Lotus of Happiness." The proximity of these two cakrams is so great that most often "no distinction is made between the *kuṇḍali* and *maṇipura-cakram*".[137]

It is from this *cakram*, descending through the throat and heart centers that "the serpent power", the *śakti* of *kuṇḍalinī*, makes its daring jump to the highest "*cakram* of command" in the head, and out through "the crown of the head to the world of macrocosmic truth and freedom.

The most vivid picture of this circulation of the life-force of *prāṇa* that I could find was in *The Gospel of Sri Ramakrishna* (Calcutta, 1836-1886), describing his own experiences:

"Once a sadhu of Hrishikesh came here. He said to me: 'There are five kinds of *samādhi*. I find you have experienced them all. In these *samādhis* one feels the sensation of the Spiritual Current to be like the movement of an ant, a fish, a monkey, a bird, or a serpent.'

- Sometimes the Spiritual Current rises though the spine, crawling like an ant.
- Sometimes, in *samādhi*, the soul swims joyfully in the ocean of divine ecstasy, like a fish.
- Sometimes, when I lie down on my side, I feel the Spiritual Current pushing me like a monkey and playing with me joyfully. I remain still. That Current, like a monkey, suddenly with one jump reaches the Sahasrara. That is why you see me jump up with a start.
- Sometimes, again, the Spiritual Current rises like a bird from one branch to another. The place where it rests feels like fire. It may hop from Muladhara to Savdishthana, from Svadishthana to the heart, and thus gradually to the head.
- Sometimes the Spiritual Current moves like a snake. Going in a zigzag way, at last it reaches the head and I go into samadhi.
- A man's spiritual consciousness is not awakened unless his Kundalini is aroused."

Returning to the analogy of Steiner's description of lotuses, or *cakram*, in the "network of the etheric body" (*nāḍi, hitā*), with the corresponding Buddhist structures, we may draw in broad lines the following scheme of their specific constituents. Steiner's "petals of lotuses", correspond to Buddho's groups of the constituents of spiritual awakening, *bodhi-pakkhiyā* (Sanskrit *bodhi-pakṣyā*), "the wings of awakening". Of the seven constituents of these "wings" in the traditional list[138] ("The Noble Eightfold Path" (the last of the "Four Noble Truths") corresponds, as explicitly stated by Steiner, to the petals symbolizing the virtues of the sixteen-petalled lotus of mental purification (*viśuddhi*). The six groups preceding this last one on the list of bodhi-pakkhiya seem to correspond implicitly, but following the same order of enumeration, to Steiner's description of the "six characteristics" of which the twelve-petalled lotus (*anāhata-cakram*) is composed.

According to the traditional Buddhist scheme the seven groups of *bodhi- pakkhiya* principles (including the Noble Eightfold Path as the concluding seventh part):

> "contain the thirty-seven qualities required for the attainment of enlightenment. They have been set forth in seven groups according to their collective and individual activities, and enumerated as thirty- seven. But, considered in regard to their psychological disposition they have been summarized under these fourteen headings"[139]:
>
> Mindfulness occurs in 8 places.
> Energy occurs in 9 places.
> Concentration occurs in 4 places, etc.

Thus, even according to this criterion, Steiner's condensation of qualities mentioned in remaining contexts and structure of other lotuses, appear justified and rational in comparison with *bodhi-pakkhiya* characteristics and also in considering the next two *cakrams.*

Describing the ten-petalled lotus (*maṇipūram*), summarized by Steiner as referring to the development of "capacities and talents" (*Fahigkeiten und Talente*), he speaks mainly of "a life in mindfulness" corresponding to the central theme of buddhist meditation - *sati-paṭṭhanam,* mentioned in our schemes as the seventh constituent of the Eightfold Path, and the first *bodhi- pakkhiyam.*

The three virtues to be developed in the six-petalled lotus (*svādiṣṭhāna- cakram*), located above the *mūlādhāra*, or the lowest "root-support" *cakram* of *kuṇḍalinī* correspond to the *hetu-paccayo*, "the root condition" (called also *mūla-hetu*) of the "wheel of existence" of the whole being-in-the-world, schematized in the formula of *paṭicca-samuppādo*, "dependent origination" of all phenomena (*dhammā*) and of the implicit wisdom of liberation (*vimutti*). These three root-conditions that have to be overcome are *"lobho-doso-moho"*, the passions of greed (sensuality), hate (mentality) and delusion (ideas). Steiner interprets them with the terms put here in brackets : *"Sinnlichkeit (Leib), Leidenschaft (Seele), und Idee (Geist)."*

7. Samañña-phala-suttantaṁ

The similes added to the description of levels of absorption in *jhānam* in *Samañña-phala-suttantaṁ* and in some other texts are also characteristic for parapsychological experiences described on various occasions by Buddho as effects of his *yogāvacaro* ascetic practices. Therefore they will be quoted here, in connection with the cultivation (*bhāvanā*) of "lotuses", understood implicitly as organs of the physiological system of *kuṇḍalinī*, presumed, not less implicitly, still in the basic *Yoga-sūtrāni* of Patanjali's school (*Patañjala-yoga*) where they refer to phenomena which Buddho described with the same terms as in the early *yogāvacaro* discourses:

First jhānam

"Just as a skillful bathman or his apprentice will scatter perfumed soap powder in a metal basin, and then besprinkling it with water, drop by drop, will so knead it together that the ball of lather, taking up the unctuous moisture, is drenched with it, pervaded by it, permeated by it within and without, and there is no leakage possible - so he does pervade his very body, drench, permeate and suffuse it with the joy and ease born of detachment, that there is no spot in his whole frame not suffused therewith."

Second jhānam

"Just as if there were a deep pool, with water welling up into it from a spring beneath, and with no inlet from the east or west, from the north or south, and the god should not from time to time send down showers of rain upon it. Still the current of cool waters rising up from that spring would pervade, fill, permeate, and suffuse the pool with cool waters, and there would be no part or portion of the pool unsuffused therewith - so he does pervade... his very body... with the joy and ease born of concentration..."

Third jhānam

"Just as when in a lotus tank the several lotus flowers, red or white or blue, born in the water, not rising up above the surface of the water, drawing up nourishment from the depths of the water, are so pervaded, drenched, permeated, and suffused from their very tips down to their roots with the cool moisture thereof, that there is no spot in the whole plant... not suffused therewith - so he does pervade his very body... with that ease that had no joy with it..."

Fourth jhānam

"Just as if a man were sitting so wrapped from head to foot with a clean white robe, that there were no spot in his whole frame not in contact with the clean white robe - just so does the bhikkhu sit there, so suffusing even his body with that sense of purification, of trans-

TABLE 2

Buddho's Noble Eightfold Path	**Steiner's analogy to *viśuddhi-cakram,* the lotus of mental purification**
1. right view	1. representations (ideas, conceptions)
2. right intention	2. resolutions
3. right speech	3. speech
4. right action	4. action
5. right livelihood	5. management of the whole life
6. right effort	6. effort
7. right mindfulness	7. accumulating experiences
8. right concentration (*samādhi*)	8. absorption
Bodhi-pakkhiya-dhammā (constituents of awakening)	Six characteristics (*Eigenschaften*) -analogy to *anāhata-cakram*
1. *sati-paṭṭhānam* (four stations of mindfulness)	1. control of mental processes (*Beherrschung des Gedankenverlaufs*)
2. viriyam (four right efforts)	2. control of action
3. *iddhi-pādam* (condensation of will, energy, thought and investigation)	3. perseverances
4. indriyam (faculties) and 5. balam (strength) in faith, energy,	4-5. faith and tolerance, strength mindfulness, concentration and in overcoming hindrances (cf. Pali *nīvaranam*, specifically the last three: sloth-and-torpor, restlessness-and-scruples, doubt)
6. *bojjhaṅgam* (limbs of awakening, specifically the last three: tranquility, concentration, and equanimity)	6. inner balance, equanimity

lucence, of heart, that there is no spot in his whole frame not suffused therewith."

The ultimate result attained by such purification of insight (*vipassanā*) is described again with a sublime Buddhic simile of a pond of lotuses in the same collection of long discourses, *Dīgha-nikāyo* XIV, *Mahā-padāna-suttantaṁ*, in the hagiography of the seventh predecessor of Buddho Gotamo, Vipassi, ninety-one aeons ago:

"As in a pond of blue, or red, or white lotuses, some lotus-plants born in the water grow up in the water, do not emerge from the water, but thrive sunken beneath; and other lotus-plants born in the water and grown up in the water, reach to the level; while other lotus- plants born in the water and grown up in the water, stand thrusting themselves above the water, undrenched by it; even so, bhikkhus, did Vipassi buddho... look down over the world with a Buddho's eye, and see beings whose eyes were nearly free from dust, and beings whose eyes were dim with dust, beings sharp of sense and blunted in sense, beings of good and of evil disposition, beings docile and indocile, and some of them discerning the danger in rebirth in other worlds, and the danger in wrong doing."

In the epic of Gilgamesh (typical also for the archetypal way of esoteric initiation as described by R. Steiner) a more hermetic symbol from the Arabian desert, corresponds to the lotus: a thorny rose. It sprouts, too, from deep subterranean deluvial sweet water, cautiously and very slowly finding its way out, hidden to the bodily eye by the arid crust of the desert[140]:

"Gilgamesh, I shall reveal a secret thing, it is a mystery of the gods that I am telling you. There is a plant that grows under the water, it has a prickle like a thorn, like a rose; it will wound your hands, but if you succeed in taking it, then your hands will hold that which restores his lost youth to a man."

"When Gilgamesh heard this he opened the sluices so that a sweet-water current might carry him out to the deepest channel; he tied heavy stones to his feet and they dragged him down to the water-bed. There he saw the plant growing; although it pricked him he took it in his hands; then he cut the heavy stones from his feet, and the sea carried him and threw him onto the shore." Later, on his return journey from the orphic nether-world (comparable also to the visit of Naciketa to the world of Yamah in *Katha-upaniṣad*) - "Gilgamesh saw a well of cool water and he went down and bathed; but deep in the pool there was lying a serpent, and the serpent sensed the sweetness of the flower. It rose out of the water and snatched it away, and immediately it sloughed its skin and returned to the well. Then Gilgamesh sat down and wept... - Was it for this that I toiled with my hands, is it for this I have wrung out my heart's blood? For myself I have gained nothing; not I but the beast of the earth has joy of it now... I found a sign and now I have lost it. Let us leave the boat on the bank and go."

The delicate buds of spiritual lotuses (*cakraṁ*) sprouting on the slender stalks and stems (*nāḍi, hitā*) twining around the creeper of *kuṇḍalinī*, rooted in the deeply submerged fertile ground (*mūlā-dhāra*), like grain buried with pharaohs in their pyramids, expecting since long millennia the help of skillful cultivation, are exposed in our age of mechanical and chemical warfare to the most brutal treatment by "psychedelic" suicides. Relentless in their eagerness to exhibit at such a high price a forceful twist on their trellis of "artificial heavens and hells" the premature opening and extinction of their exotic flowers, they are poisoned to bloom like plants exposed to piercing flashes of light at an artificial exhibition of night-flowers.

On the other hand, during the centuries of commentarial decadence, *thera-vādo* Pali Buddhism was reduced to a heteronomous belief in ritual rules and regulations, while on the side of the expanding Hinduism the penetration of *kuṇḍalinī-yoga* became increasingly a part of esoteric teaching until it was profanized into "modern techniques".

In the "commentarial developments" of the later Buddhism *yogāvacaro* practices, more specific instructions concerning postures of the body (*āsanaṁ*) of functional importance to meditation practices appear to have penetrated through such influences, directly or indirectly, thanks to their far and wide adoption by *mahāyānaṁ* religions.

P. Vajiranana's presentation of the commentarial development in Pali Buddhism is to a large extent based on a late *yogāvacaro* manual, translated for the Pali Text Society under the title "The Manual of a Mystic" (London 1916). Speaking of "the image of the meditation posture Vajiranana describes it as follows:[141]

"When this posture is assumed the right leg is crossed over the left; the feet are resting upon the upper portion of the thighs, the soles turned upwards; the hands are placed just below the level of the navel, with the bend of the wrists pressed against the thighs, bracing the upper part of the body; the spinal column is straight like a pile of coins, one coin on top of another. The diaphragm is expanded to its maximum fullness; the chin is up; the sight is fixed on the tip of the nose or else straight in front..."

To this description of the classical *yoga* details a comparison with the *Tibetan Yoga* by Evans-Wentz is added in a footnote:

"When one sits down in the Buddha-posture the right leg is crossed over the left, whereas in the posture which Hindus called Buddha-Padmasana, the left leg is crossed over the right, and this is the highest posture of Indian Yogis. A similar posture to this which is called "Siddhasana", the seat of Siddha deities or of holiness, is easier to assume and more commonly used today by practicing Yogis in India. In this posture the legs are crossed in such manner that the left heel is pressed against the region of the perineum and the right foot is placed in the fold of the left leg. These two are the most favored among the numerous postures or asanas described in Sanskrit works on Yoga. According to the Tibetan teaching Buddha-posture, Dorje-posture or Vajrasana and Siddha-posture are the three yogic (or Lamaic) postures. Straighten the body and assume the Dorje-posture. Accordingly, place the feet in the Buddha-posture. Place hands level and equiposed below navel. Straighten the spinal column. Throw out the diaphragm. Bend the neck to the shape of a hook, the chin just pressing against the oesophagus. Place the tongue upward against the roof of the mouth. The cross-legged posture regulateth the inspiration. The posture of equilibrium (Dorje-posture) equalizeth the vital heat of the body. The straightening of the spinal column together with the expanding of the diaphragm regulates the nervous fluid pervading the body. The placing of the tongue against the roof of the mouth together with the focusing of the gaze causes the vital force to enter into the median-nerve."

The reasons for such specific advice, obviously based on the heterodox tradition of *kuṇḍalinī-yoga*, were never explicated in early *thera-vādo* manuals of meditation (*bhāvanā*). They remained concealed due to the secrecy of the revelation through "direct transmission" (according to the zen-term) by a *guru's* authority.

Japaḥ - repetitive thinking

Steiner's reference to the correspondence of the "petals" of *kuṇḍalinī* lotuses to the steps and levels of Buddho's eightfold path of liberation and to other basic formations of the *bodhi-pakkhiya-bhāvanā* or "wings of meditation" had a suggestive effect also on my practice of condensing and increasing mental concentration in *sati-paṭṭhanam* exercises. When the breath concentrates more or less spontaneously, on the throat level of *viśuddha-cakraṁ*, I try to sustain the duration of its model for at least eight in- and out-breaths. (A longer spontaneous extension is always desirable on all levels.) The same intention applies to the concentration on other *cakraṁs* and the sequence of lowering the level from the throat to that of the heart and farther down, or vice-versa, of raising it in a sequence without much premeditated intention. In the early years of my regular exercises I felt a stronger need to discipline my concentration in one-pointedness (*cittass'ekaggatā*) by stricter means of repetitive thinking, corresponding to the Buddhist adaptation of the ancient *yoga* practices.

In a booklet on japah[142], M.P. Pandit (whose synopsis of *kuṇḍalinī*-yoga was quoted in the preceding section), traces the tradition of this practice of concentrative "repetition of a Mantra, a potent syllable or syllables, a word or a combination of words", back to the Rg-vedah (I, 156,3) as a form of religious sacrifice (*yajña*), which "has the potency to stamp and mould the consciousness". In Vedic contexts mantras are "terms of Call" to deities. In my Buddhist interpretation they may correspond to a still deeper notion of *karma* as formulated (implicitly) by Heidegger[143]: It is "the appeal which calls back by calling forth (*Der Anruf ist forrufender Ruckruf*"): it calls *Dasein* (the there-being of a human reality) forth to the possibility of taking over, in existing, even that thrown entity which it is."

According to Pandit's description of this practice,

> "It is usual in the traditional method of doing Japa to fix the number of times one is to repeat the Mantra at a sitting..." -"If Japa is done in the heart, there must be a strong feeling, and intensity accompanying the repetition. The Japa should rise on the crest of deep emotion. The whole of the heart must beat in unison with the Mantra which thus gathers strength, acquires a fresh life in the individual and in time begins to repeat itself spontaneously without effort."[144]

Sri Aurobindo, in his epic masterpiece *Savitri*, describes this practice of *mantra-yoga* in the following verses:

> *"As when the mantra sinks in yoga's ear,*
> *Its message enters stirring the blind obtain*

And keeps in the dim ignorant cells its sound;
The hearer understands a form of words
And, musing on the index thought it holds,
He strives to read it with the laboring mind,
But finds bright hints, not the embodied truth:
Then, falling silent in himself to know
He meets the deeper listening of his soul:
The Word repeats itself in rhythmic strains:
Thought, vision, feeling, sense, the body's self
Are seized unalterably and he endures
An ecstasy and an immortal change;
He feels a Wideness and becomes a Power,
All knowledge rushes on him like a sea:
....
(Book IV, Canto III)

Abstracting not only from the magical but also from the emotional overtones of the Hindu theistic *japa*, in the Buddhist striving towards the dispassionate coolness of reasonable clarity and insight (*yathā bhūtaṁ*) the corresponding method of repetitive thinking has, in my practice, the initial purpose of slowing down the flux of thoughts and the moving force of their existential processes (*bhavāñga-soto*). The usual practice of *japa* in Indian religions suggests rather the analogy with Coue's method of autosuggestion. Even some superficially "westernized" Buddhist authors tried to bring such "meditation" down to autosuggestive exercises (especially against insomnia!). However, the hypnotic effects of *japa* on will and consciousness are so tenuous that they vanish if even there is the slightest span or break in their automatic flow, infiltrating two rhythmic measures. The purpose of the slow and sustained repetitive thinking in serious meditation (on the level of the first *jhānam*), as I understand it, is just the opposite. It has an intentionally inhibitive function to slow down the rapid flux of superficial awareness and endeavors to *increase* the span of peaceful emptiness and silence between undesirable but unavoidable intrusions of thought and perception, which are natural influxes and discharges (*āṣavā*) from both the internal and external (*ajjhattam-bāhiram*) world. The mindful recurrence of an essential thought, or rather of a purposeful apperception, has not the purpose of increasing the pressure as in an "autosuggestive" *japa*, but rather the tendency of awakening and making die away the echo of existential worries as described in the *Cū*a-suññata-suttaṁ* (M. 121), quoted at the end of the preceding chapter. In the course of my exercises in straightening mindfulness (*sati-paṭṭhānaṁ*) - just as a fletcher makes his arrow straight" (*Dhamma-padaṁ* 33, 80, 145) - I used, when necessary, to repeat one single autosuggestive word instead of explicit verbal counting of breaths. At the beginning (during the first year of my stay at the Island Hermitage in Sri Lanka, in 1966) this was the Pali word *khantī* (Sk. *kśānti*) whose meaning I encompassed in the idea of peaceful forbearance. During the next year I substituted that idea (which is, of course, repeated only in thought) with another, which is simply the expression of the ultimate aim of all my effort: Buddho's explicit definition of the second *jhānam, tuṇhi* or silent. Besides that, I soon realized that any kind of "ritual" preparation to attune the religious mood (among which *japa* might replace the Christian prayer) would prevalently tend to reduce the starting energy on which I could already rely - *in media res.*

The most popular approach to the practice of meditation is considered to be *metta-bhāvanā* or the cultivation of friendly attitude towards all living beings. This basic virtue *mettā* (Sk. *maitrī*), precedes in Buddhism the next higher (but not the highest) sifted stage of compassion (*karuṇā*)[145], and is usually identified and reduced under western influence to the Christian virtue of love, *caritas* or *agapé*. I consider it closer in its pristine meaning to *karuṇā* than to *mettā*.

Abstracting also from such popular simplifications, I have been, and remained, deeply impressed by the *Mettā-suttaṁ*, one of the most archaic poems in the ancient Pali anthology of *Sutta-nipāto* (143-152). When the conscious repeating of words, or even of short verses in thought, became a hamper to the transition ("smooth as pouring a string of oil") in more abstract states - a tendency and normal inclination of the meditating mind - the opening verses of the following poem appeared in a fresh visual vividness to my mental grasp. I still invoke them in order to evade carefully "those evil and unwholesome states of mind that have arisen within me" and tend to become more stubborn the more directly one endeavors to eliminate them.

> 'This should be done by one with skill in good intention, in order to attain this state of calm:
>
> He should be able, straight, very straight,
> gentle in speech and mild, without conceit;
> contented, easy to support, of few needs,

of light livelihood,
calm in faculties and prudent,
not covetous nor greedily attached to families.
He should not commit any slight wrong
such that other wise men might censure him.
- In happiness and safety
may all beings rejoice. (*Sabbe sattā bhavantu sukhitattā.*)

....

The last verse, quoted in Pali, was the first Buddhist *mantraṁ* which I learned as a young convert at the end of the war in 1946. From the same time dates another mantric formula of Tibetan and strictly *kuṇḍalinī* origin: *oṁ maṇi padme hūṃ* (*Oṁ*, the jewel in the lotus, *hūṃ*).

This evocation does not pertain to the same group with preparatory and protective thoughts of meditative concentration. It is purely acoustically attuned to the intention of molding the exercise into a gradually accomplished whole - the attainment of inner equipoise. It culminates in favorable cases through a gradual alteration of the upholding level of raising and lowering breaths along the *kuṇḍalinī cakraṁs* or lotuses emerging and floating on its stream, in the sequence of vowels while descending these syllables, *oṁ ma-ṇi pad-me hūṃ*,

oṁ will resound in the upper vault of the skull,
ma will spread clearly on the horizontal level of the eyes,
ṇi will circulate around the vertically turning *cakraṁ* of *viśuddham* in the throat,
pad will evoke the fall (Sk. patanam) of the breath to the cardiac plexus,
me will extend the sinking movement of this vibration to the solar complex of the relaxing diaphragm, and
hūṃ will let it penetrate into the dark depths below that membrane screening the part of *prāṇic* organism where "each drop of cool nectar flowing down from the ambrosial Moon (*ājñā* in the naso-ciliar plexus) is swallowed by the Sun" (in the solar plexus of *maṇi-pūraṃ*[146].

With a strong enough intonation *hum* will be the longest lasting syllable, corresponding to the "ground-bass" of the will-to-live, a simile often repeated by Schopenhauer, to which the associations with Freudian sub-consciousness are here apparent.

Also from the Tibetan tradition I have adopted a shorter three-syllable form of this invocation for the specific purpose of strengthening and harmonizing the attention in *sati-paṭṭhānaṁ*.

In a commentarial work on Tsong-kha-pa's *The Three Principles of the Path*[147] there is the following mahayanic description of a Buddhist *Divina Commedia*:

> On a ray of light extending directly in front of Tsong-kha-pa are seated the *lamas* with whom you have actual dharmic connections. Surrounding Tsong-kha-pa, a multitude of *yidams, buddhas, bodhisattvas, ḍākinīs,* and protectors of the *dharma* are seated on lion thrones. On jeweled stands in front of each of them, their own teachings appear as books that have radiant light as their actual nature. On the crown of the head of each in the holy assembly is a white OM; on the throat of each is a red AH; and at the heart of each a blue HUM. From the HUM, light radiates in the ten directions..."

I apply the invocation OM-AH-HUM (mentally, and never orally) in order to attune and harmonize the breath-span. I do this from time to time when changing the key, the pitch and the length in accordance with the natural modulation of a selected "melody" which consists of ascending or descending notes along the gamut of *kuṇḍalinī-cakraṁ* knots.

Concentration on the same three note measure also helps regulate the alternating breath in both wings of the lungs. The normal disproportion of functional strength of the two halves of the body and of twin organs tends to bring about the neglect of the weaker side. Some *yoga* teachers consider it even as a normal astrological fact which corresponds to the macrocosmic and microcosmic harmony of life regulating the strength of breathing switching it every four hours from one nostril to the other. But there may be other reasons for blocking one nostril for a longer time, or for its lagging behind. In my case the right side is weaker than the left, but its functioning can regularly be equalized by proper attention. If nothing else, without any artificial means, the feeling of equal strength of alternate breathing in both lungs can be established even if the air enters only through one nostril and has to be consciously directed either to one or the other lung. The movement of inbreathing starts from the depth of the lung where its pattern is formed, and not from the nostril.

I feel that the neglect of this disproportion may be, at least partly a side-effect, its main cause being the unequal development of *iḍā* and *piñgala nādi* (as described in section 8 above). I became aware of this possibility when reading about the experience of awakening *kuṇḍalinī* by Gopi Krishna. An experience that was verified and commented upon by the well known German atomic physicist C.F. von Weizsacker, published by his *Forschungsgesellschaft fur ostliche Weisheit und westliche Wissenschaft*[148]. Later, in the biography of J. Krishnamurti by Mary Lutyens, *The Years of Awakening*[149], a report on the medical diagnosis of a hereditary deficiency which affected his nose, I found a series of suggestive symptoms connected with a psycho-physical derangement. These seemed to reveal side-effects and consequences of a brutal unnatural quack treatment that tampered with the high sensitivity of a naturally well disposed *kuṇḍalinī* organism.

Notes to Part II

1. Quotations from *Visuddhi-maggo* are adapted from Bhikkhu Nanamoli's translation, *The Path of Purification*, Colombo 1956, and later editions by Buddhist Publication Society, Kandy.

2. I owe the last two references on this subject and some more from the commentarial literature to Ven. Kheminda Thera of Vajirarama, Colombo, who has compiled a valuable concise material of references to *jhānam* in Pali sources,in his book *The Way of Buddhist Meditation*, Colombo, Vajirarama, Bambalapitiya,1980.

3. Among the most explicit on this subject was N. Hartmann's criticism of Kant, condensed at the beginning of his book *Neue Wege der Ontologie* (1942).

4. M. Scheler, *Philosophische Weltanschaung* (1954), ch. II.

5. Schopenhauer considered that the will-to-live "can be fully compared to an unquenchable thirst" and defined it as such. (*The World as Will and Representation*, Vol. I, section 57)

6. Against the prejudicial tendency under western influences to translate this term basic for the central conception of Buddhism (both in its original Pali version and in the later Mahayanist interpretations) by 'emptiness' or 'void', I wish to quote the following considerations: "Sunyata is not a container that can be emptied nor is there anything that could be taken out of sunyata. The choice of the term 'emptiness' dates back to the time when ...mind was conceived as a container of ideas" in the western analogy to Platonic philosophy. (H.V. Guenther, *Buddhist Philosophy in Theory and Practice*. Pelican Books 1972, p. 224, n. 4). The most prominent Japanese Buddhist philosopher in the 20th century, Nishida Kitaro, translates the term *Mu* in the title of his best known book, *Intelligibility and the Philosophy of Nothingness* (Tokyo,Maruzen, 1958) with its proper designation, 'nothingness'. Guenther (1.c)mentions "16 types of nothingness... in the Prajnaparamita literature".

   Another prominent Japanese philosopher, Sh. Hisamatsu, in an essay on *The Oriental Nothingness*, analyzes six meanings of this term.

7. In rejecting the "Hume-Kantian" synthetic theory of experience, Scheler underscores its "mythological" provenance and heritage in a special chapter on the "Mythology of the productive activities of our understanding" (in his main work, *Der Formalismus in der Ethik und die materiale Wertethik*). Interested in the modern aspects of the "sociology of knowl-

edge", Scheler reduces in his context this "mythology" to the Protestant mentality of its protagonists in England and Germany - Hobbes, Hume, Kant. (Wi.thout Hobbes' moral distrust of human nature, Hume's epistemological distrust in our experience would also not have appeared, nor Kant's ambition to reshape it by the interference of will.)

Scheler refers to the deep study of the Protestant mentality by Max Weber.

8. *Mahā-prajñā-pāramitā-śāstraṁ*, XL 2, quoted from the French transl. by E. Lamotte, *Le Traité de la Grande Vertu de Sagesse de Nāgārjuna*, Tome III. Ed. Institut Orientaliste, Louvain 1970

9. New York, New Directions, 1973, p. 143.

10. Cf. my article *Karma-The Ripening Fruit*, in The Wheel Publication No.221-224, Buddhist Publication Society, Kandy 1975.

11. The Sanskrit word *śramaṇa* is usually rendered *sarmanes* in Greek reports (since Magasthenes, 3rd c. B.C.). Porphiries (3rd c. A.D.) in his book *De abstinentia* calls them *samanoi* which corresponds to the Pali title *samaṇā* used for Buddho and his followers.

12. Cf. his *Studies in Philosophy*, Vol. I, p. 343, Calcutta, Progressive Publishers, 1956.

13. Cf. J.W. Mac Crindle, *Ancient India as described by Megasthenes and Arrian*, London 1877, and *The Invasion of India by Alexander the Great, as described by Qu. Curtius, Diodorus, Plutarch and Justin*, by the same author,London 1893.

14. Kant, to whom it has been reproached that he as a representative of the rationalist era was under a stronger influence of Stoical rather than Christian ethics, praised this most prominent virtue of the Stoics in one of his late treatises on ethics, in the "Preface to the Metaphysical Elements of Ethics",under the heading "Virtue necessarily presupposes Apathy (considered as Strength)", concluding that "the true strength of virtue is the *mind at rest*,with a firm, deliberate resolution to bring its law into practice. This is the state of *health* in the moral life." Nietzsche's reproach of *ressentiment* to Christianity (in *Antichrist*, section 20, and in *Ecce Homo*, "Why I am so wise",section 6) finds in the same argument of "health" and "hygiene" and advantage of Buddhism and its "deep difference from Christianity". (Cf. my forthcoming book on "The Ethos of Knowledge in European and Indian Philosophies".)

15. Nietzsche makes occasional distinction between *ephexis* and *skepsis*, at least in the gradation of terms. (Cf. his discussion upon the "ascetic ideals"in the *Genealogy of Morals*, III, 24.)

16. Cf. the *epechtic* meaning of the term *yathā-bhūtam* for things as they "actually are" in Buddho's critique of "views" (*diṭṭhi, dṛṣṭi,* doxa).

17. Cf. Buddho's often repeated formula on "the thicket of views, the wilderness of views, the contortion of views, the fetter of views" to whose analysis the first long discourse, *Brahma-jāla-suttaṁ*, in *Dīgha-nīkayo* is dedicated.

18. Cf. particularly the basic structure of *Brāhma-jāla-suttaṁ*, and my paper, "Dependence of *punar-bhava* on karma in Buddhist Philosophy", in Indian *Philosophical Annual*, Vol. I, Madras 1965.

19. In the formulation of W. Schubring, *The Doctrine of the Jainas*, Delhi,M. Banarsidass, 1962. p.164.

20. The following basic definitions are taken from Puyapada's *Sarvārthasiddhi*, Engl. transl. by S.A. Jain, Calcutta, Vira Sasana Sangha,

    1960, pp.41-43. The translation quoted in brackets is by Schubring, op. cit.,Section 76, p. 160.

21. Cf. S. Radahakrishnan's *Indian Philosophy* I, Ch. VI, 5, on this subject.

22. For my definition of the doxographic method see C. Velyachich, *Problems and Methods of Comparative Philosophy*, in *Indian Philosophical Annual* 1965.

23. Op. cit., p. 343. Underlined by me.

24. For the basic documentation on Buddho's acosmic attitude see my article *Why is Buddhism a Religion?* (Ch. II, 10), in *Indian Philosophical Annual*, Vol. VI, 1970.

25. V. Brochard, *Les sceptiques grecs*, Paris 1932, p. 60.

26. W.J. Richardson, *Through Phenomenology to Thought*. The Hague 1963. P.XXIII.

27. M. Heidegger, *Nietzsche II*, Pfullingen 1961, p. 350.

28. Candrakirti, *Prasannapadā*, edited by L. de La Vallee Poussin, p. 19.1.

29. Edmund Husserl *Ideen zu einer reinen Phanomenologie und phaenomenologischen Philosophie*, section 26. Quotations are in part from the English translation by W.R. Boyce Gibson, *Ideas: General Introduction to Pure Phenomenology*, New York, Macmillan, 1931. Paragraphs and page nos. are according to the original German first edition.

30. E. Husserl, *Cartesianische Meditationen und Pariser Vortrage*, Band I, Haag, M. Nijhoff, 1950. Pp.189 and 196.

31. Husserl, *Ideen... II*, p.. 262 (in *Gesammelte Werke*, Band IV, Haag,1952).

32. *Ideen...III*, Husserliana Band V (1952), p. 3 f.

33. *Cartesian Meditations*, II, section 20, end. Where not indicated otherwise quotations are from Dorion Cairn's translation: The Hague, M.Nijhoff, 1970.
34. *Ideen*, I, p.113.
35. *Sommaire des lecons du professeur E. Husserl, Introduction a la phenomenologie transcendentale*, in Vol. I of *Gesammelte Werke*, Haag, Husserliana, 1950. P. 195 ff.
36. *II Cartesian Meditations*, Section 15, p. 72.
37. *Ideas*, I, section 24, p. 43.
38. *Ideas*, I, section 58, pp. 110-111. section 44, p.81. Cf. also section 79, p. 157.
39. D.M. Datta, *The Chief Currents of Contemporary Philosophy*, University of Calcutta 1961, pp. 119-121. For the following references cf. also my paper, *Hegel and Indian Philosophy*, in *Indian Philosophical Quarterly*, No. 3, 1976.
40. *Some Aspects of Negation* (Cf. Datta, op. cit. p. 122)
41. *Place of the Indefinite in Logic* (Cf. Datta, op. cit. p. 121)
42. *The Concept of Philosophy* (Cf. Datta, op. cit. p. 122)
43. Cf. *Die grossen Philosophen I*, Munchen 1957, p. 132-3. English transl. *The Great Philosophers*, London 1962 (a selection from the German original), p.36.
44. *Ideas...* (English transl.) pp. 41-43.
45. Cf. the introduction to the French translation, *Idees directices pour une phenomenologie* by Paul Ricoeur, Paris, Gallimard, 1950, 3rd edition.
46. E. Fink, *Die phanomenologische Philosophie Edmund Husserls in der gegenwartigen Kritik*, in *Kantstudien*, Vol. 38, 1933 p.366.
47. *Ideen...*, *I*,p. 142.
48. Id., p. 139.
49. Where not indicated otherwise, quotations are from Dorian Cairn's translation: Edmund Husserl, *Cartesian Meditations*, The Hague, M. Nijhoff,1970.
50. *Milinda-pañhā*, 87.
51. *Die Idee der Phanomenologie, Gesammelte Werke, Band II*, Haag,Husserliana, 1950. III. Vorlesung, p. 43.
52. *Visuddhi-maggo* (V.M. in the sequel, see n.1.), IV, 31.
53. *Ideen...*, *II*, p. 262 (in Gesammelte Werke, Band IV, Haag 1952).

54. V.M., pp. 20-22 n.
55. *Ideen...*, p. 182-183.
56. *Ideen...*, I, 59, pp.113.
57. *Cartesian Meditations, First Meditation*, section 5, p. 53.
58. M. Heidegger, *Letter on 'Humanism'*, in *Wegmarken*, p. 194. (Ed. V.Klostermann, Frankfurt M., 1967)
59. V.M. XXII 5 and 44.
60. V.M. Commentary, in Nanamoli's translation, ad XXII 5.
61. According to Husserl's basic definition in *Ideen..., I*, 25, "eidetic properties adherent to determined things, to sensitive qualities, to space-forms, to determined experiences (Erlebnis), taken as such are eidetic singularities".
62. V.M. Commentary ad ch. I 53 (quoted in Nanamoli's transl.) and XV 26.
63. Examples quoted from *Visuddhi-maggo* in this preliminary analysis of basic concepts will become clearer in their organic connection from the basic text in ch. IV of this survey, *Cū*la-suññata-suttaṁ.*
64. *Logical Investigations*, Vol. II, Invest. V, section 23, p. 599, in J.N. Findlay's transl., London, Routledge and Kegan Paul, 1970.
65. *In Wegmarken*, Frankfurt M., V. Klostermann, 1967, p. 243.
66. Op. cit., p. 128-9. Underlinings are mine.
67. *Sommaire des Leçons du Professeur E. Husserl*, in *Cartesianische Meditationen und pariser Vortrage*, p. 198.
68. *Ideas...*, p.173.
69. *Ideas...*, Husserl's Preface to the English edition (1931).
70. *Cartesianische Meditationen*, p. 63.
71. *Cartesianische Meditationen*, p. 63, and *Ideen... III*, p.3f.
72. For the following quotations see Max Scheler , "Formalismus in der Ethik und die materiale Wertethik", 4th ed., Gesammelte Werke, Bd. 2, Bern, Francke, 1954. pp. 487, 304, 303.
73. Quoted from "Kant's Critique of Practical Reason and other works on the theory of ethics" transl. by Th.K. Abbott. London, Longman, 1923. P. 258 (Rosenkranz edition).
74. Cf. *Second Cartesian Meditation*, section 20.
75. *Cartesianische Meditationen*: I, section 5, p. 52. I section 1, p.44.II section 13, p.68.

76. Quotations from Pali texts are adapted mainly from the *Pali Text Society* (London), *Translations Series*. References are to *Dīgha-nikāyo* (D.), *Majjhima-nikāyo* (M.), *Saṁyutta-nikāyo* (S.), and the serial number of the *suttaṁ*.

77. Cf. *Visuddhi-maggo*, IV 93.

78. Id., IV 170.

79. Cf. The Pali Text Society, Pali-English Dictionary, under *piti*.

80. See my book *Schopenhauer and Buddhism*, Buddhist Publication Soc.,Kandy 1970, p. 65 f.

81. Compare Nietzsche's notes at the time of *The Will to Power*, in *Die Unschuld des Werdens, Der Nachlass*, edited by A. Baeumler, Vol. II, Leipzig,Kroner, 1931, "*Aus dem Gedankenkreis des Willens zur Macht*", Section 182, 186,190-210 *passim*.

82. Compare Bergson's and Heidegger's criticism of the rationalist and scientific simplification of the temporal character of existence, and also the divergence of these two authors on this point, in my article *Karma - The Ripening Fruit*, in *The Wheel Publication* No. 221-224, Buddhist Publication Soc., Kandy 1975.

83. See the quotation from Kant on the subject of "Apathy (Considered as Strength)" in the text corresponding to n. 73 above.

84. From *Sixty Songs of Milarepa*, transl. C.C. Chang, Buddhist Publication Soc., Kandy 1966, p.36.

85. Cf. Part Three, II, 2, p. 60.

86. Cf. Part One, B8, *Dhānañjāni-suttaṁ* (M. 97).

87. See on this subject the comparative study of S. Akpinar, *The Path of Meditative Absorption in Sufism*, Published in Serbo-Croat in : *Kulture Istoka 4. 1985*

88. Cf. the selection of texts on this subject in Nanamoli (Bhikkhu), *The Practice of Loving kindness (Metta)*, in *The Wheel Publication No. 7*, Buddhist Publication Society, Kandy, 1959.

89. Trevor Legget, *śaṅkara on the Yoga-sūtras (Vol. I: Samādhi)*, London, Routledge & Kegan Paul, 1981. p.142.

90. I am following here F.L. Woodward's translation of terms derived from the common stem *jhāyati*, to muse or meditate, Cf. *The Book of the Gradual Sayings*, Vol. V, p. 205.

91. K. Jaspers, *Der philosophische Glaube*. Munchen, Piper, 1951. pp.54,55,125.

92. The same instruction is repeated in the *Sati-paṭṭhāna-suttaṁ*, D. XXII,21.

93. On "the correct relation of value-universalism and value-individualism" from an analogous standpoint see Max Scheler, *Der Formalismus in der Ethik...*, 4th edition, Franke, Bern 1954, Part II, section VI, B, p. 497 f. See also references in N. Bredyaev's discussion following Jean Wahl's lecture, *A Short History of Existentialism*, on "Kierkegaard's philosophy of existence as an *expressionist philosophy...* the expression of the existence of Kierkegaard",in my study on *"Buddhism and modern philosophies of existence"* in *Buddhist and Western Philosophy*, edited by N. Katz, Sterling Publishers, New Delhi, 1981, p.334.

94. For a wider context see my article "Karma - The Ripening Fruit" in *Kamma and its Fruit*, Buddhist Publication Society, Kandy, 1975, p. 28 f.

95. Cf. T. Leggett, *śañkara* on the Yoga-sutra-s, translation of *Vivarana sub-commentary to Vyāsa-bhāsya on Yoga-sūtra-s of Patañjali. Vol. 1: Samādhi-pāda*. Routledge & Kegan Paul, London 1981.

96. *The Gospel of Sri Ramakrishna*, transl. by Swami Nikhilananda, 4th edition, Madras 1964. P. 951.

97. Quoted in the sequel from the translation by Bhikkhu Nanamoli, Colombo 1956; later editions by The Buddhist Publication Society, Kandy, Sri Lanka.

98. For the analogy with Bergson's vitalist philosophy see ch. II, 3 of the first part of this book, and for the direct application of analogous vitalistic terms to the interpretation of the Buddhist *abhidhammo* philosophy, Upajiva Ratnatunga, *Mind and Matter*, Colombo, Lake House Publishers, 1982.

99. Cf. my article *"Aniccam* - The Buddhist Theory of Impermanence" in *The Basic Facts of Existence I*, Buddhist Publication Soc., "Wheel" No. 186/7, Kandy 1973.

100 According to the commentary on *The Vaisesika Sutras of Kanada* (Allahabad ed. 1923 2) - rather a rough criticism by an opponent school which I had not in view at the time of my described experience.

101 Cf. e.g. *Vyāsa-bhāsyam* on *Samādhi-pādam* I,1; II, 28; III, 33.

102 Cf. Part II, "The Indian Origin of Pyrrho's Epoche" on these terms.

103 In section 6. "The Physiological System of Kundalini" at the end of this chapter.

104 *Visuddhi-maggo* (in the sequel V.M.), VIII, 153.

105 See basic texts and arguments on this problem in Kheminda Thera, *The Way of Buddhist Meditation - Serenity and insight according to the Pali Canon.* Vajirarama, Colombo 1980.

106 Cf. Mahasi Sayadaw, *The Progress of Insight*, Kandy, The Forest Hermitage, 1965; pp. 10-13.

107 For a more extensive and detailed presentation of basic texts, also referring to the problems discussed in the sequel of this section, see *Mindfulness of Breathing*, texts translated by Nanamoli Thera' Buddhist Publication Society, Kandy 1964.

108 Cf. Nanamoli, Mindfulness of Breathing, p. 25.

109 Nanamoli, op.cit. p.80.

110 Ibid. p. 31

111 Ibid. p. 27n.

112 V.M, ch. VIII, 172.

113 Ibid. Section 199.

114 J. Krishnamurti, *This Matter of Culture*. London, V. Golancz, 1964,pp. 133-136.

115 *Manual of a Mystic*, transl. by F.L. Woodward, London, Pali Text Soc.1962, p. 14-15n.

116 Nanamoli, *Mindfulness of Breathing*, p. 34, n.2.

117 Ibid.

118 Translated from the Burmese by U Pe Thin and Myanaung U Tin. Ed. The Forest Hermitage, Kandy 1971. Part II, pp. 24-28.

119 See references on this subject in the first chapter of Part II, and in the second chapter section 4, of Part III, in connection with the idealism of *sunna-vādo*.

120 Cf. Kant's explication of *apathy*, quoted in Part One, ch. II, (5),text corresponding to footnote 41.

121 According to W. James, *Principles of Psychology*, at the beginning of ch. XIII *Attention*: "Physiologically, then, the narrowness of consciousness seems to depend on the fact that the activity of the (cerebral) hemispheres tends at all times to be a consolidated and unified affair, determinable now by that, but determinable only as a whole.The ideas correlative to the reigning system of processes are those which are said to 'interest' us at the time;...At all times, however, there is a liability of disintegration of the reigning system. The consolidation is seldom quite complete, the excluded currents are not wholly abortive, their presence affects the 'fringe' and margin of our thought."

122 Sunlun Shin Vinay, *The Yogi & Vipassana* (*Buddhist meditation: The Sunlun Way*). Rangoon (about 1960).

123 Sh. Bh. Deo, *Jaina Monastic Jurisprudence*, Banaras 1960, p.42.

124 T.M.P. Mahadevan, *Ramana Maharshi and his Philosophy of Existence*, Tiruvannamalai, Sri Ramanasramam, 1959, p.12. See also: Arthur Osborne, *Ramana Maharshi and the path of self-knowledge*, Jaico Books, Bombay 1970. Heinrich Zimmer, *Der Weg zum Selbst - Lehre und Leben des indischen Heilegen Shri Ramana Maharshi aus Tiruvannamalai*, herausgegeben von C.G. Jung - Rascher Verlag, Zurich 1954.

125 The comparative terminology and explanation of physiological data which I follow here and in the sequel have been very carefully and critically presented by the Indian Dr. Vasant G. Rele in his book The *Mysterious Kundalini*, Bombay 1960. This and the following reference are from pp. 28 and 24.

126 The Theosophical translator and interpreter of the *Yoga-sutrani* of Patanjali, I.K. Taimni (in *The Science of Yoga*, Adyar, Madras, 1961, p. 266) formulated correctly the generally accepted traditional standpoint that "what takes place during the course of these practices, how the *prānic* currents are used to arouse *kuṇḍalinī*, how the *kuṇḍalinī* activates the *cakras* in the *suśumṇā* is not mentioned by Patanjali because all these things of a practical nature which are fraught with dangerous possibilities are taught by the *guru* personally to the *celā*."

127 Rele, op.cit. 34.

128 Ibid., p. 25-6.

129 In *Parerga and Paralipomena I*, translated by E.F.J. Payne, Oxford University Press, 1974, p. 234 f. See Annexe to this chapter.

130 The translation of upanisadic texts follows here in broad lines Radhakrishnan's stylization in *The Principal Upanisads*, London, Allen & Unwin, 1953.

131 Sir John Woodroffe (Arthur Avalon), *The Serpent Power (Kundalini Sakti)*, Madras, Ganesh, 1958 (6th edition), p. 163.

This book is quoted in the sequel from M.P. Pandit, *Kundalini Yoga - A brief study of Sir John Woodroffes's "The Serpent Power"*, Madras, Ganesh, 1962.

132 Op. cit., p.X

133 Rele, op.cit., pp.23-5.

134 Ibid, p. 50-51.

135 Rudolf Steiner, *Wie erlangt man Erkenntnisse der hoheren Welten?* My subsequent translations are from the edition 1961, Verlag Freies Geistesleben, Stuttgart; pp. 86-7.

136 On this subject of psychoanalysis see the critique by Jaspers at the beginning of this chapter, section 1, texts referring to footnote 86.

137 Rele, op. cit., p. 28.

138 Cf. E.J. Thomas, *Early Buddhist Scriptures*. London 1935, p.39f.among many other treatises on this subject cf. in connection with the presentation in the sequel, Paravahera Vajiranana, *Buddhist Meditation in Theory and Practice* (ph.D. thesis, Cantab.), Colombo, M.D. Gunasena, 1962; chapter on *Bodhipakkhiya Bhāvanā*.

139 Cf. *Buddhist Meditation in Theory and Practice*, op. cit. p. 133.

140 The following quotation is from the English version of *The Epic of Gilgamesh* by N.K. Sandars, Penguin Classics, 1964, chapter 6.

141 Op. cit. (see n. 133) p. 136f.

142 M.P. Pandit, *Japa*. Cf. pp.2, 3, 4.

143 See my paper *Buddhism and Modern Philosophies of Existence*, III (e) *Karma, "The Ripening Fruit"*, p. 362; in *Buddhist and Western Philosophy*, edited by Nathan Katz; New Delhi, Sterling Publishers, 1981.

144 Pandit, op. cit., pp. 15, 9.

145 See for further reference note 87 above

146 *Das klassische Yoga-Lehrbuch Indiens: Hatha-Yoga-Pradipika*, Aus dem Sanskrit mit Kommentaren von Hans-Ulrich Rieker. Rascher-Verlag, Zurich u. Stuttgart, 1957. P. 141.

147 See Part III, chapter on Tsong-kha-pa. The commentarial passage quoted above is from the Fourth Panchen Lama's, Tenbay Nyima, instructions for meditation, written in the early 19th century, translated in *The Door of Liberation* by Geshe Wangyal, New York, M. Girodias, 1973. P. 199.

148 See also S.F. von Weizsacker: Gopi Krishna, *Biologische Basis religioser Erfahrung* (1971). Both books were published by O.W. Barth Verlag, Weilheim/Obb, W. Germany.

149 Published by Krishnamurti Foundation, Madras 1975. Cf. chapter 17 (end) and 18 (The Turning Point), pp. 150 ff.

Part Three

The Limits of Buddhist Nihilism

Chapter One

1. Cū*a-suññatā-suttaṁ

The "Condensed Discourse on Nullity" (*Cū*a-suññata-suttaṁ*), M. 121[1] describes the levels of annulment (*suññatā*) as part of the formless (*arūpa-*) *jhānā* structure. On this level of the third *arūpajjhānam,* in the (noematic) "region of no-thing" (*ākiñcaññayatanam*), we reach a point of intersection between two terms indicating nothingness: one as 'nullity' (sunnata), and the other as the (categorial) 'region (*āyatanam*) of nothing (*ā-kincannam*)'. The specific attainment of this noematic region is described as a positive experience intended by the reductive consciousness. It is still not the ultimate aim and level of phenomenological reduction. The attainment of this state of reductive consciousness is described in this discourse by the following statement:

> "His mind is concerned only with the perception (*saññā*) of the region of no-thing. By this perception his thought (*cittam*) is penetrated, clarified, stabilized and released."

The relativity of the partial annulment in this state of consciousness is confirmed by the further statement that "only this is still non-annulled: the perception of the region of no-thing."

Of the two terms designating nothingness, as (a) 'nullity' (*suññam*, Sk. *śūnyam*), and (b) the categorial "region containing no thing" (*ākiññāannayatanam*) in its perceptive content (noema), the first term, *suññam* (designating also the numerical symbol of zero in Indian mathematics) has a wider range of abstractive intentionality, while the second, *ākiñcaññam,* is the noematic correlate of the specific function of limiting a region of "pure contemplation of cogitata as actual experiences (*Erlebnisse*)"[2] within the reach of a specific level of contemplative absorption - the 'formless region' of the third *arūpajjāhanam*. Thus, while the concept of *suññam* (*śūnyam* in the mahayanist Sanskrit philosophy) can easily find a manifold application for speculative purposes of ontological and cosmological theories, *ākiñcaññam* remains restricted to the experiential state, or region, of consciousness converging upon nullity. In this converging the consciousness still remains aware of its own transcendental identity and it is just for this reason that the reductive process of contemplation (*citta-vivekoṃ* epoché) is not yet completed nor brought down to its stand-still in "extinction" (*nibbānam, Sk. nirvāṇam*).

2. Godatta-suttaṁ

In this text the two terms designating nothingness in their ultimate intentional meaning are not joined in *Cū*a-suññata-suttaṁ*, but in one sense they are analytically disconnected as "different in their intention and in their designation", while in another they remain the same. As aspects they do not stand in a mutually exclusive, or dialectical, relation, but rather as integrative parts of a more extensive and farther extendible scope of their phenomenological horizon:

> "Once the reverend Godatto was staying at Macchikasando in Wild Mango Grove. Then Citto, the householder, came to visit him... The reverend Godatto asked Citto, the householder: - The release of mind that is bound by no limit (*appamānā*, by no thing (*ākiñcaññam*), null and void (*suññatā*), signless (*animittā*) - are these states of mind different in their intention and in their designation, or are they one and the same? - There is, sir, one aspect in which these states of mind are different..., but there is another aspect in which they are one and the same. - Thus (in the first case) a bhikkhu dwells with his mind endowed with benevolence..., with compassion..., with sympathy..., with equanimity, suffusing one quarter of the world with his mind endowed with benevolence,..., and so also the second, third and fourth quarters, ... suffusing the whole world with his mind endowed with benevolence..., that is widespread, great and boundless... - And what is, sir, the release of mind (bound) by no thing? In this case a bhikkhu surpassing all the aspects of the region of sense-consciousness, aware that 'there is no thing', reaches and abides in the region of nothing. This is called the release of mind (bound) by no thing. - And what is, sir, the release of mind by nullity

(*suññatā*)? In this case a bhikkhu goes to the forest or the root of a tree or a lonely place, and reflecting attains the insight: 'This is nothing (*suññam*) both in itself and for itself (*attena vā attaniyena vā*).' This is called the release of mind by nullity. - And what is, sir, the release of mind that is signless? In this case a bhikkhu, without thought of all signs, reaches and abides in signless concentration. In this aspect, sir, these states of mind are different as well in their intention as in their designation. And in what aspect are they the same? - Lust, sir, sets a limit. Hate sets a limit. Seclusion sets a limit. In a bhikkhu who has destroyed these intoxicants (*āsavā*), cut them at the root, made them like a palm-tree stump, unable to grow again in future, - of all the boundless states of mind's release, that of the unshakable mind's release is considered to be the supreme. In that unshakable release of mind lust, hate and delusion are truly annulled (*suññā*). - Lust is something (*kiñcanam*), hate is something, delusion is something. In a bhikkhu who has destroyed these intoxicants..., - of all these states of *mind's release in nothingness*, that of the unshakable mind's release is considered to be the supreme. (The same applies to the supreme value of) the unshakable mind concerning the *annulment* of lust, hate and delusion, and to the *elimination of their distinctive signs (nimittam)* by the ascetic who has destroyed these intoxicants. - Indeed, the *unshakable mind's release is the highest annulment (suññatā)* of lust, of hate, of delusion. This is the aspect in which these states of mind are the same in their intention and in their designation." (S. XLI, 7, 7)

In this text, too, there is a categorial relation between the two terms, 'no- thing' (*ā-kiñcaññam*[3]) and 'nullity' (*suññatā*), where the first specific term is subordinated to the second one, since it is not the highest and supreme attainment in the process of meditative isolation (*citta-vevieko*) and release (*vimutti*) of mind. Whereas the second term, nullity (*sunna*) has a wider range of abstraction evident in the concluding statement of the last quotation, it is "the supreme unshakable release of mind" (*akuppa cetovimutti aggamakkhāyati*).

3. Upasīva-mānava-pucchā

The "question of young Upasivo (*Upasīva-mānava-pucchā*, Sn. 1069-1076) elucidates *ākiñcaññam* in a broader meaning of nothingness, independent of its generic connection to the 'supreme' abstraction of nothingness in the nihilating of *suññatā*. This poetical text makes it clear that the meaning of *ākiñcaññam* is not exclusively limited to the awareness of 'no thing' in a meditative absorption (*jhānam*) but naturally extends to nothingness in its broad meaning when compared to *suññatā*. Thus the following text also confirms the synonymous meaning of both designations of nothingness:

> "I alone, O Sakko[4], aside the monk Upasivo, am not able to cross the mighty flood unaided. Tell me where is a support, O seer of all, upheld by which I may cross this flood.
>
> - In mindful contemplation of nothingness (*ākiñcaññam*), Upasivo, - said the Lord - upheld by insight that nothing is, cross the flood. Giving up lust, disgusted with talk, overcoming thirst, penetrate this enormous darkness.
>
> - And who dispassionate reverts from all craving - asked the monk Upasivo - upheld by nothing, renouncing to all the rest, released in the highest freedom from perception, would he remain undisturbed in it?
>
> - Yes, answered the Lord, who dispassionate reverts from all craving, upheld by nothing, renouncing to all the rest, released in the highest freedom from perception, he would remain undisturbed in it.
>
> - If he would remain so undisturbed for many years, O seer of all, would there for him, in such coolness released, still exist consciousness of this state?
>
> - Just as a flame blown by the force of wind, answered the Lord, goes out, and designation applies to it no more, even so the silent sage, released from name-and-form, goes out, and designation applies to him no more.
>
> - And he who attains the goal, is he no more, or is he for ever healed?
>
> O silent sage, explain this well to me, how have you perceived this truth.
>
> - There is no measuring of the man who attained the goal, answered the Lord, nor any adequate expression of his being. Where all appearances (*dhammā*) have been abolished, there all tools of talk, too, have been abolished.

4. Suññata-loka-suttaṁ

The talk on the nullity of the world" (S. XXXV, 85) is perhaps the clearest concise presentation of the thesis of *double nullity* of the world "in itself and for itself" (*attena vā attaniyena vā suñño loko*). This formulation has already been quoted, in the context of the *Godatta-suttaṁ*, and is repeated in several other texts with the same meaning. In the later *mahā-yānaṁ* philosophy this thesis has been elicited as the tenet of Buddhist philosophical idealism since Nagarjuna's logical and dialectical deduction and argumentation in his *Madhyamaka-kārikā*, to which I shall briefly refer.

"The Venerable Anando said thus to the Lord:

- 'The world is nothing, the world is nothing' - thus it is said, Lord. In what sense is the world said to be nothing, sir? - Because the world is nothing in itself nor for itself, Anando, therefore it is said that the world is nothing. And what, Anando is nothing in itself nor for itself? (The organs of) sight, hearing, smelling, tasting, touching, and the mind, their objects and the (corresponding types of intentional) consciousness, are nothing in themselves nor for themselves. That is why, Anando, it is said that the world is nothing."

5. Nāgārjuna

The following few quotations taken from an extensive treatise dating from the early period of Nagarjuna's school and attributed to Nagarjuna himself[5], may be considered as a concise elucidation of Nagarjuna's and as well as the later mahayanist doctrine of "double nihilation". They encompass the wide range of problems discussed mainly during the first millenium A.D. among various trends of idealist philosophies. There are two principal groups of this idealist philosophy: Nagarjuna's strictly dialectical rationalism of the Madhyamika school, and the idealism of the epistemological school. The latter had a wider theory of knowledge (*vijñāna-vāda*) with the thesis that all knowledge is "limited to the cognizing consciousness" alone (*vijñapti-mātram*), implying the negation or annulment of any whatsoever transcendent reality of a thing-in-itself (*sva-bhāva*).

"The two aspects of nullity (*śūnyatā*) are: (1) nullity of being (*sattva-śūnyatā*), (2) nullity of phenomena (*dharma-śunyatā*). To say that there is no self (*ātmā*) is a statement of *sattva-śūnyatā*, to say that there is no phenomenon is *dharma-śūnyatā*."

"In what concerns oneself (*adhyātmam*) Buddho always applies his knowledge that there is no self (*anātma-jhānam*), and in what concerns the outward (world) (*bahirdhā*), he always contemplates the nullity of phenomena (*dharma-śūnyatā*),"

"He sees the true character of the phenomena (*bhuta-lakṣaṇa-dharmam*) - he realizes that there is no self (*atma*) and no being (*sattvam*)." (*Mahā-prajñā-pāramitā-śāstraṁ*, Ch. XLI 9, XLI 4, XL 2)

6. Madhyamaka-kārikā

There is an evident analogy in the relation between Nagarjuna and later Buddhist epistemological schools with Kant and the post-Kantian philosophies. The terms 'in itself' (*attena*) and 'for itself' (*attaniyena*), with reference to the structures of immanent being (*sattva*) and phenomenal (*dharmā*) appearances in the transcendental constitution of the world, are analogous to the fundamental meaning of these terms in the transcendental idealism of Kantian and post-Kantian philosophies (Hegel's 'for itself' and its existential turning in Sartre's "Being and Nothingness"). The discussion of transcendental structures of knowledge in these schools consequently remains centered on the ontologically negative aspect of Buddho's fundamental teaching of nothingness.

The reduction of the transcendent to the transcendental dimension (or in Husserl's terms) of the 'external' object to the noema-correlate of the world as representation, can be explicated in modern terms through the comparison of the first chapter of Nagarjuna's *Madhyamaka-kārikā*, on the transcendental nature of the category of causality, with Schopenhauer's interpretation of the problem of thing-in-itself in Kantian philosophy. Since this analogy will be extended in some later chapters of *Madhyamaka-kārikā* (particularly on the transcendental nature of space and time), I shall begin with Schopenhauer's formulation of his basic thesis within the context of his "Fragments for the History of Philosophy"[6].

"Accordingly, the whole of our empirical knowledge is now resolved into two components both of which have their origin *in ourselves*; namely the sense-impressions and the forms time, space, causality that are given *a priori* and hence are in the functions of our intellect or brain... This *passage from the effect to the cause*, however, is the only way to reach directly from the internal and subjectively given to the external and objectively existing. But after Kant has conceded the law of causality to the subject's form of knowledge, this way was no longer left open to him. Moreover, he himself warned us often enough *against making a transcendent use of the category of causality*... But we can reach the thing-in-itself only by our shifting once for all *the standpoint*, that is to say, by starting from what *is represented* instead of, as hitherto, always merely from what *represents*."

A *prima facie* confirmation of the basic idea that the source of the components of causal effects is "in the functions of our intellect", can be found also in the following proposition (9) of the "Examination of action and effect" (*Karma-phala-parīksā*), ch. seventeen of Nagarjuna's *Madhyamaka-kārikā*[7]:

> "Therefore the continuity of thought (*cittam*) has its source in the mind (*ceta*, intellect, Kant's *Verstand*). Without this source the intended (causal) effect cannot arise."

The idealist premise of this thesis has been elicited in the first chapter of the same treatise, beginning with the examination of the problem of causal relations:

(1) "Neither from itself (alone), nor from an other, nor from both itself and an other, nor even causeless, no being has ever arisen."

(2) "In such relational conditions neither being by itself, nor being by another can be conceived."

(8) "Granted that no phenomenon has a (transcendent) support (*ālambanam*), wherefrom could phenomena without such support obtain it subsequently?"

(13) "The effect is produced from antecedents which themselves are not produced by themselves. How could effects which are not produced by themselves be conditioned by such dependant factors?"

Nagarjuna's pupil and successor Aryadeva formulated the principle of *apriority* in connection with the theory of nullity (*śūnyatā*) as follows. "He that perceives the nature of a single ens, perceives the nature of all. The *śūyatā* of one is indeed the *śūnyatā* of all."

The *apriority* of the transcendental structure of thought - of space, time and causality in the above quoted proposition (2) - is confirmed (at least implicitly) by Nagarjuna in the concluding statement:

> "There are four relational conditions:
> - (physical) cause (*hetu*)
> - (reasonable) ground (*ālambanam*)
> - (relation of) contiguity (*anantaram*)
> - (motivated by) decision (*adhipateyam*)
> - *There is no fifth (mode of) conditioning.*"

It is interesting to note that this particular apodictical categorial structure and the same quaternarian formulation of the principle of causality appears to have an almost archetypal origin in the history of logical thought. Schopenhauer, who insisted on the reduction of the whole structure of Kantian categories to the single category of causality, started, in his Ph.d. thesis, from the same fourfold branching of its "roots":

(1) the principle of sufficient reason of *becoming* - the law of *causality* in the region of the objective real world,
(2) the principle of sufficient reason of *knowledge* - the law of *truth* in the region of reason, (*Vernunft*),
(3) the principle of sufficient reason of *being* - the apriority of *insight* in the transcendental-aesthetical region of space and time,
(4) the principle of sufficient reason of *activity* - the law of *motivation* in the region of will.

In researching the historical backgrounds of this fundamental principle of sufficient reason in the analysis of causality Schopenhauer finds the fundamental quaternarian scheme in Aristotle's *Analytica posterior*, II, 11, P. 94 a 21. Here Aristotle elucidates the four kinds of causes which were defined in the scholastical formulation as *causae materiales, formales,efficientes and finales*.

Buddho was perhaps the first in the history of philosophy whose formulation of the principle of causality has remained recorded verbatim: "If this is, that becomes" (*satidam asmin bhavatiti*).

A more extensive formulation of this statement and its explanation is contained in *Majjhima-nikāyo*, discourse 38, and in *Anguttara-nikāyo*, X, 10, 92. The quoted sanskritized formulation is explicitly denied by Nagarjuna in proposition 10 of the first chapter of *Madhyamaka-kārikā*, dealing with the problem of causality:

> "The being of entities which do not exist by themselves cannot be affirmed. Therefore even the statement, 'When there is this, that comes to be', is not tenable."

This is not the only example of Nagarjuna opposing his propositions to the traditionally established initial statements of Buddho, in direct dialectical confrontation. For him all teachings not directly and explicitly based on the principle of nothingness remain below the apodicticity of transcendental insight and therefore can have only a propedeutic value - directing the common sense of "the uneducated persons who have never seen a noble man, who are not acquainted with, not trained in, their noble teaching", toward the essential turning to transcendental truth (*paramārtha-satyam*). The principle of nothingness here discussed does not mean just "non-being" in a relation of dialectical anti-thesis to "being"[8], but rather requires the act of transcending both - a solution based on the higher level of understanding.

"Paramārtha" is here translated as transcendental in the Kantian meaning of the term. This is confirmed by the *kārikās* which establish the identity of space and time through the same dialectical method. The plain literal meaning of the term, taken *prima facie* without prejudice and distortion, denotes: *arthaṃ* "purpose, end and aim[9], *param-* (Greek *para-*, Latin *trans-*) beyond or superior - *ergo*: transcending, not the 'substance' or the 'thing' (*vastu*) itself but the *intention* of the common-sense realistic meaning.

The *transcendental* intention denotes (at least in the post-Kantian European philosophy) the noetic side of the cognizing subject 'aiming at' a distinct *transcendent object* as its noematic counterpart. The advantage of the Sanskrit term *paramārtha* consists in a clearer formulation, in as far as *artha*, 'purpose' or intention, does not imply the connotation of any object, or even 'thing' in itself, and thus remains unprejudiced by the scholastically overloaded meaning of the equivocal 'transcendentality' in European philosophy.

Thus, in explicitly Kantian terms of our interpretation, there is a correspondence between the transcendental level of the *category* of causality with logical necessity and the apriorism of 'transcendental aesthetic' on the ontological level of space and time.

Ch. XXVII formulates the transcendentality of *space* through the examination of seeing and views *(dṛṣṭi-parīkṣā), kārikā* 21, in terms analogous to Kant's first antinomy on space:

> "If the world has limits, how could there be another world? On the other hand, if the world has no limits, how could there be another world?"

It may be interesting for our comparison to note that Kant in the formulation of his first antinomy refers to the "limits" of the world "in relation both to time and space".

In his "examination of arising and dissolution" (*saṃbhava-vibhava parīkṣā* M.k. XXI, 2) Nagarjuna affirms the transcendental origin of the conception of time:

> "The existential continuity within the three temporal moments (past,present and future) is not possible. And how can there be existential continuity (of phenomena) which are not (appearing in the sequence of these) three temporal moments?"

Superficial interpreters tend to identify this statement, taken out of its context within the systematic whole of Nagarjuna's dialectics, with Zeno of Elea and his "deduction of our usual conception of *motion ad absurdum*".[10] Yet, Nagarjuna has dedicated, besides the quoted proposition and a few more in several other chapters, an entire chapter of his investigations (ch. XIX, *kāla-parīkṣā*) to the conception of time. Here, the systematic deduction of a purely transcendental character of both time and space is based on the concluding proposition (6) where the transcendentality of time and of space as implied in proposition (4) is elicited from the principle of ontological ideality of the being of entities, or the primordial buddhist theory of *śūnya-vāda*. The following is a condensed rendering of Nagarjuna's investigation of the ideality of time (M.k. XIX, *kāla-parīkṣā*):

1. If the present and the not yet occurred (future) events were dependent on the past, both the present and the future should have happened in the past time.
3. And yet the present and the future cannot be conceived without the past.
4. The same procedure can be applied to other pairs of reciprocal relations (in time and space), such as the upper, lower, middle, equal etc.
5. Time without stability cannot be grasped; yet there is no stability in time. How could our understanding grasp the ungraspable time?
6. If time is conditioned by being, how can 'time' be conceived without 'being'? But since there is no 'being' at all, how could there be a 'time'?

Chapter XI, 2 of the same work rejects Buddho's principle of "the middle" (*madhyam*) in its often abused generalized form[11]. This rejection is based on the same criterion as affirmed in proposition (4) above. The treatise is nevertheless entitled *Madhyamaka kārikā*, or "Verses of the Middle Path" giving Nagarjuna's school of dialectical idealism its name *mādhyamikā*:

> "Since there is nothing primordial nor posterior, how could there be a middle (*madhyam*). Statements on the sequence of first, simultaneous and following states cannot be adequate."

Nagarjuna's criticism of the "middle way", as a method often wrongly used for generalization in the traditional exegesis of Buddho's doctrine, is based on his principle of relativity of truth, formulated in his distinction of common-sense knowledge, *saṁvṛti-satyā*, which is an apparent or "undisclosed truth, a heuristically admitted mode of agreement, or "thought-construction" (in Inada's translation), and transcendental insight (*paramārtha-satyā*). Chapter XXIV of *Madhyamaka-kārikā*, "The Examination of the Noble Truth" (*ārya-satyā*), is dedicated to this distinction of two modes of truth, empirical and transcendental. Proposition (11) contains the positive designation of 'the middle way' as "annulment (*śūnyatā*) applied... in following the middle way and in discarding the beliefs in being, in non-being etc." Proposition (18) states:

> "We declare that whatever is of dependent (relational) origination is naught (*śūnyatā*). It is a mode of agreement (a thought-construction: *prajñaptir-upādāyaṁ*), and this is *the middle path* (*pratipat-sa-ivamadhyamā*)."

The postulate of a higher level of epistemological criticism follows rationally from the skeptical realization that the empirical apperception of events consisting of syntheses of sense-data cannot form a sufficient and reliable basis of things as they are (*yathā bhūtā*). In his *Repudiation of Contests*[12] Nagarjuna asks,"if every cognition of an object depends about (reliable) sources of knowledge (*pramānam*), on what do these sources depend?"

In applying this principle, Nagarjuna's commentator Candrakirti concludes,"our assertion cannot be refuted on the ground of immediate experience, because even the reliability of that experience has not been proved."

Thus the causally dependent origination, the basic categorial structure of human understanding (the same as in Schopenhauer's revision of Kant's "Table of the Categories"), from whose critical examination Nagarjuna started, ultimately brought him in the "Examination of the Noble Truth" (ch. 24) to the conclusion that causal dependence was the rational proof of ontical nullity or nihilation both of the subject and the object of knowledge. In Candrakirti's formulation it is "due to the non-existence of a being in itself (*asati bhāva svarūpe*)." In the same connection Nagarjuna's statement in the quoted chapter (XXIV,14) remains one of the most famous formulations of the Buddhist nihilist *ontology* (and certainly not of any "agnostic" epistemology).

"All is logical to him for whom nothingness is logical.
Nothing is logical to him for whom nothingness is not logical"

This conclusion implies premises deduced in earlier chapters that can be summarized for our purpose in the following points:

(1) The idea of an *absolute* becomes meaningless if there is nothing to set against it. "If the existence of the composed is not demonstrated, how could the existence of the not composed (elements of aggregates) be demonstrated?" (M.k. VII, 33) The principle of "existence in mutual dependence" (*paras parāpekṣikī siddhi*), formulated in M.K. VIII, 12, is explained as "existence of the relative as such, independent on any reference to the absolute"[13]

(2) Candrakirti, in his answer to criticism of the teaching of nothingness (*śūnya-vāda*) with reference to M.K. XXIV[14], says: "As a victim of your own discursive thought you super-impose on the term 'nullity' the wrong interpretation of 'non-being'."

This reconfirms our earlier reference(see note 8) on the same mistake repeated by Hegel in his criticism of Buddhist logic on this point.

(3) For the same reason the nihilism of *śūnya-vāda* cannot be considered nor maintained on the same level of knowledge as another form or 'model' of world-view - *dṛṣṭi* (Greek *doxa* or dogmatic stand- point as defined by Husserl):
Annulment (*śūnyatā*) of all (*world-*) views is postulated by the Victorious Ones (*buddhas*) as the way to release. Incurable indeed are those who take *śūnyatā* itself as a view." (M.k. XIII, 8)

Thus we come again, at the end, to the refrain which is often repeated (and often misused by exegetes, especially of theravado or "hinayanist" Buddhist schools and "modern" westernized indologists with the intention to tabuize all mention of Buddhist nihilism):

"If I neither admit a thing's reality,
nor unreality, nor both,
then to confute me
a long time will be needed."

This version was formulated by the best known Sinhalese follower of Nagarjuna's Madhyamika school.[15]

7. Vasubandhu

Since the beginning of the first millenium of our era a critical and dogma- free development of Buddhist philosophy began with Nagarjuna's dialectical turn to the strictly idealist position. This was based on Buddho's original teaching of *śunya-vāda* or ontological nihilism as elicited in the preceding sections of this survey. This turning already implied and further influenced a historical divergence of two possible approaches to the original teaching of Buddho.

The first was the school of *abhi-dhammā* (corresponding to the Greek meaning of *peri phainomena*) which developed still within the Pali *ti-piṭakam* canon soon after Buddho's death. The traditional method of *phenomenological analysis* (*vibhajja-vādo*) of constitutive elements distinguished within the subject-object split by the cognizing consciousness (*vijñānam*).

The second approach was from the *suñña-vādo* nihilistic ontology as the principle of purely rational dialectical deduction. It appeared necessarily as a later phase, established by Nagarjuna on a philosophically independent criterion. It abstracted *a limine* from the *abhidhammā* reduction of instantaneous events-in-process to statically isolated quasi-elements (*dhatu*) which threatened to disgregate the fundamental continuity (*santānam*) of the "flux of life-articulation" (*bhāvanga-soto*) into an atomistic conglomeration. Potentially it was still further reducible to the scheme of mechanicist materialism (which ultimately happened, too, at least according to its 'scientifically modernized' interpretations in terms of western popular science in the 19th century - and later.)

This danger was clearly anticipated by *Vasubandhu* (fourth century of our era) under the influence of his elder brother Asanga, the founder of the second school of transcendental idealism, *vijñāna-vāda* "theory of knowledge".

Vasubandhu was the last and philosophically most conspicuous systematizer of the *abhi-dharma* (phenomenological) teaching in its encyclopedically integrated sanscritized form, elucidated in the nine extensive studies of his *Abhidharma-koṣa*. His conversion to *mahāyānam* Buddhism under Asanga's influence, unanimously understood and interpreted from various standpoints in Indian tradition, has raised superficial doubt and positivistic criticism of recent European indologists[16] concerning Vasubandhu's personal identity. For on the one hand he was the author of a famous "hinayanist" compendium, and, on the other hand, after his conversion to *mahāyānam*, he wrote two short, but not less fundamental works (one in twenty, the other in thirty theses - *Vimśatikā* and *Trimśikā*), on the basic tenets of the school founded by his brother Asanga, *vijñāna-vāda*.

This shift of Vasubandhu and those of his time appears natural after Nagarjuna's extreme position in idealist dialectics. The counterpart of the same heritage, which had remained neglected and even rejected as superfluous by Nagarjuna, needed to be incorporated in some way resulting in a broader synthesis of the two philosophical systems. The apparent inner contradiction between the older school, already immobilized in the statics of a dogmatic tradition, and the impetus of a new unprejudiced revolt had to be overcome just at the time when Asanga attempted another independent approach to the whole problem.

In short, the reintegration of the essential results of phenomenological analysis of structures and processes constituting the cognizing consciousness (*vijñānam*) following the *abhi-darma* method with the logical premise of transcendental idealism deduced from the ontological principle of *śūnya-vāda* was a task that could be successfully undertaken only by such a deep knower, analyst and reconstructer of the primordial foundation as was Vasubandhu. The principles of the *abhi-dharma* method were laid down by Buddho himself as the orientational basis for the integration of his teaching, while the *śūnya-vāda* was elicited from Buddho's initial statement by Nagarjuna.

Far from raising doubts about the reconcilability of the two sides of the same encompassing problem - *abhiharma* analytic and *śūnya-vāda* dialectic - which was ripening just at this historical junction under the roof of the same family of Buddhist scholars, Asanga and

Vasubandhu, I would rather suggest a better analogy. As more than a daring conjecture, the model for which I am pleading, for immanent philosophical reasons, should suggest a classical turning point reached in maturation crises. This model emerges as an essential necessity on all historical medians of the *philosophia perennis.*

Would it not be less daring (or at least less harmful for the immanent integrity of the great philosophers) to compare Vasubandhu's "conversion" with the split of A.N. Whiteheads's philosophy in "two halfs", according to his own statements about their difference[17], coinciding with the transition from his English to his American phase? The first period started with *Principia Mathematica* (1910) and continued with the use of "symbolism of *Principia* to restate the Newtonian theory" in three subsequent books published between 1919 and 1922 (*An Enquiry Concerning the Principles of Natural Knowledge, The Concept of Nature, The Principle of Relativity*). Then he realized that "Einstein's contribution was a brilliant mathematical theory", and gave up his efforts to save Newton by merely "restating" his theory in "proposing alternative theories". Thus, when he realized that Newton's "scientific materialism broke up from the inside" in the twentieth century, Whitehead conceived a new "scheme of ideas" which he named "the philosophy of organism".

> "The doctrine that I am maintaining is that neither physical nature nor life can be understood unless we fuse them together." "The reason for this blindness of physical science lies in the fact that such science only deals with half the evidence provided by human experience.

"Whitehead's "second half" denotes a transition from science to philosophy.

> "Thus as disclosed in the fundamental essence of our experience, the togetherness of things involves some *doctrine of mutual immanence*[18] How to understand this process of coordinating?"

The principle of relativity, as taken over from Einstein, was broadened in the "second half" of Whitehead's "transition from science to philosophy" so that "the principle of relativity applies the *doctrine of the relativity of all things* to the very definition of 'being'. The being of any kind of entity is its potentiality for *being an element in a becoming.*[19]

These statements (including parts that might be relevant for an extended analogy, here underlined) suffice to explain my analogy. Although I am restricted here mainly to the formal structure, the possibility of an extended comparative study of analogous motives may appear appropriate even after a few implicit hints. Whitehead's judgment on "the weakness of this positivism" seems especially relevant here as it caused his more emphatic turning to the "second half" of his "philosophy of organism" by breaking the framework of the first phase of his inquiries limited to "scientific materialism": an idea that mankind "could neither live with nor live without"[20]

> "The weakness of this positivism is the way in which we all welcome the *detached fragments* of explanation attained in our present stage of civilization." "The notion of life should involve the notion of physical Nature." "Sense perception is only one factor" in " the general observation of mankind." "It discloses no aim."

The same can be stated also, and not only in a purely formal manner, of Nagarjuna's motives to break the static atomisation of the *abhidharma* analytic.

In the case of Vasubandhu and the school of *vijñāna-vāda* epistemological idealism, it is important first to underscore that they never abandoned, nor deviated from, the central importance of *śūnya-vāda* idealism and its theses of "double nullity" - both of the cognizing self, or subject, and of the cognized object.

The explication of this thesis in the development of the *mahāyānam* idealism can be followed in the symptomatic modifications of the basic tenet of Buddho's formulation of "three characteristics" (*ti-lakkhaṇam*) of all existence, defined as transient and therefore as suffering and consequently void of any selfhood:

> *(sabbe saṅkhārā anicca ti-*
> *sabbe saṅkhārā dukkhāti-*
> *sabbe dhammā anattā ti-*
> *Dhammapadam 277-279)*

Prof. E. Lamotte, in his translation of the extensive commentary of the mahayanic text basic for Nagarjuna's school, *Mahā-prajñā paramitā-sūtraṁ*[21], paid special attention, in a lengthy note (vol. III, PP. 1368-70), to the mahayanic modification and extension of this fundamental criterion, whose ultimate version in Nagarjuna's school was:

"Impermanent are all formations.	*(Anityā sarva-samskāarā*
Painful are all formations.	*dukhā sarva-saṃskārā*
Null and void are all entities.	*śūunyā sarva-dharmā*
Void of any selfhood are all entities.	*anātmāna sarva-dharmā*
Appeasement is extinction."	*śāntaṁ nirvāṇaṃ)*

In comparing this Sanskrit version with the Pali quoted above, the interposition of the third statement in the Sanskrit version between the second and the third Pali propositions is essential for the emphasis of "double nullity". This interpolation is where *śūnyaṃ* or nullity of all entities, of phenomena (*dharmā*) as objects, precedes the negation of the selfhood (*ātmā*) as subject of the cognizing consciousness (*vijñānaṃ*).

Vijñāna-vāda or "theory of knowledge" (the German word *Er-kenntnis* corresponds etymologically better to the Sanskrit *vi-jñānaṁ*) designates the school of Asanga and Vasubandhu which they define as *vijñapti-mātrā*. As an approximate interpretation in terms of modern transcendental idealism I would define the term as the immanence of objective contents (*noemata*) within the constitutive structures of cognizing consciousness alone. *Mātrā* means 'limitation' or 'restriction' to the immanent constitution within the cognizing consciousness. The term *vijñapti* expresses the negation of a transcendent 'in- itself' (*sva-bhāva*). We must analyze the meaning of this term in its contextual and historical usage. According to D.T. Suzuki[22] *vijñapti* is "literally, 'that which is taken hold of'." The same author refers to Vasubandhu's *Triṁśikā*[23] *vijñapti* as "representation". The meaning of *idam* ("this") in Vasubandhu's statement, in *Triṁśikā*, verse 17, *idaṁ sarvaṁ vijnaptih-mātrakam*, implies "that which is discriminated as 'This is the self' and 'That is external reality,'" that is, this world where the subject is distinguished from the object."[24]

Another text quoted by Suzuki in the same connection, *Sagāthakam*, includes *vijñapti* in the definition of thought (*cittam*). This is analogous to Descartes' *Cogito* (and its various versions specified by Husserl):

"Mind (*cittam*), discrimination, *representation* (*vijñapti*), will(*manas*), consciousness (*vijñānam*), the storage (*ālaya*) (of sub-conscious karmical "seeds" of actions), that which makes the triple world, all these are synonyms of thought (*cittam*)"

In the *Laṅkavatāra-sūtraṁ* (the basic mahayanam text of the zen teaching elicited by Suzuki) the term *vijñapti-mātrā* is not used, but, the same basic idealist doctrine is designated as *citta-dṛśya-mātrā* 'that which is seen in thought only'. This more explicit term corresponds even better to my comparative analysis, at least in so far as it is more explicitly comparable to Schopenhauer's "*Vorstellung*", more correctly translated by "representation" than by "idea".[25] Thus despite some variations among various schools of the idealist theory of knowledge (*vijñāna-vāda*) concerning their metaphysical superstructures[26], the term "mind-only" (*citta-mātrā*) is "the principle of unification in which all representations (*vijnapti*), cogitations (*mananam*), discriminations (*vikalpa*), and a world of particulars (*viṣaya*), leave no traces".[27]

The conclusion, concerning the reductive analysis of a *Cogito* leaving "no trace" is explained more explicitly in *Triṁśikā*.

> "When the cognizing consciousness (*vijñānam*) takes no hold on an objective world, it abides in the *vijñapti-mātratvā*, for when there is nothing to be grasped, there is no grasping."

Nominalist conceptualism is common to Indian idealist philosophies, and particularly to Buddhism, since Buddho in his analysis of the five constituent factors (*pañca-khandhā*) of phenomenal being had classified all psycho-physical aggregates (*sankhāraā* in the meaning closest to the German *Gestaltungen*) in "names" (*nāmam*) and "forms" (*rūpam*). In terms of this nominalist conceptualism, the intention and purpose of all this phenomenological analysis is to show that "he who sees that all is name-only (or concept of our representation in a meaning comparable to Schopenhauer's theory of intelligence), sees that all is *vijñaptimātrā*. According to *Triṁsikā*, "As he abides in names, what is attained by means of representation (*vijñapti*) is cut off."[28]

The commentator of Nagarjuna, Candrakirti admonished the *vijñānāvādins* of the danger of hypostatising nullity into a negative entity. For Nagarjuna had warned (in M.K. XIII, 8, quoted at the end of section 6 above) that "those who take nullity (*śunyatā*) itself as a view (*dṛṣṭi*) are incurable". Nonetheless, such a "negative absolute" reappears as a ghost of nihilism in some recent attempts to vedantisize and/or to christianize this central conception of Buddhist philosophy.[29]

"If our adversaries define nullity as an entity (*dharma*, consisting of) the absence-of-entity, how should this not imply that the absence-of-entity has the character of entity, too, and how could nullity be considered as non-composed if it were an entity (*dharma*)?"

"Some (of our adversaries) hypostatize as 'non-composed' the space,the stop of recurrence (*rebirths*), the extinction (*nirvāṇam*). Others hypostatize nullity (*śūnyatā*) by defining it as 'thatness' (*tathatā*).It has been shown (*ādarśitaṁ*) by us that nothing of all that does exist if the existence of composed entities has not been proved."

(*Prasannapadā*, 174.12, 176.9, ad M.k. VII, 32- 33)

Vasubandhu specifically applied the same argument against the atomistic theory[30]:

"The objection that aggregates of atoms are objects of perception is untenable because atoms themselves have not the quality of aggregates." (*Triṁśikā*, 1)

"A particular entity is neither simple nor multiple from the standpoint of atomism, nor is it an agglomeration of atoms. Thus (the hypothesis of) the ultimate atom (*paramāṇu*) offers no solution." (*Viṁśatikā*, 11)

As for the basic argument, insisted upon by Candrakirti, concerning the subjective aspect of the "mind-only" theory, it seems that Suzuki in his differential analysis of standpoints adopted by different schools of *vijñāna-vāda* (referred to in note 26) above wished to reconfirm for his Lankavatarah-zen tradition the thesis rejected by Candrakirti.

"The mind is what is left behind when all forms of discrimination are rejected as leading to spiritual bondage and defilement. It is thus *something that has been here even prior to all discrimination,* that is, even before the duality of subject and object had come to exist. The *Laṅkāvatāra* does not advocate *nihilism pure and simple;* it tries to take hold of something beyond this world of particularisation."[31]

However, the founders of *vijñāna-vāda* were never explicit in denying, or even attacking, Nagarjuna's principle of *śūnya-vāda* but remained in a defensive position against imputations by the elder school of rationalist idealism. Within the limits of mahayanam religions their deviation to transcendental-logical analysis of the actual structures of cognizing consciousness and its noematic contents remained a marginal problem, inflated first by "modern", predominantly outsider, exegetes, as I shall try to show in the concluding chapter of this survey.

Regardless of the question of how far Suzuki's insistence on a dogmatic deviation from the initial thesis of both Candrakirti and Vasubandhu has been influenced by modern western pressure based on more or less dubious later religious traditions, there remains a deeper purely philosophical problem which may have caused later misunderstandings between the two original schools. This problem concerns the authentic difference between a purely formal-logical dialectical approach and the subsequent re-evaluation of transcendental-logical criteria of phenomenological *abihi-dharmā* analysis on a higher level of criticist idealism. For a *prima facie* comparative orientation I would venture to say that in the free development of Buddhist philosophy the speculative position corresponding to Hegel's dialectic preceded Kant's critical correction of speculative metaphysics. And he who cannot realize the advantage of the more natural Indian model should study Schopenhauer's extensive Kantian argumentation against "those three sophists" - Fichte, Schelling and above all, Hegel.[32]

On the Indian side, the sequence of the development traced above can be properly appreciated only by entering *in medias res* of the *vijñāna-vādī* transcendental analysis of the process of knowledge and its constitution, *vijñapti-mātrā*, viz. within the critical limits of the cognizing consciousness alone, as intended by Asanga and Vasubandhu. Here only a few glimpses can be added as direction for further deeper and purely philosophical study, concerning mainly problems of the *ontology of ideal being* and the central problem of Buddhist phenomenology in all its aspects. This was neglected by Nagarjuna and critically re-established by Asanga and Vasubandhu, beginning with Buddho's own interpretation of the "stream of existential articulation" (*bhav-añga-soto*) and the immanence of its entire karmic configuration (*sañkharo*, better translatable with the German term *Gestaltung*), according to the *pricipium individuationis* analyzed as the vicious circle of *paṭiccā-samuppado* (Sanskrit *pratītya-samutpāda*). The difference between the original Pali canon and the later Sanskrit schools of idealist philosophy found its fundamental expression in the thesis of the former that the *thusness* (*tathatā*), or the existential support of entities was the circle of interdependent arising (*pratītya-samutpāda*), while according to the thesis of the latter even this constituent principle had to be reduced to the zero point of *śūnyatā*. Not the opposition of these two principles, but the reductability of the first to the second, was formulated by Nagarjuna in M.K. XXIV, 18 (quoted in section 6, above). There, he says,"We declare that whatever is of dependent (relational) origination is naught (*śūnyatā*)."

Candrakirti in his commentary upon M.K. VIII, 11 (*Prasannapadā* 188.10) says:

> "We do not conceive a being-in-itself (*sva-bhāva*) in any entity,considering that they (all entities) are produced by dependent origination."

8. Asaṅga (4th century of our era)

Asanga intended to reconstruct the phenomenological analysis of *abhi-dharmā* structures from the same vantage-ground as the *mādhyamika* school by defining the constitution of all phenomena as *abhūta-parikalpa*, or unreal representation, due to "dependent origination totally bereft of any characteristic mark of objectivity".[33]

> "Because the types of knowledge by which the image is represented give the incentive to look at it, they act as support for (the image) arising in the form of an object."

Thus the question about the structure and formation of phenomena turns explicitly to the question "What is the cognizing consciousness, or the scope of *cogito - citta-matrā*?"

According to Vasubandhu's *Abhidharma-kośa* (II, 34), thought (*cittam*), mind (*mano*), and consciousness (*vijñānam*) are synonyms." This corresponds, in the broad lines of these categorial terms, to the specifications and aspects of the Cartesian *Cogito* as elicited in various contexts by Husserl. In the basic term of the vitalist idealism of his system Asanga formulated a still broader scope of the term *cittam*, requisite for the reduction of all constituent elements (*dhātu*) of the subjective and objective world-horizon to the "mind-alone" (*vijñapti-matrā*). This *ālaya-vijñānam*, or "treasury consciousness" is the sprouting-ground of all the "seeds" (*bījam*), literally the same as the *logos spermatikos* of the Stoics:

"*Cittam* (the Cogito) is the treasury consciousness of all the seeds (*sarva-bījakam ālaya-vijñānam*) impregnated by impressions[34] (*vāsanā*) of formations (*skandha*), of elements (*dhātu*) and of layers (*āyatanam*)."
Asañga, Abhidharma-samuccaya I, 1)[35]

According to *Lañkāvatāra-sūtram*[36]:

"The seven *vijñānas* (types of consciousness) which are the waves of the ocean, rise in conjunction with thought (*cittam*). Manifold are the waves evolved in the ocean; likewise indeed the *ālaya* sets in motion a variety of *vijñānas*. *Cittam, mana and vijñāam* are spoken (as different) because of appearances; in fact the eight (*vijñānas*) have no specific qualifying marks: there is neither that which qualifies nor that which is qualified."

The concluding statement of this description confirms again, as the most typical refrain of the whole mahayanam philosophical literature, the principle of double nullity.

For the essential *vitalist turning* in Asanga's departure from Nagarjuna's purely speculative rationalism, it may be characteristic to note Stcherbatsky's suggestion about the rendering of *karma*. Accordingly, the principle of psycho-physiological conditioning *hetu-pratyaya* (corresponding under the term *visayah* to Schopenhauer's *principium individuationis*), is "biotic force", while: "causal conditioning (*hetu-pratyaya*) is the treasury-consciousness impregnated with favorable impressions." (*Abhidharma-samuccaya,* I, 2)

Asanga reconstructed the traditional scheme of *abhidharma* elements by expanding it to one hundred analyzable structural units and by so doing he outlined his ideal horizon. The early Pali *abhidharma* compendium[37] started, in the first of its seven books, *Dhamma-sangaṇī,* with a complex of experiential structures altogether containing eighty-nine elements. The third book, *Dhātu-kathā* or "the statement of elements" is entitled *khanda-āyatana-dhātu-kathā* or "the statement of groups, bases, and elements"[38] It discusses in the structure of phenomena in their mutual relations of "inclusion and noninclusion", "association and dissociation", divided in "dyads and triads" of 125 interrelated units, classified in fifteen organic wholes or "matrixes". It includes in its schemes such groups as the physical elements (earth, water, fire, air), sense, psychical faculties, types of consciousness and volition, as well as subjective elementary incentives in the biotic process of causation, and also regions of ideal being as the four basic existential truths concerning the problem of suffering, the components of meditative absorption, and others.

What is essential for our investigation of the historical development of these classifications and their strata with interconnections of their complexities, are the critically unsifted common-sense criteria applied both in the analysis and the synthesis of distinctions and connections of "elements" (*dhātu*). Thus "the four primary physical elements (earth, water, fire, air) are designated as "underived", while "twenty-three phenomena, to wit: the five physical sense organs, visible object, sound, smell, taste,... vitality, bodily intimation, verbal intimation, space,... subsistence, decay, impermanence, nutriment", are considered as "derived" from the four primary physical elements. Five sense organs are considered as "own" or subjective, and their objects as "external"[39]. These five objects are defined as "not karmically acquired", which implies the status of material reality in-itself on the objective side, facing the ideality of the "self" (*an-ātmā*) on the subjective side. Material "reality" remained an inert fossil of substance, while mind, as the incomparably predominant factor of incessant transformation in the stream of events was analysed away, reduced into the sets of pure functions. Buddho's following statement being characteristic of this attitude, negates an "underived" soul although it by no means implies the thesis of realistic stability, or even inertness of "underived" substance:

> "It would be better for the unlearned worldling to regard his body,built up of the four elements, as his Self, rather than his mind. For it is evident that the body may last for a year, for two years, for three, four, five, or ten years, or even for a hundred years and more,but that which is called thought, or mind, or consciousness, arises continuously, during day and night, as one thing, and passes away as another thing."(*Saṁyutta-nikāyo*, XII, 62)

On higher levels of real and ideal being, complexities grouped according to the generic provenance from their "matrixes" are not specified with reference to such realistic dichotomies. Since they pertain prevalently to "matrixes" of purely ideal being of transcendental structures, they are considered in their pure state of phenomenal events and beyond the dichotomic postulates of common-sense realist ontologies. ("Modern" positivistic perspectives prefer to speak of a pluralist, rather than a dualist, ontology of the early Buddhist world-view. But this could not bring its historical development any closer to a solution of the fundamental epistemological problem.)

A critical reduction of these realistic dichotomies, in their inconsistent applications to the epistemological principle of *vijñapti-mātratā*, has elicited criteria for essentially different structures of complexities exclusively derived from the transcendental subject of cognizance.

In the definition of Asanga's *cogito - cittam*, as quoted above, this encompassing mental principle comprises the formative process of "aggregation" (*skanda*) with its "content laden" (*hyletic*, in Husserl's terminology) elements, "sprouting" in particular regions (*āyatanam*) and on specifically determined levels of their confluent being. The biotic causal conditioning (*hetu-pratyaya*) of their emergence in consciousness is predetermined and treasured in the depth-consciousness of *ālaya-vijñānam*. In his *Mahāyāna-saṃgraha* (II,2) Asanga deduced, from the analysis of the structural gradation of understanding, a table of eleven categories which, in short, is threefold: (1) dependent, (2) represented (intuited in the meaning analogous to Schopenhauer's *Vorstellung*), (3) fully accomplished. Both the first and the second are described as "dependent". Their "seed" forms "the basic cognizance", corresponding to "unreal representation" limited to a frame of eleven categories of understanding:

1 - the cognizance of the body,

2 - of the innate psycho-physical principle,

3 - of the subject of experience (*bhoktri*, lit. the "enjoyer", or "eater" of food, the term for experience in Indian philosophy is "eating", or enjoyment of food-stuff),

4 - of the object of experience (*bhoga*),

5 - of the act of experiencing (*bhogi*),

6 - the cognizance of time,

7 - of the number,

8 - of place,

9 - of discourse (language),

10 - of the difference between oneself and the other,

11 - the cognizance of the good and the bad way, of disappearance and arising (or of death and birth).

The first five categories designate the *psycho-physical* level of empirical knowledge, the next five the *transcendental level*, and the last one the *axiological level* of ideal being.

The highest level of fully accomplished cognizing consciousness, which, according to Buddho's often repeated statements, is characterized by "abandoning the good and the evil" (*kusala-akusala* or *puñña-pāpa-pahayam*) is consequently explained in Asanga's context from the highest principle of *śūnyatā*. To the question concerning the perfect accomplishment of the cognizing consciousness Asanga's answer is: "It is the total absence of the sign of a dependently conditioned (relational) object. "*Mahāyāna-saṃgraha*, II, 4)

In *Abhidhamma-samuccaya*, II, a "triple nullity (*śūyatā*)" is distinguished concerning the object of cognizance:

1 - nullity concerning the non-being (*abhāva-śūnyatā*) in general,

2 - nullity concerning the not-being-there (*tathābhāva-śūnyatā*) in particular,

3 - nullity of the material world (*prakṛti-śūnyatā*) in its totality.

The first has to be understood as a formal logical principle (*parikalpitā*), the second as relational (*para-tantram*), and the third in a total or absolute sense (*pari-niśpannā*).

From the standpoint of uncritical naive realism, in as far as it was implicit and further developed in the Pali *abhidhammā* literature, the *vijñapti-matrā* turn to gnoseological idealism could not avoid being misunderstood as a hypostasis of "mind only" against the increasing realistic insistence on the static "underived" and "gross" material substance (*sthūla-śarīraṁ*). This took the place of a consequent annulment of both premises of possible hypostatizing in a dichotomic realism. So the *vijñāna-vāda* idealism was accused of the worst heresy of soul-theory (*ātmā-vāda*) earlier than the not yet eliminated nor challenged hypostasis of matter. Thus the adjustment to the double nullity, undertaken by Asanga, was not properly understood neither by *abhidharma* realists nor by mystically disposed idealists following the mahayanic tendency that became stronger as mahayanam religions continued to extend beyond their Indian birthplace. Vasubandhu, in his fifteenth proposition of *Triṁśikā* had to confess the apprehension of being misunderstood by philosophically uneducated dogmatics:

> "The consciousness of self-assertion is deep and subtle. It flows as a stream with all the (karmic) seeds. I have not published this(before) because of those whose mind is not developed, so that they would erroneously imagine that this (subtle depth-consciousness) means the Self (as soul-substance)."

There is an analogous statement by Buddho in the elucidation of the same danger in *Saṁyutta-nikāyo*, XLIV, 10, 10:

> "Then Vacchagotto the wanderer went to visit the Lord... and said:
>
> - Now, Master Gotamo, is there a Self? At these words the Lord was silent.
> - How, then, master Gotamo, is there not a Self? For the second time the Lord was silent. Then Vacchagotto the wanderer rose from his seat and went away. Not long after the departure of the wanderer, the venerable Anando said to the Lord:
> - How is it, Lord, that the Lord gave no answer to the question of the wanderer Vacchagotto?
> - If, Anando, when asked by the wanderer: "Is there a Self?", I had replied to him: "There is a Self", ... would my reply be in accordance with the knowledge that all things are impermanent?
> - Surely not, Lord.
> - And, Anando, when asked by Vacchagotto the wanderer: "Is there not a Self?", had I replied that there is not, it would have been more bewilderment for the bewildered Vacchagotto.
>
> For he would have said: "Formerly indeed I had a Self, but now I have not one any more."

Far from being any mysteriously ambiguous explanation of "Buddho's silence", the rational background of this statement only presupposes that nullity or nihilation of both the subjective ("internal") and objective ("external") counterparts to "consciousness alone", (i.e. of both the Self and the Universe), can qualify the sufficient reason for a negative answer to these questions which transcend the horizon of dogmatic vedantist religion. Buddho's discourses with his own disciples challenged the prevalent dogmatic ambience exemplified by Vacchagotto and made possible its assimilation. To that end our previous Pali texts were selected and quoted. (Cf. *Anurādha-suttaṁ*, S.XXII, 86,) *Yamaka-suttaṁ*, S. XXII, 85, and the section on existential fear, referred to also in *Vacchagotto-suttaṁ*, in *Ala-gadd'ūpama-suttaṁ*, M.22)

Asanga's analysis of *abhi-dharmā* phenomenological structures and their elements from the standpoint of their integration in "mind only" (*vijñapti-matrā*) start from such deeper questions about the transcendental functions of mind:

> "How does the representation represent (phenomena)? What is its (functional) support, what the comprehension (or grasp) of signs, what its clinging thereupon, what the verbal expression?..."

The answer is: "The representation represents while finding its support in names (or nominalistic concepts) comprehending its signs in their dependent being, clinging thereupon by its views (opinions, *dṛṣṭi*, Greek *doxa*), finding verbal expression in (mental) reflection... and so it attributes the presence to an object which is not present (as such)."

In the next chapter (III,8) of *Mahāyāna-saṁgraha*[40] the following question is raised. "How does this penetration (of an apparent object) occur in the cognizing consciousness?" It is answered in the following way.

> "It penetrates in the pure consciousness through (the category of) duality, supplying it with image-and-glance and manifold configurations, provided that name, object, designation of being,specification of particulars, essence and accidence, these six (categorial) designations of objects are no-objects."

The table of eleven categories quoted above from *Mahāyāna-saṃgraha* and referring to the lower two regions of representation dependent on sense-data interpreted categories 3-5 in terms of "experience" understood as "enjoyment" in "food-stuff". In contradistinction to this sphere of sensuality the superior and highest level of fully accomplished consciousness is characterized in *Abhidharma-samuccaya* (I, 2) by another criterion of dichotomy: that of the external and internal intent of the cognizing mind. The first is the psycho- physical need of "food" and "enjoyment". The second is characterized by the opposite intention toward abstention and inhibition (Greek *epochá*) on which the categorial structures and their regions in contemplative absorption (*samādhi*) are "rooted":

> "What is the division according to extroversion?

- It is prevalently the division in the region of desire (*kāmāvacaram*).

What is the division according to introversion?

- These are all the regions of concentration (*samādhi-bhūmi*)."

Here a rather unexpected suggestive analogy with modern western philosophy requires a digression:

In the early Pali sources, the same as in other classical systems of Indian philosophy, "the nutriments of life"[41], or objects of experience, are four: (1) edible food, (2) sense-impressions, (3) conative action, (4) the nutriment of consciousness.

Psycho-physiological theories of experience, based on existential incentives of hunger and thirst, food and its enjoyment, appear in modern European philosophy in some of Nietzsche's interpretations.[42]

In England S. Alexander in his main work, *Space, Time and Deity* (1920) elicited an extensive theory of experience based on the same principle of "enjoyment", coming suggestively close to the Indian models to which he, however, never refers explicitly. The distinction between the "enjoyment" and "contemplation" refers to the difference between subjective knowledge and objective knowledge. Alexander calls the former "enjoyment", and the latter "contemplation". Space-Time as "a system of motion" is the "stuff of matrix (or matrices) out of which things or events are made..." "Empirical things come into existence, because Space-Time of its own nature breaks up into finites..." "Time is enjoyed in the enjoyment of material acts." "Man can only *enjoy* consciousness... gods or God can know it as an object of contemplation."

Nearly at the same time as Alexander's system of emergent evolution, G. Santayana's *Scepticism and Animal Faith* (1923) appeared in New York as an introduction to his voluminous system of philosophy. In the chapter on Indian Origins of Pyrrho's *epoché* and its revival in the twentieth century, in the second part of this book, I tried to explicate the postulate of the Pyrrhonian skepticism as the basis of the reductive method of *epoché*. In its Indian antecedents it appeared more natural than in the extant fragments of Phyrrho's intention to apply it to the *ethos* of knowledge, of which the primary purpose of *epoché* was to check exactly that inborn lack of criticism which Santayana in his peculiar context (explicitly even less of Pyrrhonian than of Indian and Buddhist casual inspiration) defined as the "Animal

Faith". Concerning the limits of the specific subject of this digression I wish to add only one remark suggestive for the new vitalist theory of experience, in contradistinction from the earlier scientific positivism:

> "...what concerns me, even in the purest dialectic or the most desultory dream,... is not to explore essence, but to gather experience. The psyche below is busy selecting her *food,* fortifying her cave, and discriminating her friends from her enemies; and in these meanderings of mine over the realm of essence, in spite of myself, I am only her scout. By experience I understand a fund of wisdom gathered by living."[43]

From the standpoint of Nagarjuna's "purest dialectic", Candrakirti's criticism of *ālaya-vijñāṇaṁ* refers principally to the problem of essences and their ideal being in a way which seems not at all incomparable with Santayana's exploration of the ontological function of essences - his central preoccupation in the quoted book.

Vasubandhu, having adopted the idealist standpoint of *vijñāna-vāda* and rejected the atomistic alternative as inadequate for the analysis of phenomena, had also to give up the rest of the theory of structural elements on which the classical tradition of the Pali *abhidhammā* was established. So, from the idealist vantage ground, there remained as an alternative only the theory of the "flux of being" (*bhavāñga-srotaṁ*) as the bearer of articulation of phenomenal events according to the *ksaṇika-vāda* theory of momentariness. The basic and specific premisses of the Pali *abhidhammā* exegesis and the most original and outstanding contribution of the Buddhist thought to Indian philosophy were the ideas of the existential flux and that of the momentariness of its formations. The atomic theory was, on the other hand, a much older, pre-vedic tradition of the universal proto-culture, well known between China and Greece. Buddho also used it conventionally without critical discrimination despite his acosmic attitude and the radical turning of his philosophy of existence (explicated by him as the philosophy of suffering - *dukkham*). From this intrinsic structure in the course of time the remainder of atomistic belief was bereft of an independent development. Nagarjuna stated it most clearly and explicitly in his bold rejection of some formulations involving realist implications (as mentioned above, in section 6). Understood as concessions to *puthujjanā*, "uneducated persons", not yet ennobled by Buddho's "noble teaching" (to whom, as we have seen Buddho often referred in his discussions), such statements, inconsistent with the later rationalist idealism, were misused by the preachers after Buddho's death in order to reconcile themselves with the cheap and mean compromise conceding a "double truth" preached by Buddho to two different classes of hearers. The "morale" of this explication was exaggerated beyond all limits of shameful restraint in the later non-Indian religious dogmatism in the struggles between sects not only against authentic Buddhism, but also against the historical Buddho himself, as well as sectarian quarrels among themselves. I shall revert to the initial dogmatic root of all these heretical sects at the end of this section, in order to show how they were reflected in the mirror of the early *vijñāṇa-vādī* philosophers.

In his criticism of the traditional theory of elements (*dhātu*) Vasubandhu asks his opponents:

> "Why do you not admit that (the modifications) of your knowledge change due to your actions? Why do you imagine 'elements'?"
> "These actions are pervaded by the stream of your knowledge and by nothing else. Why do you not admit that it is just there, where this pervasion occurs, that also its fruit appears, viz. a corresponding change of knowledge?" (*Viṁśatikā*, 6-7)

In consequence of this de-atomization of phenomenological analysis of the transcendental structure of knowledge Vasubandhu had, on the other hand, to reject as "excessive" the doctrinal oversimplification of Nagarjuna's school formulated in the statement:

> " 'Both self (*ātmā*) and phenomena (*dharmā*) are pure imagination: they do not exist as transcendent entities (*paramārtha*). Consequently the intended object (noema) has to be considered the same as the intending subject.' This doctrine is exaggerated and should not be admitted." (*Triṁśikā*, p. 64)

I am not reticent to extend the analogy with Husserl's transcendental idealism to Vasubandhu's interpretation of intersubjectivity as empathy (*Einfühlung*):

> "It is by a mutual influence that communications (between individuals) are reciprocally determined."
> "For those who know the mind of another (being), it is not a knowledge conform with the knowledge of an object. Why? Here the case is the same as in their knowledge of their own mind."
> (*Viṁśatikā*, 18, 21)

Here the difference between the knowledge of another person's *mind* and the knowledge of an external *thing* presents an argument against the "exaggeration" of the dialectical theory of identity of the knower and the known. The recognition of this difference is purely phenomenological, concerning two correlative structures, and need not imply the reality of the knower as an "absolute" entity against the purely phenomenal, i.e. "relational"[44] status of the known (*noema*). Unlike most European theist standpoints in the confrontation with this implication of "*ego sum*"[45], authentic Buddhist idealism has never renounced the consideration of the absolutization of the knower's "self" (*ātmā-vāda*) as the worst heresy of its Vedantist opponents. Yet, mutual accusations for this heresy have continued throughout the scholastic period, and until today, to be imputed on both sides, the Buddhist and the Vedantist, even to the greatest exponents of idealist schools. As Candrakirti was the first to accuse Asanga of hypostatizing the subject of knowledge as a negative absolute, so in the Vedantist camp Samkara had to defend himself and the earlier founders of his school against accusations of being a surreptitious Buddhist nihilist.[46] In this way the problem was pushed always more and farther into the field of religious dogmatics. On the Buddhist side it coincided fortunately with its transplantations to always more distant foreign countries and cultural ambiences, as far as Japan, until the colonial pressure, mainly at the beginning of the twentieth century, brought it back to the Buddhist world at large, via India, where it still lingers thanks to non-Buddhist influences. I will discuss the relevance of this issue to the present day. Even the basic *mahāyānam* texts, such as the *Lañkāvatāra-sūtraṁ* in Suzuki's interpretation, quoted by those who wish to reestablish the belief in a permanent and 'absolute' self-principle or soul by hypostatizing consciousness as the subject of thought (*cittam* = *cogito*), contain, on the other hand, discoverable to other, differently minded authors, statements whose obvious and contextual purpose is to exclude such insinuations. Thus in *Lañkāvatāra-sūtraṁ*[47] is the statement:

> The thinking and its thought, mind, and the consciousness together with its subconscious store (*ālaya-vijñā*ṇAṁ) -se three aspects are synonymous with thought (*cittam* = *cogito*).

"In *Abhidharma-samuccaya*, Asanga, in answering some questions, states[48]:

" - What is the definition of the *aggregate* of consciousness (*vijñāṇa-skandha*)?

- It is the thought *(cittam)*, mental organ (*mana*) and also consciousness (*vijñāṇaṁ*).
- And what is thought *(cittam)*?
- It is the store-consciousness (*ālaya-vijñāṇaṃ*).
- It consists of the six groups of consciousness: visual consciousness, auditory, olfactory, gustatory, tactile and mental (*mana*-) consciousness."

In *Mahāyāna-sūtrālañāara*, one of the oldest texts of the same school, in Ch. VI, 8, it is stated:

"The *bodhisattva* having the insight that there is nothing beyond the thought (-consciousness, *cittam*), and also the non-being of even that thought, ... and since there is no other substrate of the object than that thought, the *bodhisattva* has thus attained the insight in the non-being of all that which exists only within the limits of thought (*citta-mātrā*)."

The commentary upon this statement explains further that through this insight into the 'essence' of *non-being* (*nastitvam*, not yet *śuūnyatā*) the *bodhisattva* (the not yet fully awakened one) reaches the "element" of truth (*dharma-dhātu*). In the mahayanic theological doctrine of trinity (*tri-kāya) dharma-dhātu*, the first of three ideals or symbolic "embodiments" of Buddho's 'eternal' virtues, is the embodiment of truth in his doctrine (*dharma-kāya*). The other two transform this (exclusively) mahayanic trinity into an increasingly anthropomorphised shape: *saṁbhogya-kāya* as "the body of enjoyment, or recompense" for the well-deserved bliss (cf. *ānandha* in the *vedānta*) and the third embodiment, the *nirmāna-kāya*, is "usually translated as... body of transformation or simply assumed body".[49]

This is how the dialectical turn to the religious purpose occurred, and also the implicit reason (as I shall try to show it presently) why it was grafted just here, on the allergic spot where the annulment of the Self and Soul entity is most explicitly confirmed in the thesis of *pure Cogito (cittam) - non sum.*

At the end of *Triṁśikā* the "non-being" is explained as the "Revolution of the Recipient" (as Silvain Levi translated *ālaya-paravṛtti*). Proposition 30 of *Triṁśikā* defines this "recipient" as *ālaya-vijñāṇaṃ*, "consciousness containing all the seeds".

Here the question arises:

"- But what has one to eliminate in order to accomplish this revolution of the recipient?

- The answer is:

- By the elimination of the two kinds of turbulence

- the turbulence of obstructions, consisting of passions, and the turbulence of obstructions consisting of the knowable (objectification)." "having eliminated these obstructions and accomplished the revolution of the recipient

- this is what is called the totality of entities (eliminated) by the great sage. It is called the totality of entities because, without abandoning the transmigration (of rebirths), he remains without passions, and consequently, obtains the mastery overall entities."

In the explanation of *Triśikā* (19), it is said:

"Actually the agent producing the transmigration consists of actions and passions. Of these two passions are of principal importance. It is only by the prevalent influence of passions that the act is enabled to project a new existence... And thus passions are the root of functioning of transmigration (rebirth), because they are the principal motive."

In this version the analogy of "obstructing passions" with the Freudian *libido* is suggested more explicitly.[50] The "revolution of the recipient", understood as the emptying of subconsciousness, in its fundamental Buddhist function, means the cleansing of the polluting affluxes (*aśravā*) of "obstructing passions". In its originally Jain meaning, taken over by Buddho, this term (Pali *āsavo*) is of central importance for Indian atheistic religions, understood and defined as the "way of purification" (Buddho's *visuddhi-maggo*). In the beginning of one of the oldest poetical texts of the Pali canon, *Muni-suttaṁ* (*Sutta-nipāto*, I, 12, 208), its title reminiscent of the common pre-Vedic origin of both Jainism and Buddhism, even this radical danger of *āsavā* affluxes of karmic matter, considered as dirt obstructing the penetration of truth (*dhammo*) by "right views", is exposed in harsh terms to a radical extirpation."

"He who destroys the sprout and does not let it thrive, and who would never again produce a new birth, he is called a silent sage, going alone. That great sage has discerned what the peaceful way is".

The ascetic extremism of this early attitude, later suspected of "heretical" Jain influence, seems to be not merely forgotten, but rather rejected with equal violence, prevalently in popular religion, among which excels *Vimalakīrti-nirdeśa*.[51] It was the *bodhisattva-vow* which, also at the end of the theoretical text of *Triṁśikā*, redirected the intention of the "revolution of the recipient" towards a dogmatically constructive, dialectically and morally higher, practical aim.

The *bodhisattva* vow contains the renunciation of the attainment of the final "extinction" - *nirvāṇaṃ* - "until I relieve all living beings from misery". On the other hand, this noble decision of self-sacrifice presupposes the reintroduction of the following cosmological belief:

> "the firm conviction that the sum-total of good deeds prevails over the sum-total of bad deeds. The evolution of the world process is an evolution of moral progress. When all good deeds will have brought their fruition, Final Deliverance will be attained in Nirvana."[52]

This optimistic interlude in the doctrine of nothingness may almost remind us - *mutatis mutandis* - of Descartes' reversal of the skeptical outset of his *Cogito* into the emphatic affirmation of his - *ergo sum!* The irrational element of religious pressure is comparable, not only between these two instances of skeptical idealism, but also among some historical missing links, such as was the disputed Muslim theological authority of Al-Ghazali (11th c.) in his autobiographical meditations in *Al-munqidhu min aḍ-ḍalāli* (Deliverance from Error).

Returning to the concluding argument of Vasubandu in *Triṁśikā*, we find the elucidation of the attainment of *bodhisattva* in the statement that:

> "... having eliminated the obstructions of the passion of cognizing,and accomplished the revolution of the recipient, it is said that this is (the attainment of) the essential totality, because *without abandoning the transmigration* (of rebirths) he will remain dispassionate and will consequently acquire the essential predominance over the totality of being."

Asanga (in *Mahāyāna-saṃgraha* IX) designates this "revolutionary" achievement as *apratiṣṭhita* or "unstable" *nirvāṇaṃ*[53] This status of instability of a *bodhisattva* is explained and dogmatically justified in connection with the fundamental doctrine of psychological idealism as understood and applied in *mahāyānam* religions. The *vijñapti-mātrā* limitation of all existence to the illusory knowledge of "mind-only", or its metaphysical nescience (*avidyā*), reveals, through penetration by a higher religious wisdom - (*prajñā*)[54], the ultimate "identity of *saṁsāra* and *nirvāṇaṁ* (*saṁsāra-nirvāṇa-samatā*), or the identification of the phenomenal flux of existence with its extinction in conceptual nullification of both.

E. Lamotte, in his introduction to the *Vimalakīrti-nirdeśa*, concludes his analysis of the dialectical predicament of *bodhisattva* as follows:

> "Thus, while remaining in *nirvāṇaṃ*, the *bodhisattva* is manifesting the *saṁsāra*. He knows that there are no beings, but he strives nevertheless to convert them... He remains always apart of the triple world (*traidhātuka*), and yet he does not abandon its beings.[55] Such dogmatic postulates, among others, may have led to the "modern" tendency to translate and interpret the "nullity" of *śūnyatā* with mere "emptiness" of the *ālaya-vijñānaṁ* "recipient".

Apart from such theological speculations peculiar to mahayanic religions, it should not be forgotten that the ideal of *bodhisattva* is far from being exclusively, or even originally, of mahayanist invention. It is a common ideal of all Buddhists (although not implying necessarily a *bodhisattva*-vow). Its most popular and oldest version is contained in the most voluminous literary work of the early Pali scriptures, *The Jātakas*, 547 tales of Buddho's previous births since the legendary time, eons ago, when under *buddho* Dipankaro, his twenty-fourth predecessor in the buddhahood, he made the vow one day to become a *buddho* himself. Thus according to the *thera-vādo* Pali tradition, the number of lives remaining to be spent by a *bodhisattvāh* for the welfare of the suffering humanity is proportioned to a purely human and individual progress of a single mind "striving with diligence" towards the attainment of his own ultimate goal of "extinction without remainder" (*anavasesa-nibbānam*). Yet in the ascending series of his lives towards this ideal a bodhisatto sacrifices himself always again not only for the benefit of his own perfection, but also in order to help other beings bound to the worldly existence to attain the same ideal of perfection (*pāramitā*). And the purely human limit of his altruistic task and capacity for teaching is brought out by Buddho's saying in *Dhammapadaṁ*:

> "You yourself should make an effort. The Awakened Ones can only show the way."[56]

Chapter Two

- But, monks, while I speak thus, and teach thus, there are some ascetics and brahmans who accuse me with false, vain, lying, untrue intention: "The ascetic Gotamo is a nihilist. The intention of his teaching is destruction, the loss, the non-existence of any being."
- Yet, I expound now, the same as I did before, only what is suffering and what is the cessation of suffering.

Alagaddūpama-suttaṁ, M. 22 1.

1. Tsong -kha'-pa'

In Tibetan Buddhism the fascinating clearness of Tsong-kha-pa's statements on nothingness and the double nullity of the cognizing self and the cognized object, the doctrine of *śūnyatā,* Tibetan *stong-nyid,* in the lapidary formulation of his didactical poems, has contributed perhaps more than all the rest of the quoted documentation, to impress the understanding of *śūnya-vāda* teaching in my mind, at least as far as "inference for one self" (*svārthānumānam*) requires according to the basic rule of Dignaga's logic. Here are a few salient points on our subject from Tsong-kha-pa's didactic poems and hymns[57]:

"Nullity is free of assertions.

....

nullity refutes the extreme of non-being,
when you understand the arising of cause and effect
from the viewpoint of nullity,
you are not captivated by either extreme view.

Son, when you realize the keys
of the Three Principles of the Path,
depend on solitude and strong effort,
and quickly reach the final goal!"
(The Three Principles of the Path)

The three guiding principles are: renunciation, the awakening thought (*bodhi-cittaṁ*) and the understanding of nullity.

In the Pali text quoted in Part I, 3 (*Sutta-nipāto*, 1069-1076), the key term designating nothingness was expressed in a wording less ambiguous than the Sanskrit, and if possible, more suited to the "modern" materialistically minded substantialist, even trans-substantialist, prejudiced reader. Here, the typical statement of the transcendental reduction (Pyrrho's *epoché* with its essential ethical implications), is expressed in the first quoted line, "nullity is free of assertion". Instead of *suññatā*, "nullity", the Pali term used in the afore mentioned text, is *ākiñcaññaṁ*, plain and simple "nothing". As far as it can be expressed in reifying terms of the English language the conclusion is: "Where all appearances have been abolished, there all tools of talk have been abolished too."

Hegel's reduction of the Buddhist theory of nothingness to the alternative of 'being' or 'non-being'[58] is also precluded a limine with unmistakable clearness by which Tsong-kha-pa in the quoted statement 'sublated' and resolved this speculative alternative in the 'nihilation' on the higher level of the nullified 'Absolute'.

Commenting on the verses of Tsong-kha-pa's poem *The Foundation of all Excellence*:

> "Having realized that there is no security in the pernicious perfections of *saṁsāra* (stream of existence) may I be strongly intention the bliss of liberation."

Kushri Kabchu Sudhi reminds the reader that "metaphysical ignorance (*avidyā*) is confused about the cause and effect of *karma* and about the nature of 'just-thatness' (*tathātvam*) which is nullity."

In connection with the essential qualities of Buddhist meditation whose purpose is expressed in Tsong-kha-pa's verses in the same text:

"May I quickly produce within myself
the path that unifies tranquility and insight"

The commentator advises the reader to "learn the good path of the Conqueror, which unifies appearance and nullity, perceiving that from the perspective of attainment, all is null and void of self-nature, and from the perspective of appearance, all is like a magician's illusion."

Commentarial texts also contain several exhortations against intolerance. A quotation from the *Kṛṣṇayamātri-tantra* contains the precepts:

> "Do not despise your own or other's religion."
> "Do not trouble the existence of worldly people."
> "Do not discriminate between the teachings."
> "It is wrong to despise the wisdom of women."

2. Chatral Rimpoche and Thomas Merton

The didactic expression of the doctrine of nothingness in Tsong-kha-pa's version and in the development of his school is based on the tenets of Nagarjuna's *Madhyamaka-kārikā*. His purpose is not to indulge any further in eliciting the speculative argumentation of Nagarjuna's dialectical theses. The peculiar freshness of Tsong-kha-pa's clear statements (if I may apply to his exegetical work, the title of the best known commentary of the same fundamental text, Candrakirti's *Prasannapadā*) fascinated me at first by the ethical turning of their pedagogical intent. Yet, as an outsider to the Tibetan Buddhist tradition, I succeeded in finding the deepest core of this fascinating tendency only in an indirect transmission formulated in an equally clear and lapidary statement of a contemporary Tibetan refugee hermit in India.He conveyed it though a no less exceptionally sensitive and worthy representative of western hermitic tradition survived in the Cistercian Trappist order, *Thomas Merton*[59].

After his visit to the Dalai Lama in 1968, Merton visited also a few Tibetan hermit-scholars in the Himalayas, among whom he mentions Chatral Rimpoche in the Darjeeling area. The essential teaching of *śūnyatā*, for me, too, became the principal *clé de Voute* after this revelation which transpired thanks to through Merton's Christian propensity:

> "... the Risen Christ, suffering, compassion for all creatures, motives of 'helping others', but all leading back to *dzogchen*, the ultimate

emptiness, the unity of *śūnyata* and *karunā*, going beyond the dharmakaya and 'beyond God' to the ultimate perfect emptiness."

In another place, looking for a Christian analogy with the Asian *Ethos of Knowledge*, Merton notes:

"... *veritas caritatis* - 'the truth of charity', *caritas veritatis* -'the charity of truth' - The foundation for it is, of course, in the *Confessions* of St. Augustine. The Cistercian mystics emphasize the former... whereas the school of St. Victor... give priority to truth and consequently emphasize the intellectual aspect of love."

In order to reduce this problem to its essential Buddhist import, we may agree with Merton:

Only through the pure virtue of *karunā*, compassion, Christian *caritas* can the truth of nullity of existence in its deepest being transpire and reach the level of wisdom (*prajñā*) beyond the horizontal reach of mere mundane knowledge (*laukika-jñāṇam*) and *vice-versa*, the intellectual understanding of nothingness (under any whatsoever nominal designation) can reward as a ripe fruit (*phalam*) the wayfarer on the path of purification (*visuddhi-maggo*) only as a gift to his empathy, in the most spontaneous ethical emotion of compassion.

Nagarjuna's most superficially understood and terrifying *dictum* can be rightfully applied to all other forms of "realizing" the truth of nothingness: "Incurable indeed are those who take nullity itself merely as a *view*" (*dṛṣṭi*, Greek *doxa*, opinion). (*M.K.* XII, 8)

In reexamining this problem of the Buddhist Ethos of knowledge, I reverted to the available texts, beginning with Tson-kha-pa's poems, quoted above, rather than the objective documentation.

In the description of "The Three Principles of the Path" Tsong-kha-pa says:

"Thus, from the outset seek renunciation.

....

Renunciation without pure bodhi-mind
does not bring forth the perfect bliss
of unsurpassed awakening.

....

Though you practice renunciation and bodhi-mind,
without wisdom, the realization of Nullity,
you cannot cut the root of saṁsāraah."

In his commentary on this poem the fourth Panchen Lama, Tenbay Nyima, says: "To generate *bodhi*-mind you must first achieve *equanimity* (*upekṣā*) toward all living beings."

Equanimity is the fourth and highest of the "four immeasurable virtues" (*apramāṇam*) requisite for the cultivation of mind through meditation. The first is *maitrī* or friendliness. The second is *karunā* or compassion, which we are discussing now in relation with Thomas Merton. The third is *muditā* or joyful empathy. The fourth is *upekśā* or equanimity, *apatheia* in the Stoical meaning as understood by Kant and quoted in our earlier context.[60]

The commentary explains the connection of *upekśā* with the preceding lower stages of sublimation of virtue in the maxim:

> "I will never feel close to some beings and help them, while feeling distant from others and harming them. I will learn to have equanimity toward all living beings."
>
> In "The Concise Meaning of the Stages of the Path" it is said:
>
> *"Wisdom is the eye which sees profound nothingness, the path*
> *that completely uproots saṁsāra (the stream of existence).*
>
> ....
>
> *But by wisdom set apart from abiding tranquility (upekṣā),*
> *though you analyze intensely, you do not expel the passions.*
>
> ....
>
> *Seeing this, understand how wonderful is the effort*
> *that conjoins intense insight and abiding tranquility."*

In "The Foundation of All Excellence" it is confirmed that "bodhi-mind alone, without cultivation of three moral practices, does not lead to awakening."

The circle of interconnections among "the three principles of the path", consisting of all the mentioned elements of the ethos of knowledge, reaches its closing point in the commentary on "The Foundation of All Excellence" in the advice to the meditator: "You should also focus on the meaning of *nothingness*, for having focussed on that, one can accomplish the abiding *tranquility*."

The essential terms joined at the closing point of the circle of interconnection are, on the side of wisdom, the insight in the depth of nothingness, and on the side of virtues their ultimate synthesis in *upekṣā*, the perfection of equanimity.

Karunā, compassion, remains included in this synthesis. In the quoted texts I found *karunā* for the first time in the explanation of "the guiding principle of method" describing the interdependence of the first two principles of the path, renunciation and bodhi-mind:

> "To produce bodhi-mind and right view, you must renounce *saṁsāra*, for if you do not desire to liberate yourself from *saṁsāra*, you can not produce the love, *compassion* (*karunā*), and bodhi-mind which desire to liberate other living beings."

3. Atīśa

The inquiry into the humanistic aspect of this specific problem of the ethos of knowledge should be pursued on a deeper historical level, a level which the Tibetan Buddhist tradition formed in the pre-scholastic period. The work of Tsong-kha-pa marks the high scholastic accomplishment of Nagarjuna's dialectical rationalization of problems representing an advanced stage of generalized categorial regions both of axiological and noetic components of metaphysical structures pertaining to the Buddhist ethos of knowledge. On the basic level of phenomenological analysis of material value components implied in such high structures of "immeasurable" (*apramāṇam*) attainments, "beyond the good and the evil" (*puṇya-pāpa pahāya*), one thing remains requisite. This is found in explicit terms in Atisa's message, brought from Indian Mahayanam to Tibet in the eleventh century.[61]

The missing link which Atisa emphasized in his practical teaching was the fundamental importance of compassion (*karunā*), rather than the ultimate attainment of perfection in equanimity (*upekṣā*). In explaining the basic teaching of Buddho (*Buddha-dharma*) to his first three Tibetan disciples, (one of whom was Drom, who was to become his successor), he answered their initial questions on "the highest teaching of the path."

> " - What is the final goal of the teaching?
>
> - It is the possession of the essence of nullity and compassion" (*śūnyatā* and *karunā*).

Atisa's successor, Geshe Drom, explained the same fundamental thought of the school with reference to "the method of practice which includes the essence of all the paths to omniscient buddhahood".

"Nullity is the absolute bodhi-mind; it is the realization that all phenomena are by nature without truly existent arising. Compassion is the relative bodhi-mind, it is great compassion extended to all living beings who have not yet realized this fundamental arising" (in merely interdependent phenomena without ontical background, considering the double nullity of both the subjective and the objective substratum of being-in-itself and being-for-itself).

Therefore:

"You must at the same moment of perceiving nullity, generate special compassion toward all living beings, who are not negated by your perception of nullity. At the time of generating relative bodhi-mind,deep compassion toward all living beings, you must also see the nondifferentiation of self and others."

In the following short statement another follower of Atisa, Geshe Sah-bo- gay-pa, explains the link between compassion and equanimity in the progress of liberating the mind by tranquilizing it.

"One who finds happiness in (the relief of) nullity does not cling to the self (being)."

4. More Recent Analogies

An analogical explanation to the first part of this statement, concerning finding happiness in the relief of annulment, can be found in Schopenhauer's aesthetical theory of catharsis, which is the context of an extensive and detailed comparison of Indian and Christian asceticism[62]:

And we know that these moments, when, delivered from the fierce pressure of the will, we emerge, as it were, from the heavy atmosphere of the earth, are the most blissful that we experience. From this we can infer how blessed must be the life of a man whose will is silenced not for a few moments, as in the enjoyment of the beautiful, but forever, indeed completely extinguished, except for the last glimmering spark that maintains the body and is extinguished with it. Such a man... is then left only as pure knowing being, as the undimmed mirror of the world... He now looks back calmly and with a smile on the phantasmagoria of this world which was once able to move and agonize even his mind..."

Let us now turn to the second part of Sha-bo-gay's statement - not clinging to one's own self - , considered in the context of Buddho's negation of selfhood (*an-ātmā*) as an ontological doctrine that reaches far beyond the *ethical problem* and maxim of *ab*-negation of selfishness in 'practical' activity.

I maintain that an analogy with the contemporary impact on ideological prejudices of our 'modern' civilization should be sought, from the bias of some 'modernized' Indian standpoints, in the religious and quasi-religious motives of the pre-revolutionary outbreaks of Russian anarchistic nihilism at the middle of the nineteenth century. This analogy, on the shortest and therefore most neglected Indo-Russian link (via Tibet) between the East and the West of our Euro-Asian continent, should not be considered superficially, and treated as a revival of the *uccheda-vādo*[63] scare-crow "destructive" materialism as the mere *tertium comparationis*. While drawing this analogy, in order to realize more adequately the depth of the religious substructure breaking out in this phase of pre-socialist utopia, we should cross the Russian border to India and to the twentieth century. For this purpose its span should be extended over two generations, from Bakunin (1814-1876) to Sri Aurobindo (1872-1950).

Bakunin was an eye-witness of the 1848 revolution in Paris which greatly impressed and stimulated his revolutionary activity. In 1836, at the outset of his career, he wrote:[64]

"The goal of life is ... *God who lives in mankind* and is exalted with the exaltation of man."

During this idealistic period of his activity he consistently confirmed and explicated the same principle:

> "My individual self now seeks nothing for itself,
> its life from now on will be a *life in the absolute*."
> "There is no evil, everything is good."

Modern Russian philosophers have paid particular attention to the influence of Fichte's political philosophy on Bakunin. At the beginning of the 19th century in Germany, Fichte, in his early work, was a staunch defender of the French revolutionary ideology. Two works bearing this out are "Summons to the rulers of Europe for the restoration of freedom of thought suppressed by them until now" and "A contribution to the setting right of public statements on the French revolution".

Zenkovsky showed how "Bakunin derived from Fichte not only a mystically interpreted immanentism but also the principle of a personalistic ethics".[65] As "an ardent defender of personalism against collectivism" Bakunin considered that "Communism is not a real, living union of free men, but an intolerable coercion, a herd of animals pressed together by violence".[66]

D.I. Pisarev, Bakunin's contemporary, considered as one of the most prominent representatives of the typical Russian "nihilism", was compared with Nietzsche by T.G. Masaryk on account of his extreme individualism.[67] Zenkovsky prefers to compare him rather "with that other *nihilist genius, Leo Tolstoy*".[68] Pisarev's thesis that "the fullest manifestation of humanity is possible only in the *integral personality*" sounds almost like a premonition of the broadest ideal formulated during the first world war in Sri Aurobindo's visionary analysis of the perspectives of anarchism in *The Human Cycle*, as we shall see later.

However, Bakunin also became famous for a gloomier analogy with one of the central motives in Aurobindo's interpretation of the Indian myth of the annihilating dance of the god destroyer Siva, *śiva-līlā*. In Bakunin's wording:

> "Let us have confidence in the eternal Spirit which destroys only because it is the inexhaustible and eternally creative source of all life. *The joy of destruction is at the same time a creative joy*."

In his later anarchistic phase Bakunin answers, already in 1849, to a question:

> "You are mistaken if you think that I do not believe in God, but I have wholly given up comprehending him through science and theory... I seek God in man, in human freedom, and now I seek God in revolution."

Ultimately his "nihilism" culminated in eliciting a rational "ontological proof of atheism":

> "If God exists man has no freedom, he is a slave. But man can and must be free, therefore God does not exist... The existence of god is logically bound up with the self-abdication of human reason."

Thus the anarchistic "nihilism" progressed in the 19th century from a "destructionist" vantage point, based on the pantheistic belief in the "Absolute", towards a materialist ontology whose historical modification suggests a remarkable analogy to the old dogmatic misunderstanding of the *uccheda-vādo* destructionist materialism in

Buddhist history. In the dogmatism illicitly imposed on Buddho's open minded, critical and even skeptical, attitude to religion, this dogmatic tendency tries, up to today, to reduce by a surreptitious dialectical 'sublation' Buddho's original idealist conception of *suñña-vādo* (later Sanskrit *śsūnya-vāda*) to the scare-crow heresy of destructionist materialism. (*Uccheda-vādo*, dubbed "annihilationism" in "modern" westernized interpretations is a barbarous cosmogonical representation totally foreign to any Indian world-view and peculiar only to the Biblical religions). The enormous dialectical contrast between these two antitheses becomes evident on both sides of our analogy in their practical, moral and social intent:

(a) The reaction against the anarchist nihilism appeared in the historical ambience of Russian mysticism also in the context of a remarkable criticism - not merely a negative rejection - of Buddhism in the work of the last defender of the Russian mystical religion, Vladimir Solovyof. Just as in the precedent of Hegel's critique of Buddhist logics[69] (and Hegel's influence on Bakunin was also remarkable) Solovyof, from his monotheistic standpoint, was unable to clearly distinguish the essential dialectical difference between the destructive 'annihilationism' of the anarchist revolutionaries and the quietist religious nihilism of Buddhist idealists, a nihilism from whose fundamental realization, as the next step on Buddho's "noble eightfold path", follows the ethic of *ahiṁsā* - non-violence as the "*supreme law*" (*ahiṁsā* paramo dharma in its primeval Jain formulation).

Solovyof's analysis of Buddhism[70] brought him to the conclusion:

> "Buddhist religion signalizes a new stage in the history of the world - the universal as opposed to the particular, tribal or national stage. It is clear, however, that the universality of Buddhism is merely abstract or negative in character."

(b) The analogy to all these phases on the Indian side of the Himalayas, hardly one generation later, is astonishing. It appears at first glance as a historical process of retrogression from Bakunin's to Solovyof's vantage point.

At the end of the nineteenth century, the first Indian missionary in America and then also in Europe, Swami Vivekananda, showed, on the one hand, the Hegelian influence on his approach to the historical heritage of Indian culture and its actual mission and value for the spiritual regeneration of the West. On the other hand, in his analysis of the early Buddhist history from the same viewpoint (perhaps for the first time applied by an Indian philosopher of history, in a lecture in San Francisco in 1900), Vivekananda drew a conclusion corresponding in its main intent to the quoted statement by Solvyof.

(1) "Within every man there is an idea; the external man is only the outward manifestation, the mere language of this idea within.Likewise, every nation has a corresponding national idea. This idea is working for the world and is necessary for its preservation... The reason that we Indians are still living, in spite of so much misery, distress, poverty and oppression from within and without is that we have a national idea, which is yet necessary for the preservation of the world."[71]

(2) "The life of Buddha has a special appeal. All my life I have been very fond of buddha, but not of his doctrine. I have more veneration for that character than for any other - that boldness, that fearlessness, and that tremendous love!... (He) brushed aside all the priestly doctrines and practices and made man stand on his own feet.It was necessary for him to go against the accustomed ways of the people: he had to bring about revolutionary changes... Buddhism apparently has passed away from India; but really it has not. There was an element of danger in the teaching of Buddha... In order to bring about the tremendous spiritual change he did, he had to give many negative teachings. But if a religion emphasizes the negative side too much, it is danger of eventual destruction... It so happened in India that as time went on, the followers of Buddha emphasized the negative aspect of his teaching too much and thereby caused the eventual downfall of their religion... The negative elements of Buddhism - there is no God and no soul - died out..."[72]

Aurobindo Ghose took an active part in the political life of Bengal in 1900, at the age of thirty, as an outstanding intellectual leader of the typical Bengali anarchist movement. About ten years later, released from prison, he emigrated to Pondicherry, a French colonial possession in South India, and spent the remaining forty years of his life there as spiritual teacher in his Ashram. In his voluminous philosophical work *The Human Cycle,* written during the first world war, he dwelled more deeply upon the spiritual sublimation of the anarchistic ideal of free life in a state of utopia in whose realization on the human level he could hardly believe. His positive valuation of the progressive stages of "certain forms of anarchism" starts from "philosophies like Nietzsche's", recognizing that "certain forms too of imperialism have been largely influenced and strengthened by this type of ideas, though not actually created by them", - from "the idealistic anarchism of the thinker which is rather the old individualism of the ideal reason carried to its logical conclusion."[73]

In "the rational age" (Ch. XIX, p. 215f) "the progress of the reason as a social renovator and creator, if we may judge from the modern movement", ... is

> "destined to pass through three successive stages which are the very loci of its growth, the first individualistic and increasingly democratic with liberty for its principle, the second socialistic..., the third - *if that ever gets beyond the stage of theory* - anarchist in the higher sense of that much abused word, either a loose voluntary cooperation or a free communalism with brotherhood or comradeship and not government for its principle".

This "third form of society" is "founding an essential rather than formal liberty... in a free community". It is *"the ideal of intellectual as of spiritual anarchism"* (p.226).

In evaluating the historical symptoms and trends indicating such possibilities it has to be taken clearly and boldly for granted that:

> "This intellectual and vital dissatisfaction may very well take under such circumstances the form of anarchistic thought, because that thought appeals precisely to this *need of free variation* in the internal life and its outward expression which will be the source of revolt, and *anarchistic thought must be necessarily subversive of the socialist order*". (p. 236) "Anarchistic thought, although it has not yet found any sure form, cannot but develop in proportion as the pressure of society on the individual increases, since there is something in that pressure which unduly oppresses a *necessary element of human perfection*... But there is a higher, an *intellectual anarchistic thought* which in its aim and formula recovers and carries to its furthest logical conclusion a very real truth of nature and of the divine in man..." (p. 241).

> "For perfectly spiritualized society will be one in which, as is demanded by the *spiritual anarchist*, all men will be deeply free" (p.288)

Thus Sri Aurobindo's visualization of the way leading to an ideal of anarchism seems to be comparable, at least at an understandable distance and to a point indicating a dim future state, to the way that might have led some Russian anarchists from Bakunin's towards Solovyof's position.

Chapter Three

Conclusion

The essential difference between the Buddhist understanding of nothingness (Pali *suñña-vādo* and *akiñcaññāyatanam*) from the criticist standpoint of its rational idealism, and all other theories of "nihilism" considered here, not only from the European, but also from Asian biases, consists in the basic principle that in authentic Buddhism nihilism and anarchism are clearly determined as ontological and logical contrasts excluding each other *a limine* (as stated in texts by which this part of our survey was initiated).

Nothingness, nullity, and consequently any authentic (viz. not dialectically sophisticated, as it sometimes happens also in mahayanic speculations) nihilism excludes the logical possibility of destructive action (*ucchedo*) as the primordial metaphysical error of illusion (*avijjā*). This follows from the anti-ontological standpoint of *nihilation* (the term opposite to "*an*-nihilation" as used for materialistic destructiveness) of both the world as object "in itself" (*attena*) and the cognizing subject "for itself" (*attaniyena*).

Applied to the actuality of our present existential situation this can be summarized in the following manner:

> Ontological nihilism excludes, in theory, and tends to preclude, in practice, political anarchism. It is the deepest intention of the Buddhist *ethos of knowledge* to disclose the irrational absurdity of anarchism from the vantage ground of the Buddhist strictly rational, cool (*sīti-bhūto*), non-emphatic and non-exstatic analytical approach (*vibhajja-vādo*) to all world-views (*diṭṭhi*).

Even the historical validity of this Buddhist *ethos* of knowledge can be easily confirmed nowadays on the level of purely empirical experience. This, of course, should not be understood too hastily, as it often occurs to ideological simpletons, as the denial of its metaphysical depth, as if any religion, or even philosophy in its full sense, could exist, or even appear, without this depth-dimension, in advertising to be purely "pragmatic", "utilitarian" and practical as a "multipurpose" technique - but aimless in itself.

It was for this reason that the interpretation of the basic virtue of *karunā*, compassion, as understood by a representative of the strictest Catholic order of ascetic monks, Thomas Merton, was chosen as the starting point of the concluding part of the present survey.

The teaching of non-violence as the highest law of Jain religions (*ahiṁsā* paramo dharma) since the pre-buddhist millennia of that universal religion, has remained not less essential also the Buddha-dhammo, despite the neglect of his later followers to recognize its pivotal importance on the second step of his "noble eightfold path of liberation". The first step in this structure just as the first *jhānam* in our earlier analysis, was meant to establish correctly the horizontal level of orientation - *sammā-diṭṭhi*, the right, i.e. purposefully intended, view-point, in the same meaning as in the Pyrrhonian philosophy of *epoché* indicated the first rule of the *ethos* of knowledge: abandoning all dogmatic views - *doxa*. Buddho clearly defined this specific intention in his First Sermon where, abandoning the dialectical opposition of any claim to the "only right" against all the wrong, dogmatic heretical "tenets", a clear orientation is singled out in an existentially purposeful direction, abstracting from, and not refuting dia-logically, all other meaningful but heterogenous interests in scientific or religious "world-lores" (*lokāyatam*):

> " - What, now, is Right Understanding?- To understand suffering, to understand the origin of suffering, to understand the path that leads to the extinction of suffering.
>
> - This is called Right Understanding."

To make the next, second, correct step - *sammā-saṁkappo* - right intention, on this selective vantage ground it is requisite to adopt *ahiṁsā*, non-violence, as the supreme law of all further exploration and cultivation of a noble character on the *selected* ground (*bhūmi*) of the *ethos* of knowledge:

> " - What, now, is Right Intention?

- Intention free from lust, *intention free from ill-will, and intention free from violence* (*avihiṁsā-sankappo*)."

The ultimate attainment on this path of meditative ennobling of mind, the eighth step, is *sammā-samādhi* - defined as the "one-pointedness of mind" attained by "right concentration". - But, unfortunately, as a symbol of the mental disease of "technicality" in order to increase speed on the long run towards cosmical extensions, even this ultimate step of spiritual perfection has been disclaimed as technically superfluous by a whole trend of Buddhist meditation gurus among other technicians engineering modern "multipurpose" shortcuts to Nirvana. The procedure has been technically termed as the process of dehydration of insight (*sukkha-vipassanā*).

Footnotes to Part III

1. The text is found at the end of the chapter on *Husserl: The Meditating Philosopher*.

2. E. Husserl, *Cartesianische Meditationen* (C.M.) II, section 19, p.18.

3. Apart from some obvious ill-will in the attempts of translators to reduce the Buddhist meaning of nothingness to a psychologically less important euphemism or *horror vacui* (expressed with the English word "emptiness"), a specific difficulty in translating the term *ā-kiñcaññam* into English consists in the fact that in the English language there seems to exist no imaginable possibility of representing any idea or concept whatsoever which before being expressed at all should not be preliminarily converted and transformed into a "thing". Thus even the nullity implied in the more specific term *ākiñcaññam,* which literally should be translated as *"no-what"*, can express its nullifying function only as a "thing". Other European languages, even when they have no linguistically comparable correlative term to be negated as *ākiñcaññam,* at least do not least depend on an obligatory reification of the fictitious substratum of each metaphysically and ontologically dubious "what", with whose obvious doubtfulness all genuine philosophy - Eastern or Western - does and has to begin. Thus the French *rien,* even though it has no positive correlate, is not to be grafted on any "thing" for that reason. To the German *nichts* corresponds, although in a somewhat archaic form, the possibility of opposing an indefinite concept of *"ichts"*, used occasionally also by modern existential philosophers. The Slavic languages, which are even closer to Sanskrit than modern Indian dialects, not only in their complex grammatical form, but to a considerable extent also lexigraphically, have no such problem when expressing the negation of "what" (*kiñcaññam*). They use most natural and common word *"ni-sta"* (in the spelling of my Yugoslav mother-tongue) - "no-what", which in its primeval commonsense excludes any association whatsoever a transformation or adaptation of "what", dubious in and by itself, when connected to any pre-established "thing".

4. Buddho's family name.

5. Quoted in the sequel according to the translation by E. Lamotte, *Le Traité de la Grande Vertu de Sagesse de Nagarjuna,* Tome III. ed. Institut Orientaliste, Louvain 1970.

6. In *Parerga and Paralipomena,* Vol. I. Transl. by E.F.J. Payne, Oxford University Press 1974. P. 93

7. For the Sanskrit text I have used: *Mūlamadhyamaka-kārikās de Nāgārjuna avec la Prasannapadā Commentaire de Candrakīrti*, publie par Loues de la Valee Poussin, Bibliotheca Buddhica IV, St. Petersbourg 1903, and also Kenneth K.Inada, Nagarjuna: *A Translation of his Mūlamadhyamakārikā* (containing also the Sanskrit text in Latin transcription), Tokyo, The Kokusedo Press, 1970.

   Consulting Inada's translation I could not adopt the philosophical terminology of his interpretation. Additions in square brackets are mine.

8. Cf. in my article "Hegel and Indian Philosophy" the ch. on "Hegels interpretation of the Buddhist theory of nothingness", in *Indian Philosophical Quarterly*, Vol. III, No. 3, 1976.

9. I. Apte's *Sanskrit-English Dictionary.*

10. Th. Stcherbatsky, *The Conception of Buddhist Nirvana*, Leningrad, 1927, p. 140.

11. On the original *historical* meaning of the designation "the middle way" in Buddho's first sermon, see Part One of this book, "Why is Buddhism a Religion?"

12. Cf. Stcherbatsky, op. cit., p. 141.

13. Cf. Candrakirti, *Prasannapadā Madhyamakavṛtti*, douze chapitres traduits du sanscrit et du tibetain... par Jacques May. Colection Jean Przyluski, tome II. Paris, Adrien Maisonneauve, 1959. P. 154, n. 463.

14. *Prasannapadā*, 490.6, in May, op. cit., p. 222.

15. Cf.Stcherbatsky, op. cit., p. 95.

16. Cf. Erich Frauwallner, *Die Philosophie des Buddhismus*. Akademie-Verlag, Berlin (East) 1956. P. 350 and 385. The same orientalist has also cut Nagarjuna in two persons.

17. *In Modes of Thought* (1938). Quotations here and in the sequel are from *Classic American Philosophers*, New York, Appleton - Century - Crofts, 1951. P.428.

18. id., p. 434.

19. *Process and Reality: An Essay in Cosmology* (1929). Op. Cit., p.407.

20. Op. cit., pp. 397, 426-429 (from *Nature and Life*, 1934). Underlinings are mine.

21. E. Lamotte, *Le Traité de la grand vertu de Nāgārjuna*, tome III. Publications de l''Institut orientaliste de Louvain, 1970.

22. D.T. Suzuki, *Studies in the Lankavatara Sutra*. London, Routledge and Kegan Paul, 1957. P. 281.

23. Op. cit., p. 280.
24. Id., p. 279.
25. E.F.J. Payne in his translation of Schopenhauer's *Welt als Wille und Vorstellung* (Dover Publications, New York 1966) has corrected this basic term, replacing by "Representation" the vaguer English meaning of "Idea" used in earlier translations and references.
26. See Suzuki's insistence on a specifically different interpretation of the principle "Mind-only" in *Laṅkāvatāra-sūtraṁ*, op. cit. p. 279.
27. Id., p. 282.
28. This and the precedent quotation (from Asvaghosa's *Sūtrālaṁkara*) are taken over from Suzuki, op. cit., p. 280.
29. Cf. *L'Enseignẹment de Vimalakīrti*, traduit et annote par Etienne Lamotte. Introduction. II. L'absolu dans le mahayana. Universite de Louvain. Institut Orientaliste. Bibliotheque du Museon, Vol. 51, 1962. See also Andre Bareau, *L'absolu en philosophie bouddhique* ... Paris, Centre de documentation universitaire, 1951, where "the escape from the absolute" is singled out as characteristic for the history of Buddhist philosophy. (P. 284)
30. The following quotations from *Viṁsatikā* and *Triṁśikā* are adapted from Sylvain Levy, *Materiaux pour l'etude du systeme Vijñaptimātra*. Paris 1932.
31. D.T. Suzuki, op. cit., p. 279.
32. *Parerga and Paralipomena*, Vol. I, p. 182, essay *On Philosophy at the Universities*. Transl. by E.F.J. Payne, Clarendon Press, Oxford 1974.
33. Cf. Asanga's *Mahāyāna-saṃgraha*, II, 2 and 4. My quotations of Asanga here are an adapted paraphrase from E. Frauwaller's German translation in Die *Philosophie des Buddhismus* (See n. 16 above) where not differently indicated.

    The original Sanskrit texts were not available for me when writing this survey.
34. This difficult term, characteristic of the whole Indian philosophy, inseparably connected with the theory of *karma*, is explained by Suzuki (op. cit., glossary, p. 438) as follows: "perfuming impression, memory, habit- energy,... memory-seed. Every act, mental and physical, leaves its deeds behind, which is planted in the *Alaya* for future germination under favorable conditions..." The very name of the contemporary "depth psychology" expresses the idea of *ālaya-vijñānam*, translated by Sylvain Levy (op. cit. passim) as "*notation de tréfonds.*" Comparative studies and books on this analogy, mainly with Freudian psycho-analysis, are appearing more frequently since E. Fromm, D.T. Suzuki, R. de Martino, *Zen*

Buddhism and Psychoanalysis. New York, Harper, 1960. In the area of Pali Buddhism the most extensively documented is perhaps the Ph.D thesis by Padmasiri de Silva, *Buddhist and Freudian Psychology*. Colombo, Lake House Publishers, 1973.

35. Quotations of this work are adapted from the French transl. by Walpola Rahula, *Le compendium de la super-doctrine (philosophie) (Abhidharmasamuccaya) d'Asanga*. Publications de l'Ecole francaise de Extreme-Orient. Vol. LXXVIII, Paris 1971.

36. Suzuki, op. cit., p. 171-2.

37. For the elements required for the present survey cf. Nyanatiloka, *Guide through the Abhidhamma-piṭaka*, Kandy, Buddhist Publication Soc., 1971 (3rd ed.).

38. Id. p. 52f.

39. Id., p. 21.

40. The following quotations from *Mahāyāna-saṁgraha* are my reconstruction with additions based on E. Frauwallner's German translation, quoted in n. 33 above.

41. Cf. selected texts on this subject in Nyanaponika Thera, *The Four Nutriments of life*. Buddhist Publication Society, "Wheel" no. 105/6, Kandy 1967.

42. Cf. Nietzsche, *Die Unschuld des Werdens. Der Nachlass*, "Aus dem Gedankenkreis des Willens zur Macht". Bd II, Leipzig, Kroner, 1931. Sections 182-200, *passim*.

43. G. Santayana, *Scepticism and Animal Faith*. Second ed. Dover Publications, New York 1955. P. 138.

44. Stcherbatsky (in *The Conception of Buddhist Nirvāṇa*), in the obvious intention to avoid as much as possible the 'nihilistic' predicament, translates, if nothing else Nagarjuna's *śūnyatā* with "relativity". Thus he identifies the correct criterion of a syllogistic premise with the actual predicate of the conclusion, leaving the conclusion to be implicitly guessed by the learned reader, while the correct deduction of the term *śuūyatā* states explicitly that *because* all entities are relative, *therefore* they are nothing in and by themselves (*sva-bhāva*).

45. It has often been stated (also by the English translator of Husserl's *Logical Investigations*, J.N. Findlay, London, Routledge and Kegan Paul, 1970, p. 25) that Husserl, in his earlier phase, in the first edition of *Logische Untersuchungen* (1901), "says that he is unable... to detect an abiding subjective center involved in all his conscious references", but later, already in the second edition of the same work, he denied this negative

position and "gradually came to recognize an integral status of the ego. *In Ideen I*, he posited the indubitable reality of the ego (in the Cartesian way) in relation to the contingent world". (Debabrata Sinha in "Philosophy and Phenomenological Research' vol. XXIII, No. 4, 1963, p. 575) - In the first edition Husserl stated (Invest. V, section 8, p. 549 in Findley's transl.): "I must frankly confess, however, that I am quite unable to find this ego, this primitive, necessary center of relations." In another reference to the same subject (on p. 541 n.1) he added: "In the First Edition the name 'phenomenological ego' was given to the stream of consciousness as such.' The same had been and remained the Buddhist attitude from the very beginning of Buddho's statements on this "stream" as *bhavāñga-soto* until today. (Cf. references to this term in our preceding text.)

46. Cf. T.M.P. Mahadevan, Gaudapada, *A Study in Early Advaita*, University of Madras, 1960, Ch. IX.

47. Nanjo Sanskrit ed., Tokyo 1923, p. 274.

48. Cf. Walpola Rahula, op. cit. (n. 35 above), p. 17.

49. For the explanation of these terms see Suzuki, op. cit. p. 308 f.

50. Cf. Padmasiri de Silva, *Buddhist and Freudian Psychology* (Colombo, Lake House, 1973), Ch. IV, sections II-IV.

51. Cf. *L'Enseignement de Vimalakīrti*, traduit et annote par E. Lamotte, Louvain, Biblioteque de Museon, Vol. 51, 1962. For our reference is particularly interesting *Appendice II*, by Paul Demieville, "Vimalakirti en Chine".

52. Th. Stcherbatsky, *Buddhist Logic*, Vol. One, p. 134. (New York, Dover Publications, 1962). The same cosmological theory was known also to Schopenhauer (probably from his Russian sources of information on mahayanic religions in the proceedings of the St. Petersbourg Academy):

    "In Buddhism the world comes into being in consequence of an inexplicable disturbance (after a long period of calm) in the crystal clearness of the blessed and penitentially obtained state of Nirvana and hence through a kind of fatality which, however, is to be understood ultimately in a moral sense, although the matter has its exact analogue and corresponding picture in physics, in the inexplicable arising of a primordial nebula, whence a sun is formed. Accordingly, in consequence of moral lapses, it also gradually becomes physically worse and worse until it assumes its present sorry state." (P.P.II, section 156) The same story can be found, related in mythological extension, also in one the "Long Discourses" of Buddho in the Pali Canon (*Dīgha-nikāyo* 27).

53. In Frauwallner's translation "das nicht feststehende Nirvana" (op. cit.. see n. 33 above, p. 346.).

54. *Laṅkāvatara-sūtraṁ*, 42-7. Cf. Suzuki, op. cit.,, p. 346.
55. Op. cit., p. 36.
56. On the *bodhisatto* tradition in the *thera-vādo* Buddhism see *The Bodhisatta Ideal* by Narada Thera, Vajirarama, Colombo 1963. A comparative presentation is given in the exhaustive study on this subject, *The Bodhisattva Doctrine in Buddhist Sanskrit Literature*, by Har Dayal, London, Kegan Paul, 1932.
57. The following references are from Geshe Wangyal, *The Door of Liberation*, Ch. 4-7. N.Y., M. Girodias, 1973.
58. Cf. text referred to in n. 8, Ch. I above.
59. *The Asian Journal of Thomas Merton*, A New Directions Book, N.Y. 1973, pp. 143, 292.
60. See Part II, ch. 3, "Husserl: 'The Meditating Philosopher'," text corresponding to footnote 73.
61. The following quotations are my adaptations from Geshe Wangyal, *The Door of Liberation* (cf. ref. in note 57, above), ch. 3. "Kadampa Precepts",pp. 390, in E.F.J. Payne's translation, Dover Publications, N.Y. 1966.
62. *The World as Will and Representation*, Vol. I, Fourth Book, Chapt. 68, p.390, in E.F.J. Payne's Translation, Dover Publications, N.Y. 1966
63. Cf. Part II, ch. i, on *jhānam*.
64. Subsequent references are from V.V. Zenkovsky, *A History of Russian Philosophy*. 2 vols. English translation. New York 1919.
65. Op.cit. pg. 248
66. Op.cit, pg. 255
67. T.G. Masaryk, *The Spirit of Russia: Studies in History, Literature and Philosophy*. 2 vols. English translation New York 1919.
68. Op. cit. p. 338.
69. Cf. Hegel's Logic in the *Encyclopedia of the Philosophical Sciences* (1817), Ch. VIII, sections 87-88. See also the chapter on Buddhism in my paper *Hegel and Indian Philosophy*, No. 3, 1976.
70. V. Solovyof, *The Justification of the Good* (London 1918), Part III, Ch. 2, pp. 227-237.
71. *The East and the West*, 5th impression, 1955, by Advaita Ashrama, Calcutta.

72. "Buddha's Message to the World" in *The Complete Works of Swami Vivekananda*. Advaita Ashrama, Calcutta, 3rd ed. 1959, Vol. VIII, p. 199.

73. *The Human Cycle*, quoted in the sequel from Sri Aurobindo Library edition, New York 1950. p.60.